Dogs
&Art

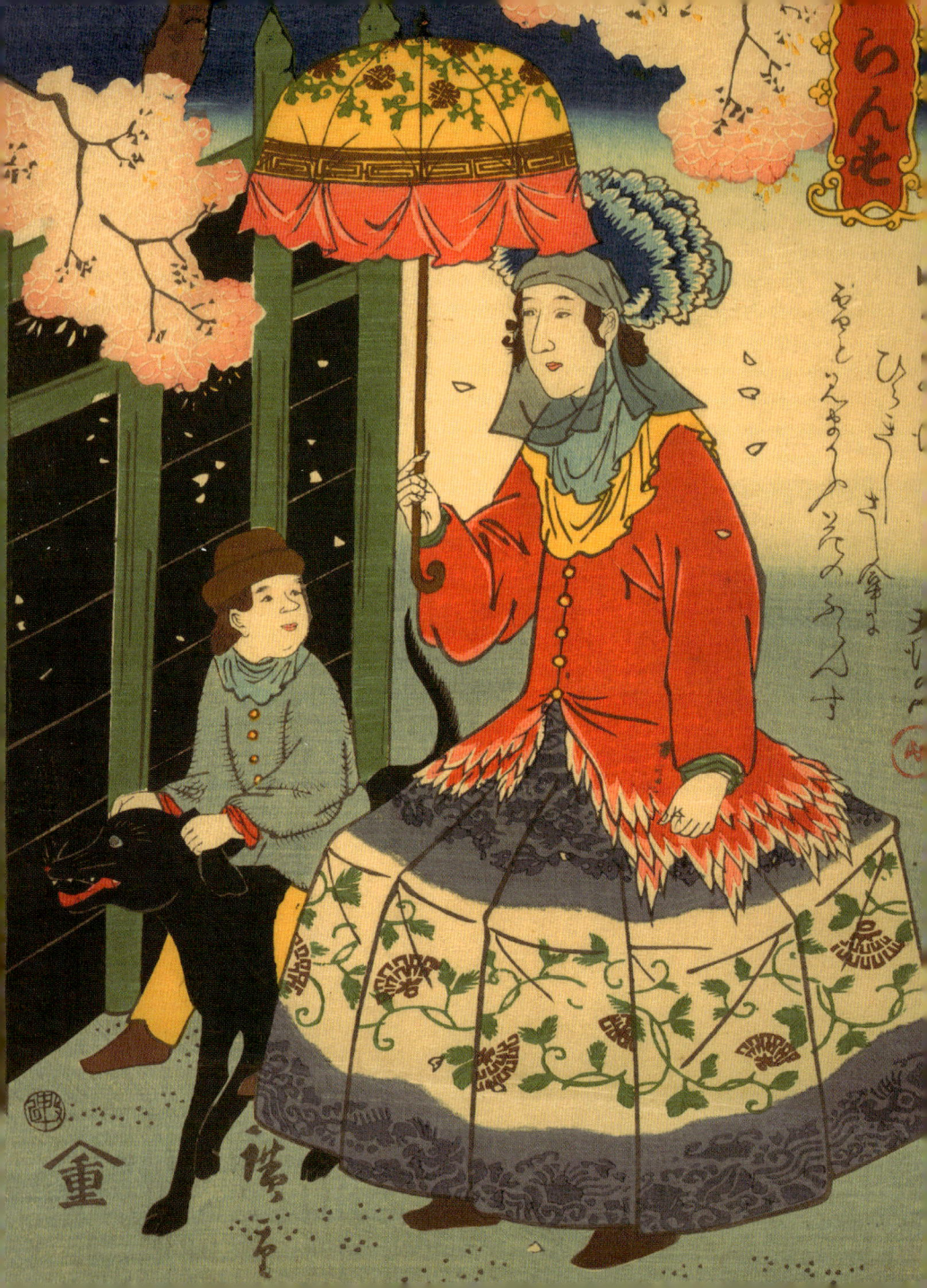

Dogs & Art

50 MASTERPIECES & THEIR DOG BREEDS

Susie Hodge

G:

Contents

Introduction

"You think dogs will not be in heaven?
I tell you; they will be there long before any of us."

Robert Louis Stevenson (1850–94)

Whether as cherished family pets or watchful guardians, dogs have been companions or working animals throughout much of human history. Because of this, a huge number of artists have represented them, emphasizing their abiding qualities, especially those of loyalty, fidelity and unconditional love. From the earliest cave drawings to contemporary installations, dogs have been an almost constant source of artistic inspiration, and many artworks express the nobility of individual breeds.

Early domestication

Archeological evidence suggests that dogs are among the earliest animals to have been tamed by humans, and were first domesticated from wolves about 15,000 years ago. The earliest known dog-like fossils date back more than 30 millennia. Although the 32,000-year-old paintings on the walls of the Chauvet cave in the Ardèche valley, southeastern France, include images of at least 13 different animal species, not one depicts dogs. But on the ground at the back of the cave, the footsteps of a child have been discovered, and alongside these are the pawprints of a wolf or large dog. This proves that dogs, or their close relatives, have been human companions for at least 26,000 years – a companionship that has continued unbroken throughout the ages.

As humans transitioned from hunter-gatherers to settled agricultural societies, the relationship between humans and dogs evolved. Ancient civilizations, among them the Egyptians, Greeks and Romans, all had domesticated dogs that helped them

UNKNOWN ARTIST

The King in the Form of Anubis

Late 18th Dynasty, New Kingdom, c. 1232–1223 BCE (from the tomb of Tutankhamun)

Wood lined with stucco and tar, decorated with gold, silver, calcite and obsidian

107⅔ × 25 × 20 in (273.5 × 63.7 × 50.7 cm)

Egyptian Museum, Cairo, Egypt

to hunt, herd and guard, and that probably also lived with them as pets. Certain breeds, including greyhounds and mastiffs, appeared during these times. In medieval Europe, dogs continued to be important animals, working on farms and taking part in hunts. Specific breeds started to be bred selectively for certain tasks, including guarding, herding and hunting, and prized dogs were often kept by royalty or the aristocracy. By the nineteenth century ownership of dogs had increased hugely, and the present-day form of dog shows and breed standards emerged. This led to the creation of many of the dog breeds we recognize today, and in the twentieth century dogs became progressively integrated as household pets and companions. They also continued to work, including in such new roles as guide dogs, police dogs, and search and rescue dogs. Advances in veterinary medicine have improved dog health and longevity. Dogs remain among the most popular pets in the world,

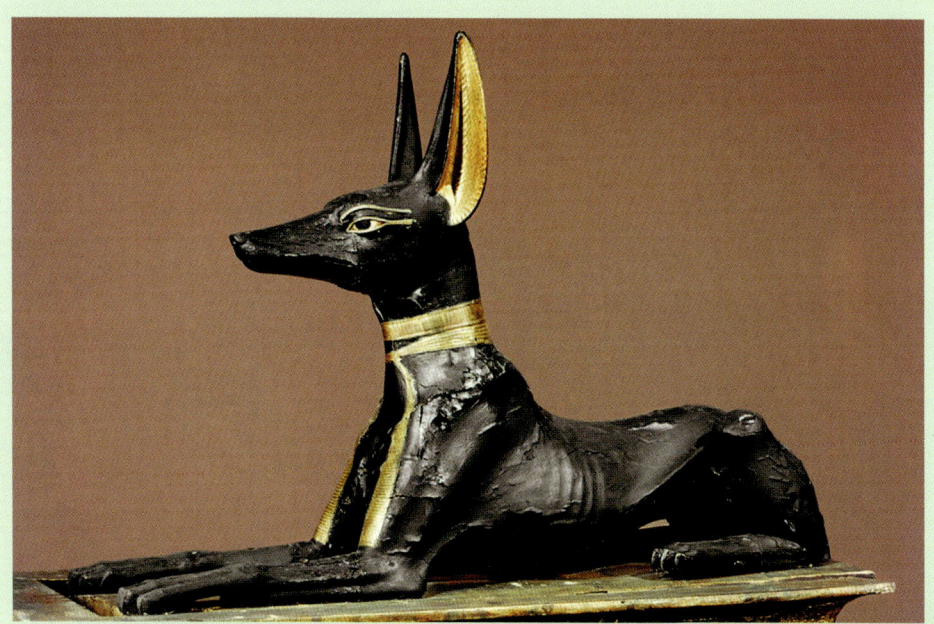

and there are hundreds of recognized breeds divided into groups, such as sporting, working, herding and toy dogs.

The history of dogs in art

Humans' long association with dogs has naturally been reflected in the art they produced. In ancient Egypt, dogs were highly regarded, domesticated, and lived with people as companions, guards and hunters. The Egyptian god Anubis, who was believed to be the protector of souls, was usually depicted as a man with a dog's head, or as an entirely canine figure (see page 7). In wealthy Egyptian families, when a beloved dog died, the family had the animal mummified. In the ancient Mesopotamian

EAGLE PAINTER
Heracles and Cerberus
C. 525 BCE
Yellow micaceous clay and paint
16½ in (42 cm) high
Musée du Louvre, Paris, France

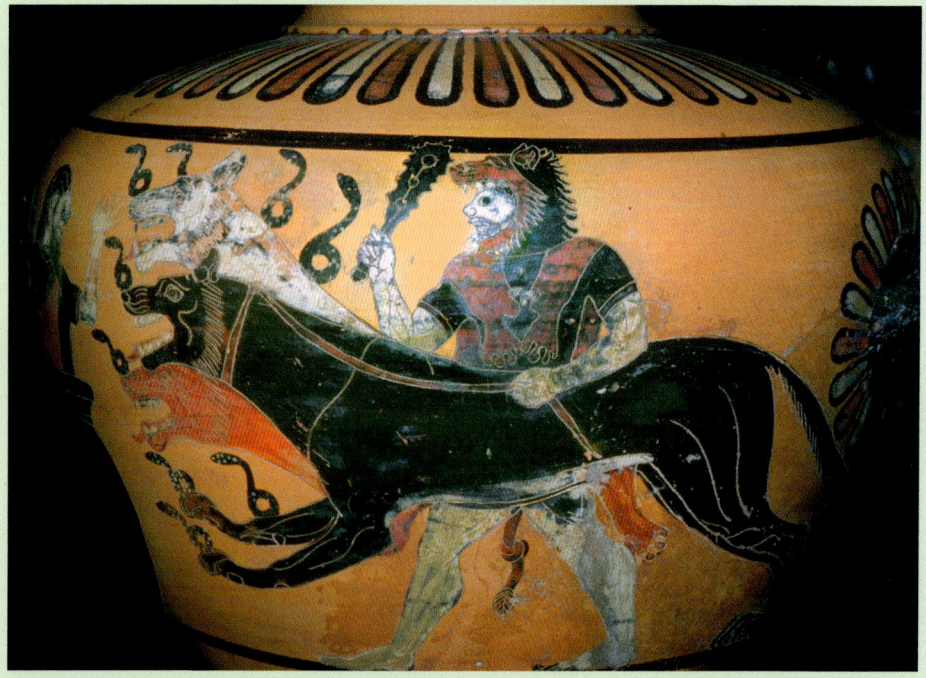

Epic of Gilgamesh (2150–1400 BCE), dogs feature as companions of the goddess Innana (Ishtar), who travels with seven hunting dogs. Unearthed from the ruins of the ancient Assyrian city of Nimrud, the "Nimrud Dogs" are a remarkable pair of carved stone statues that date from the ninth century BCE. These imposing canine figures once stood guard at the entrance to the palace of the Assyrian king Ashurnasirpal II, their fierce expressions and muscular forms embodying the power and might of the Assyrian empire.

The ancient Persians associated dogs with divinity. A dog's soul was thought to comprise one-third wild beast, one-third human and one-third divine. The Avesta (Zoroastrian scriptures) has a section known as the Vendidad, which describes the way dogs should be handled, the penalties for those who abuse them, and how the treatment of dogs will affect a person's final destination in the afterlife. Persian dogs were used in hunting, as guard dogs, for herding sheep and as companions.

The representation of dogs in ancient Greek and Roman art shows that these animals were loved for their loyalty, character and energy. The Greek goddesses Artemis and Hecate had dogs, and Artemis (Roman Diana), the goddess of the hunt, was usually seen with a hunting bow, a quiver of arrows, and dogs. Hecate kept black Molossian dogs. In literature, the most famous ancient Greek dog was the three-headed Cerberus, guardian of the gates to the underworld realm of Hades. Dogs are featured on ceramics, such as the Caeretan black-figure hydria vase of Heracles and Cerberus dating from about 525 BCE (opposite). The hero of Homer's *Odyssey*, King Odysseus of Ithaca, had a faithful dog named Argos that was the only member of his household to recognize him when he returned from his long adventuring.

The Mayan culture of South America bred dogs as food, as guardians, as pets and for hunting. Dogs were also associated with the gods, and were believed to conduct the souls of the dead across water to the afterlife, the underworld of Xibalba. In this role they appear in underworld scenes painted on Mayan pottery. Once a deceased soul had arrived in the dark realm, the dog would guide them through the challenges presented by the Lords of Xibalba, and eventually to paradise. The Aztecs shared similar ideas. According to their myths, dogs pre-date the present race of human beings, so should be treated with the greatest respect. The Aztec people buried dogs with their dead and imagined their god of death, Xolotl, as a huge dog.

During the Middle Ages in Europe, dogs were portrayed in religious art, serving as symbolic representations of the Christian virtues of fidelity and obedience. The collection known as *Les Très Riches Heures du Duc de Berry* (opposite), created in the fifteenth century by the Limbourg brothers (active 1385–1416), for example, depicts a noble hunting hound, emphasizing the dog's association with the aristocratic pursuits of the European elite.

Naturalistic portraiture flourished in the Renaissance, and dogs were frequently included in intimate depictions of family and domestic life. For instance, in the fifteenth century in northern Europe, dogs were often included both to suggest domesticity and to symbolize faithfulness and devotion. At around the same time in Asia, a Chinese emperor of the Ming dynasty who loved dogs also painted them and became famous for his lifelike depictions (page 19). Some years later Titian (page 37), a giant of the Venetian Renaissance, created paintings that included small dogs, such as a Maltese and a papillon, to denote loyalty and love. Another enormously influential painter – this time of the Baroque – Diego Velázquez (page 60), featured a huge Spanish Mastiff in a royal portrait, for similar reasons.

As the centuries passed in Europe, portraits of prominent figures in society often included their pet dogs, since the animals helped both to calm the sitter and to convey human qualities of dependability, love and affection, while also symbolizing devotion and allegiance. As new art movements, such as Realism and Impressionism, came to prominence in the nineteenth century, dogs continued to feature as artists sought to capture notions of spontaneity, naturalness, comfort and artlessness. For instance, the French artist Édouard Manet (page 108) was one of the first to depict scenes from his own life just as it was, without idealism. To this end, he painted the modern urban landscape around

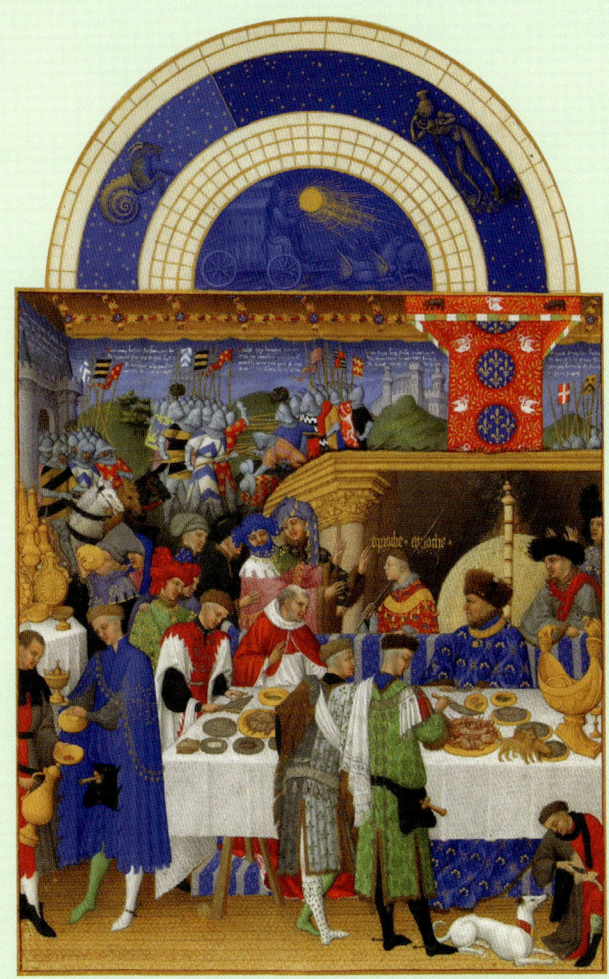

LIMBOURG BROTHERS

Janvier (January), from *Les Très Riches Heures du Duc de Berry*

c. 1412–16

Tempera on vellum

12 × 8½ in (30 × 21.5 cm)

Musée Condée, Chantilly, France

him, and his family, friends – and pets. His paintings of little dogs are captured with lively, quick brushwork. Another artist who used animated, loose brushwork was John Singer Sargent (page 118). Although he did not fit into any particular category or movement, Sargent captured the personalities and characters of the dogs belonging to his friends and sitters through confident flicks of his brush. As art evolved in the twentieth century, greater expressiveness and individualism allowed further attributes, such as strength, vigour and playfulness, to be highlighted in depictions of dogs.

In 1951 the Swiss artist Alberto Giacometti (1901–66), one of the most important sculptors of the twentieth century, produced *The Dog* as both an illustration from memory and an expression of his emotional state. The Mexican artist Frida Kahlo (page 139) is well known for having led a very traumatic life. She loved all the animals she kept, and she often painted her favourite hairless Xoloitzcuintli dog, a breed that was cherished by the Aztecs.

All artists who depict animals have their own ways of working, especially when it is their own pet. For instance, David Hockney (b.1937) kept a separate palette ready so that he could paint his dogs Stanley and Boodgie at any moment, usually when he saw them sleeping; otherwise, they would simply follow him around the studio and never sit still.

In most societies across the world, the dog remains a popular and versatile subject for art, and artists are constantly exploring innovative ways to depict the canine form. The stainless-steel *Balloon Dogs* series by Jeff Koons (b.1955), for example, was made between 1994 and 2000, with different coatings creating different colours. Consequently, the enduring legacy of the dog in art continues to evolve, reflecting the multifaceted relationships between humans and their steadfast four-legged friends.

Pet, worker, symbol

This book delves into the rich and varied history of dogs in art, exploring how these remarkable animals have been depicted and celebrated by painters, sculptors, printmakers and other visual artists. Spanning continents and millennia, it explores the versatility of the dog as a subject – whether portrayed as a precious family pet, a heroic working companion, or a powerful symbol of the natural world or wider society.

Within the pages that follow are 50 works of art, all of which include one or more dogs – each a different breed. From ancient Greek mosaics to dynamic Futurist paintings, and from the couch of a Renaissance goddess to the expressive brushstrokes of a twenty-first-century master, the book includes a broad variety of images, uncovering the deep and durable connections between humans and canines. Every artwork is examined and analysed in a text that considers the artist, their style, methods, rationale and ability, and their technical expertise in capturing the unique energy, personality and physicality of individual breeds. A description of the featured dog breed is also offered. Because dogs have evolved, and since most breeds were not categorized specifically before the nineteenth century, some of the breeds shown in early artworks do not correspond with contemporary varieties.

Whether you are a devoted dog lover or art enthusiast (or both), or simply curious about the myriad ways in which humans' beloved companions have inspired creative expression, this book will enlighten and captivate you. Prepare to be enthralled by the enduring legacy of the dog as the ultimate artist's muse.

Overleaf
JACOPO BASSANO
Two Hunters Tied to a Tree, 1548–9, page 40

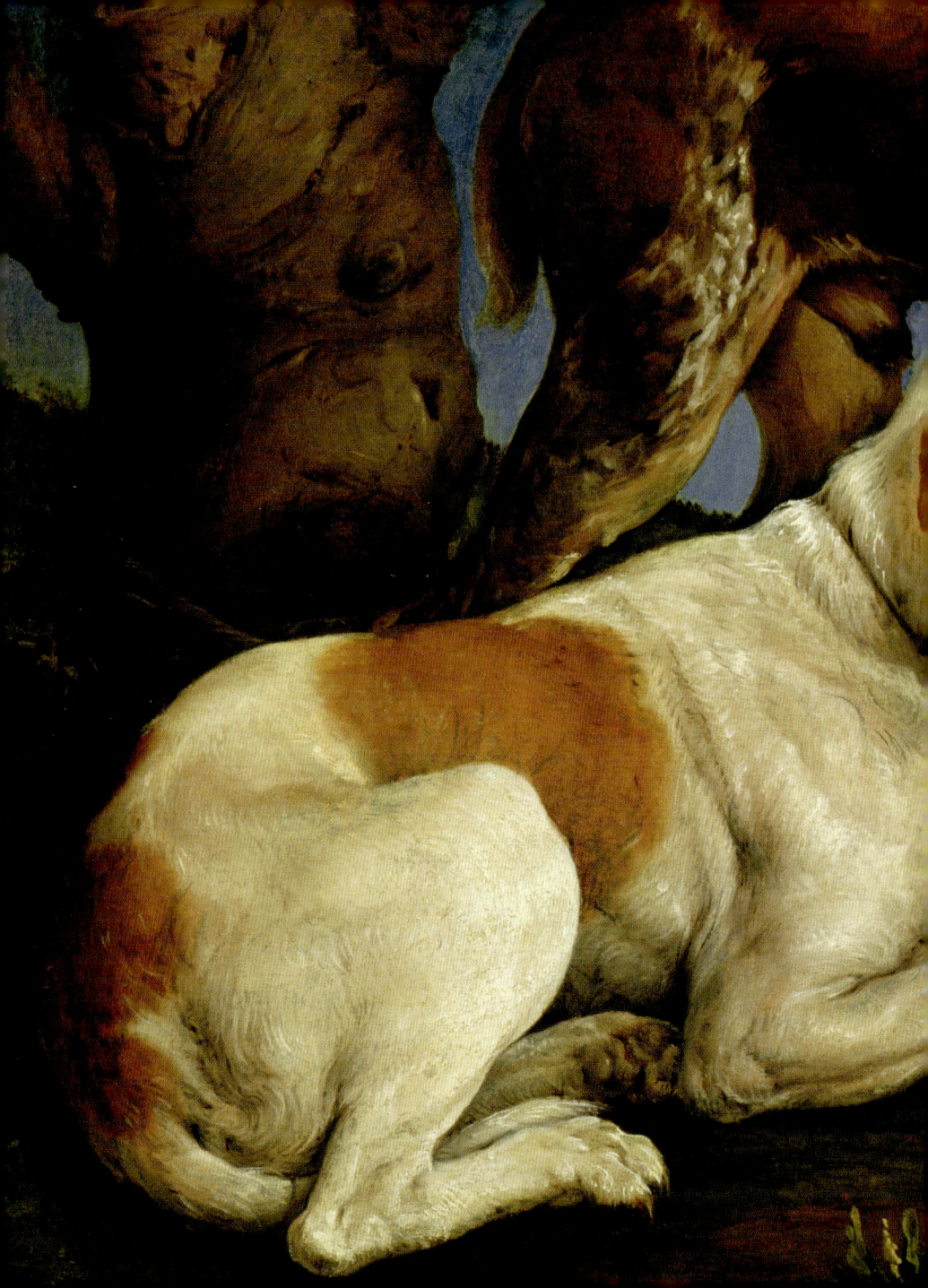

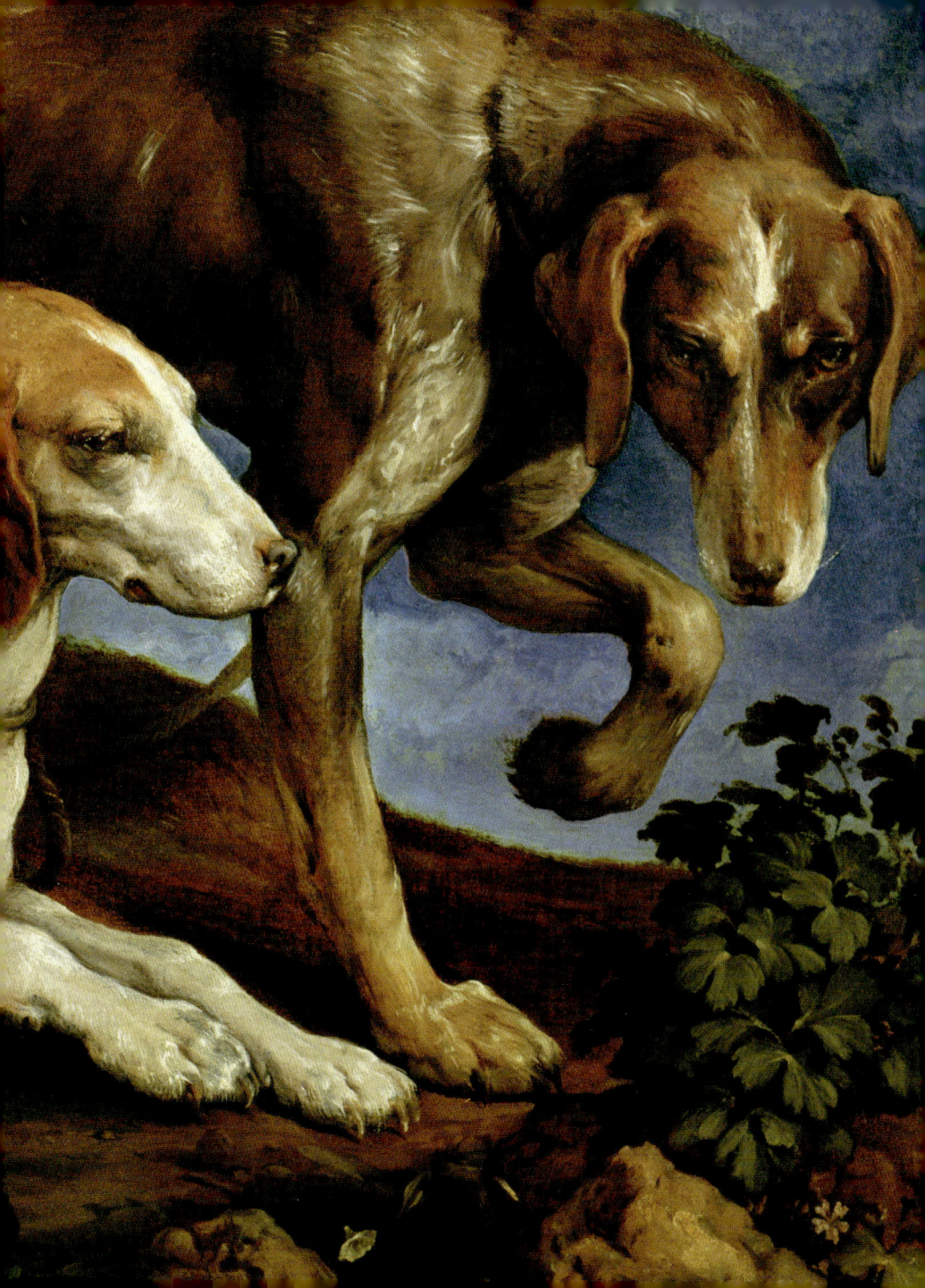

Naturalistic

Excavated from the grounds of the New Alexandrian Library in Egypt in 1993, this Ptolemaic mosaic depicts a dog sitting next to a gilded metal Greek *askos* vessel (for holding water or wine) with looped handles. With bright eyes, the dog looks lively, but also perhaps guilty. It might be a household owner's pet that has just knocked over a container of wine, or the image may suggest that a banquet has been held. Despite the age of the work and the rigidity of the tesserae (tiny squares of stone, tile or glass), the dog appears soft, spirited and lifelike, sitting at a three-quarter angle, its spotted coat and red collar carefully depicted. The variety of tesserae conveys a naturalistic sense of three dimensions and soft fur. The Ptolemaic empire was an ancient Greek culture based in Egypt during the Hellenistic period (305–30 BCE), and this mosaic once decorated a floor in the royal quarter of Alexandria. Using the tiniest tesserae, it was created using the Opus Vermiculatum (worm-like) technique that was developed in Greece during this time. This method of laying mosaics emphasized outlines, allowing artists to build up minute details and emulate the illusionistic approach of Hellenistic painting.

1

UNKNOWN ARTIST

Ptolemaic Roundel

C. 200–150 BCE

Mosaic

Dimensions unknown

Greco-Roman Museum, Alexandria, Egypt

LACONIAN HOUND

Dogs may have been introduced to the ancient Greeks by their Egyptian trading partners, since the Egyptians revered many animals. Hunting dogs were important in Greek society, and the most popular were Laconian hounds, pictured here. Used for hunting deer and hares, these dogs were usually either tan with white markings or black with tan markings. They were athletic and energetic with a keen sense of smell and short, sleek fur. Friendly, affectionate, courageous and intelligent, they were sometimes impatient but never vicious. Traditionally, they hunted in pairs or small groups.

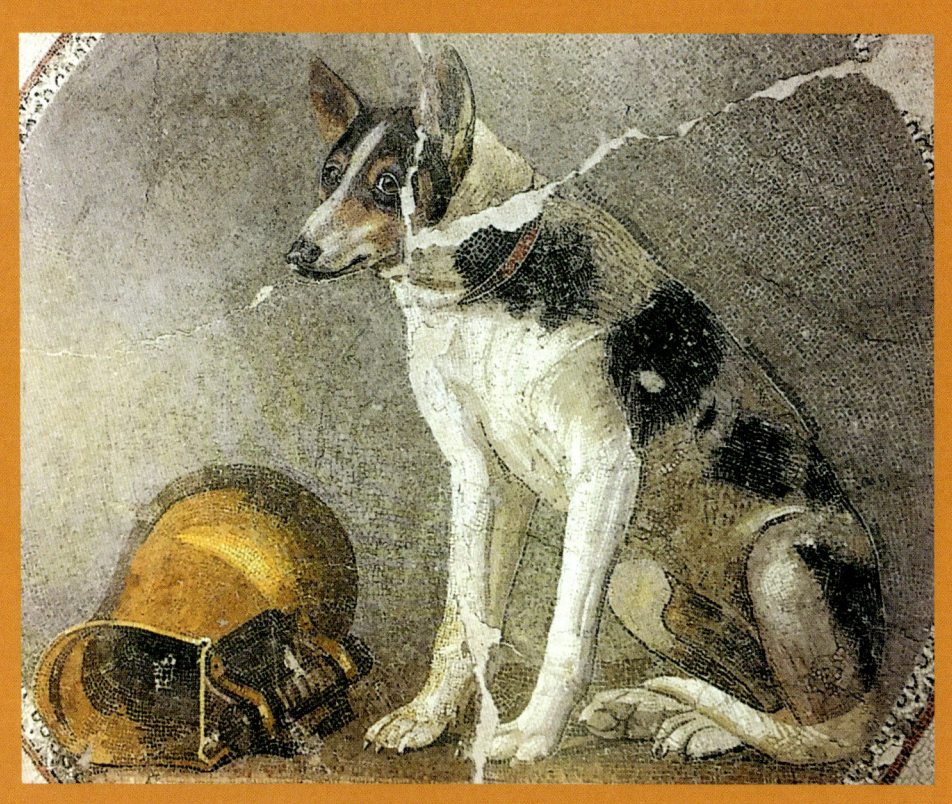

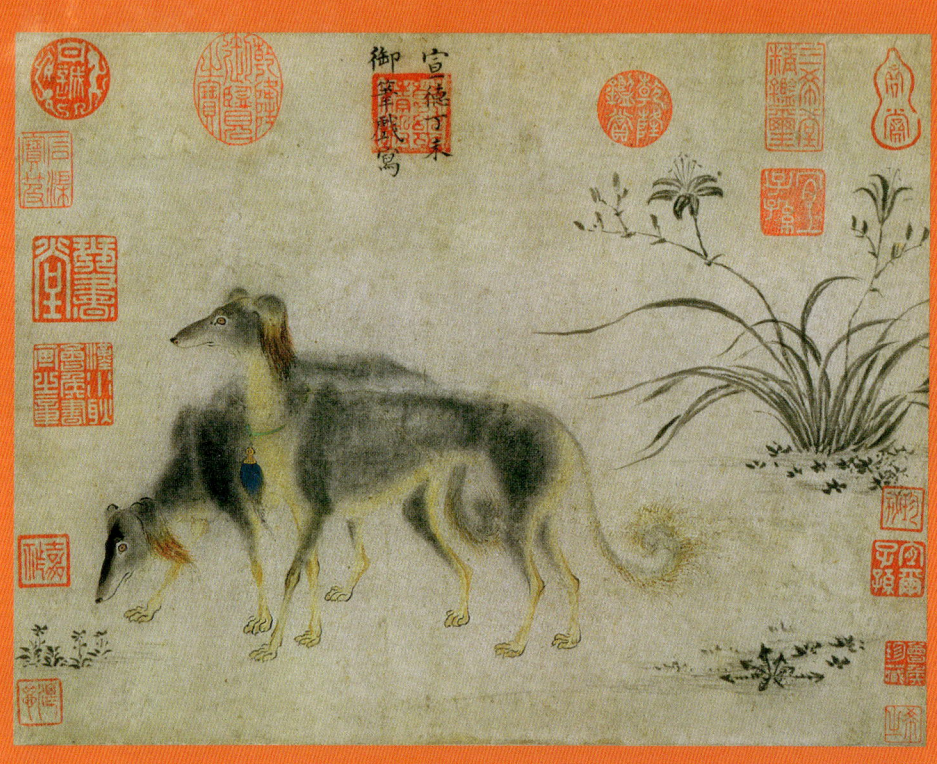

Imperial elegance

Chinese emperors were expected to be cultured gentlemen who enjoyed hobbies including painting, calligraphy and collecting art. Often known by his temple name, Xuanzong, or by the name of his reign, Xuande, the fifth Ming emperor, Zhu Zhanji (1399–1435), was one of the few emperors who – as well as being an avid collector – displayed genuine artistic skill. He specialized in painting animals, and his art is often categorized as being part of the Zhe school, since other artists of this style worked at his court. Emperor Zhanji loved dogs, and they were a favourite subject for him to depict. This sensitively painted image uses minimal marks, including fine lines and velvety areas that convey the contrasts between the softness of the dogs' fur and their clear, watchful eyes. As emperor, Xuanzong could make up his own rules about the art he produced. The dogs have been drawn from direct observation, with fine, flowing lines depicting fur, eyes, ears, tails and paws, as well as some flowers and plants. In black ink, he wrote the inscription "playfully painted [by the] imperial brush". Red seals were added in later years by imperial Chinese owners of the painting, until the eighteenth century.

2

ZHU ZHANJI

Two Saluki Hounds

1427

Ink on a paper album leaf

10¼ × 13⅔ in (26.2 × 34.6 cm)

Arthur M. Sackler Museum, Harvard University Art Museums, Cambridge, USA

SALUKI

A hunting dog that developed from sighthounds (dogs that hunt by sight rather than scent), the Saluki can run after prey at astonishing speed. Sensitive, intelligent and gentle, these dogs are naturally resolute hunters. With their long, narrow heads, large eyes, drooping ears, long legs and lengthy, curving tails, they are most closely related to the Afghan hound (sometimes called the Gazelle hound). The Salukis in this painting were probably Emperor Zhanji's personal pets. Thanks to their graceful appearance, dignity and loyalty, these dogs were often owned by the aristocracy. A similar breed appears on Sumerian wall carvings (in what is now Iraq) dating from 7000–6000 BCE. These dogs were first seen in China during the Tang dynasty (618–907).

Symbolizing faithfulness

A man and a woman wearing expensive clothes stand in a room. Jan van Eyck (active 1422–41) painted this small work in intricate detail. On the floor, the man's pattens (overshoes) point towards the outside world, while the woman's point into the room. She is not pregnant, but fashionably holding up her long gown in front of her. The man is probably the Italian merchant Giovanni di Nicolao di Arnolfini, and the woman is either his late wife, who died in childbirth the year before this was painted, or his second wife, whom he married several years later. The large bed is covered with expensive red woollen cloth, costly oranges are on the windowsill, and a brass chandelier hangs from the ceiling. On the wall is a convex mirror that reflects two men, and above it is written "Johannes de Eyck fuit hic. 1434" (Jan van Eyck was here. 1434). This is the first depiction in fine art of a dog that many people consider to be a Brussels griffon. The breed was not recognized in Europe until 1880, however, so it could be a Smous, a common, rough-coated stable dog that may have been slightly larger than the modern "griff". Whatever the breed, the little dog shown here represents faithfulness.

3
JAN VAN EYCK
Portrait of Giovanni Arnolfini and His Wife
1434
Oil on oak
32⅓ × 23⅔ in (82.2 × 60 cm)
The National Gallery, London, UK

Overleaf: detail

BRUSSELS GRIFFON

The little wiry-haired dog in this painting is probably an ancestor of the Brussels griffon or griffon Bruxellois, the earlier Smous or affenpinscher-like dogs known as *griffons d'écurie* or wire-coated stable dogs. Their descendants originated in Brussels in the early nineteenth century, beginning as rat-catching dogs kept in stables by coachmen and developing into sophisticated lapdog companions for the wealthy. There are three varieties of the "griff", with different coats and colours: the griffon Bruxellois, the griffon Belge and the Petit Brabançon.

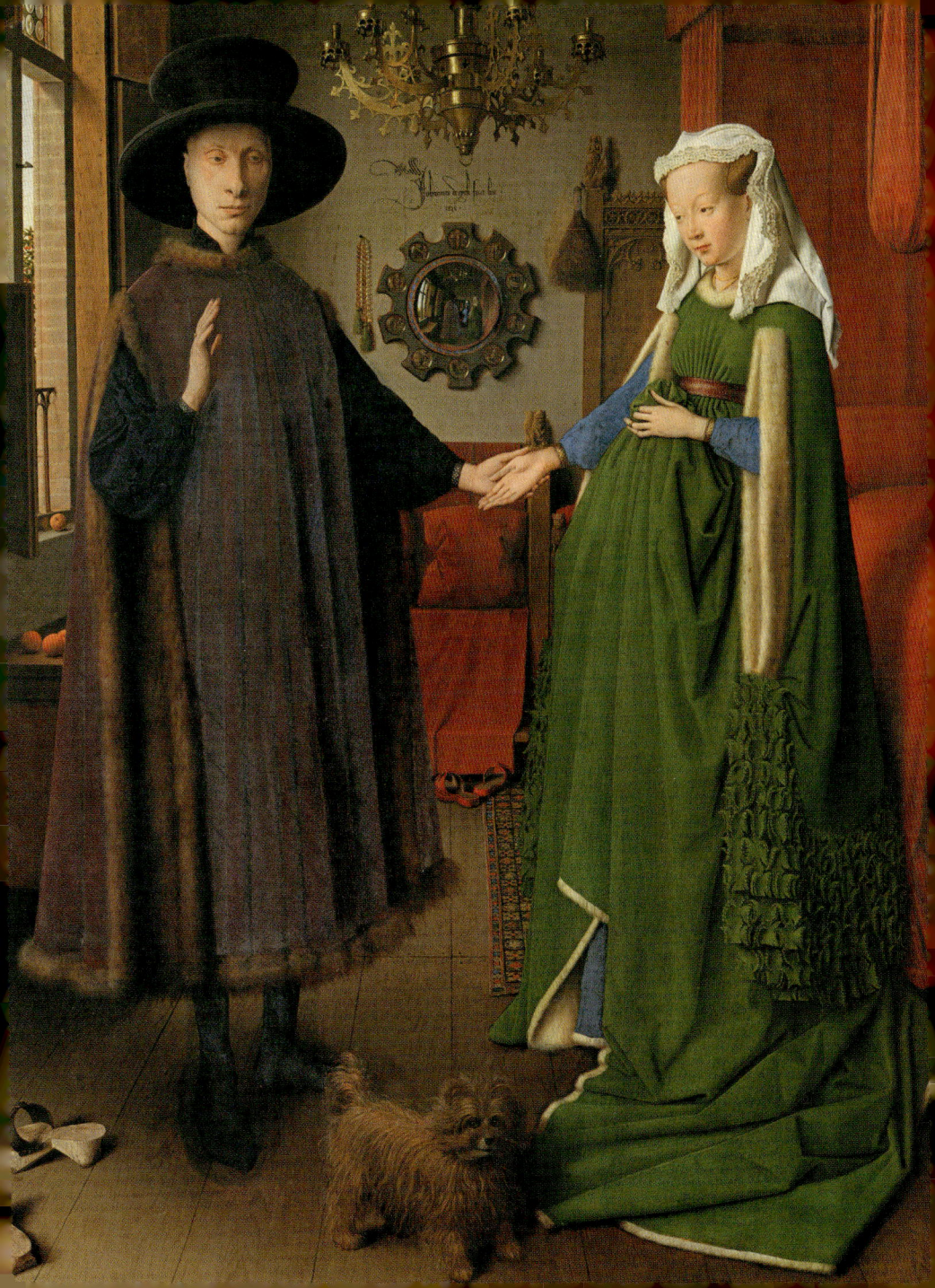

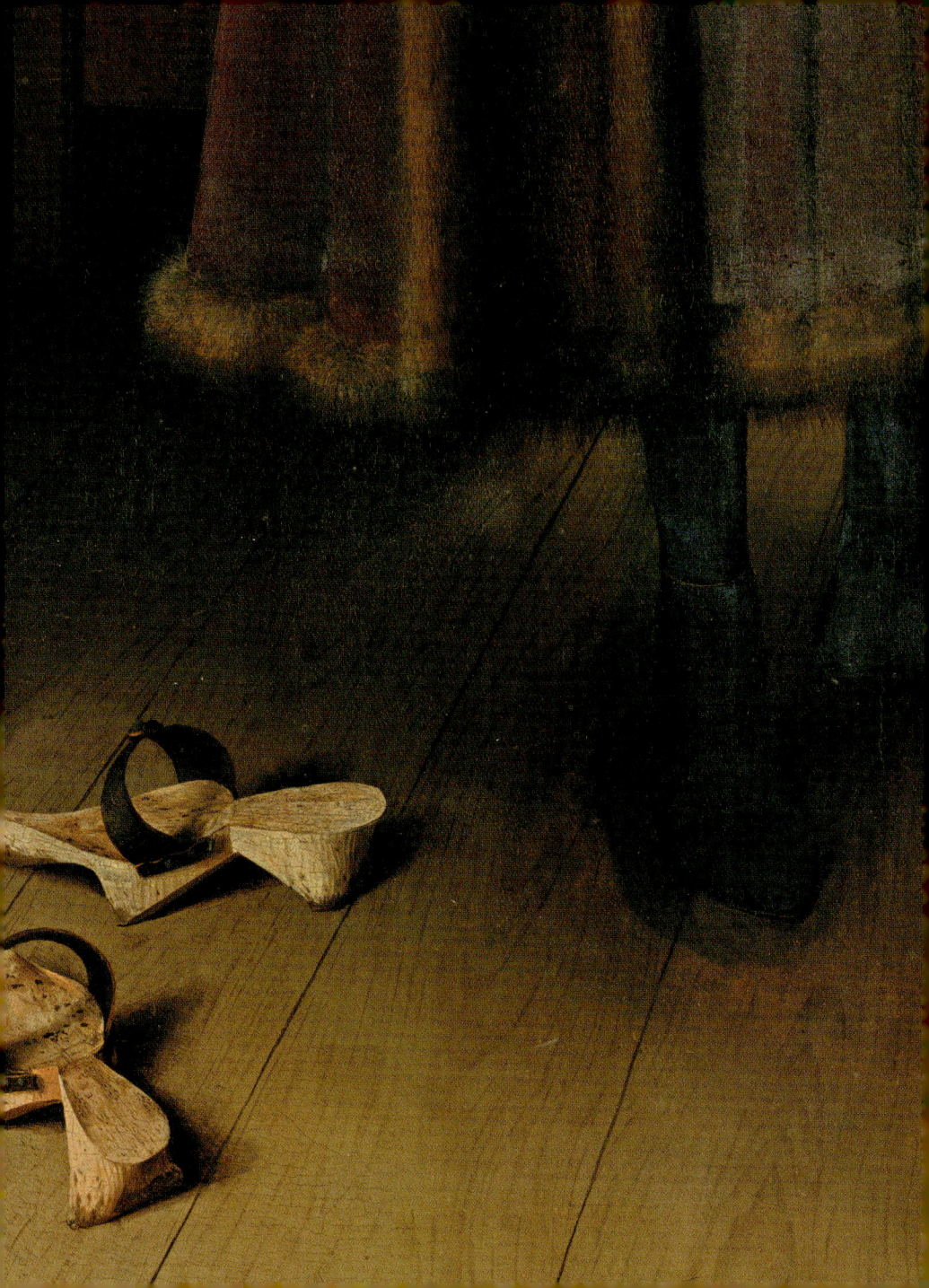

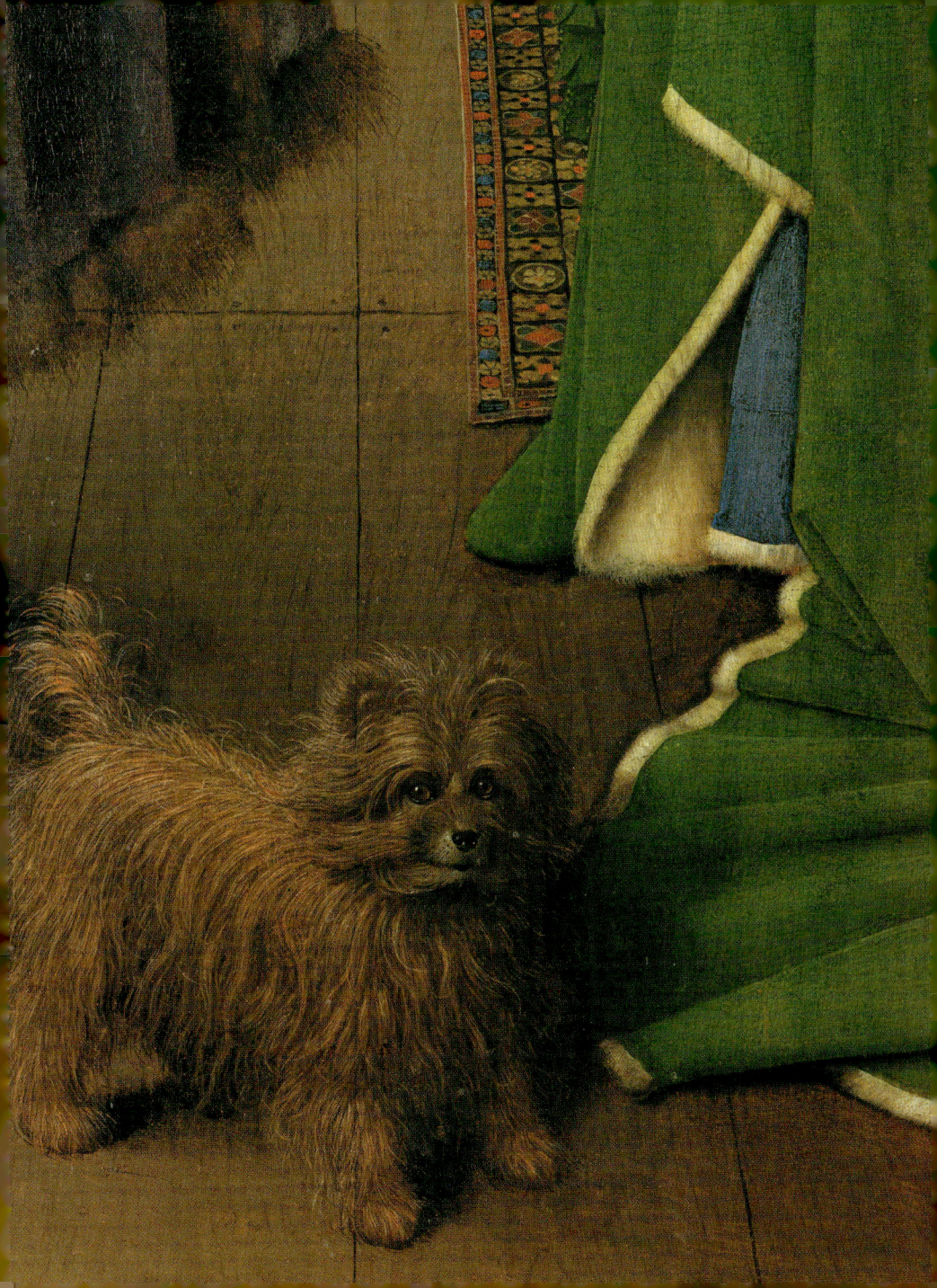

Deer chasing

The oldest and most conservative of all dogs, the greyhound has appealed to artists throughout the centuries, appearing in ancient Greek and Persian art. By the Middle Ages the breed had come to symbolize power, pageantry and majesty. This painting by the Italian artist Pisanello (c. 1394–1455) depicts the vision of St Eustace, a Roman general named Placidus, who converted to Christianity and changed his name after seeing a stag bearing a crucifix between its antlers. Here, in the midst of a lush forest, he sits on his horse before the stag; two greyhounds lead the way, and other dogs surround him. Pisanello has rendered the foliage, the animals' textures and the effects of glowing light in meticulous detail. There is no sky and no horizon. St Eustace is portrayed as a fashionable contemporary huntsman, wearing a golden tunic and blue headdress, and the animals – the stag, hunting dogs and various birds – are depicted in varying sizes to suggest the effects of perspective, all with fur, feathers and expressions delicately rendered. Pisanello was especially famous for his ability to depict animals, as can be seen here in the elegant lines of the greyhound.

GREYHOUND

The greyhound has altered little during the 7,000 years in which the breed has been prized for its speed and kept by humans for hunting, hare coursing and racing. Since their depictions in ancient Egyptian, Assyrian, Greek and Persian art, these dogs have been tall, muscular and smooth-coated, with thin tails, long, powerful legs and deep chests. They are a gentle, quiet and intelligent breed, rarely bark and come in some 30 colour variations, including white, brindle, fawn, tan, black, red and grey. They live well as pets in calm environments and can be trained as service dogs for people with disabilities.

4

PISANELLO
*The Vision of
St Eustace*
1438–42
21½ × 25¾ in
(54.8 × 65.5 cm)
Egg tempera
on wood
The National
Gallery, London,
UK

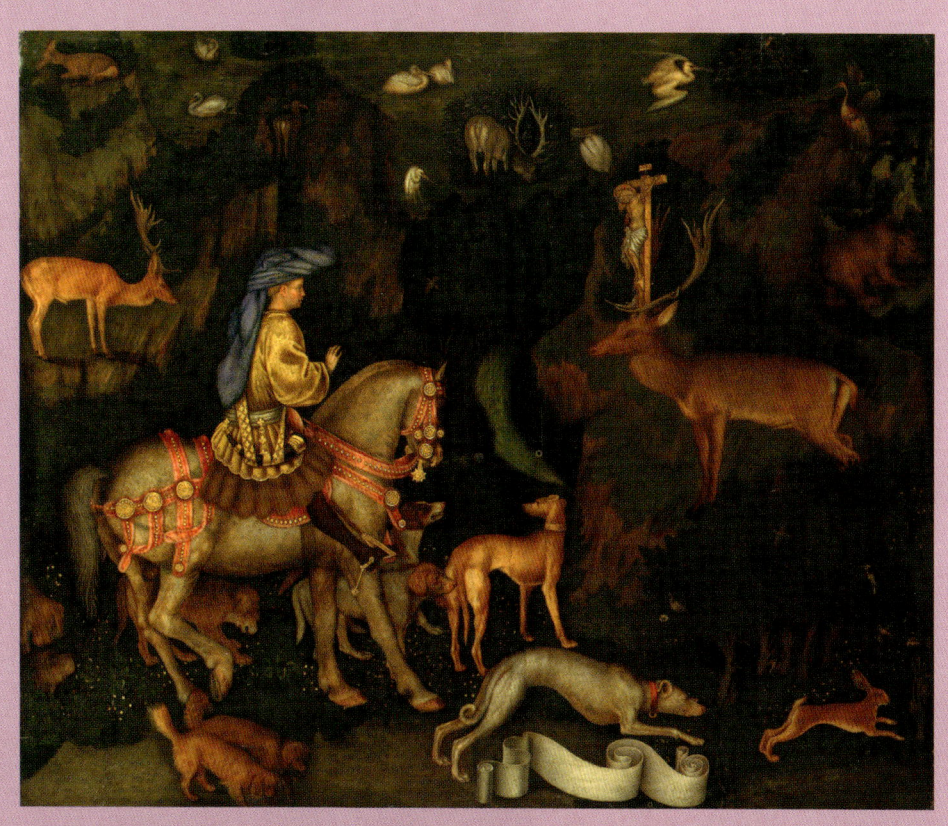

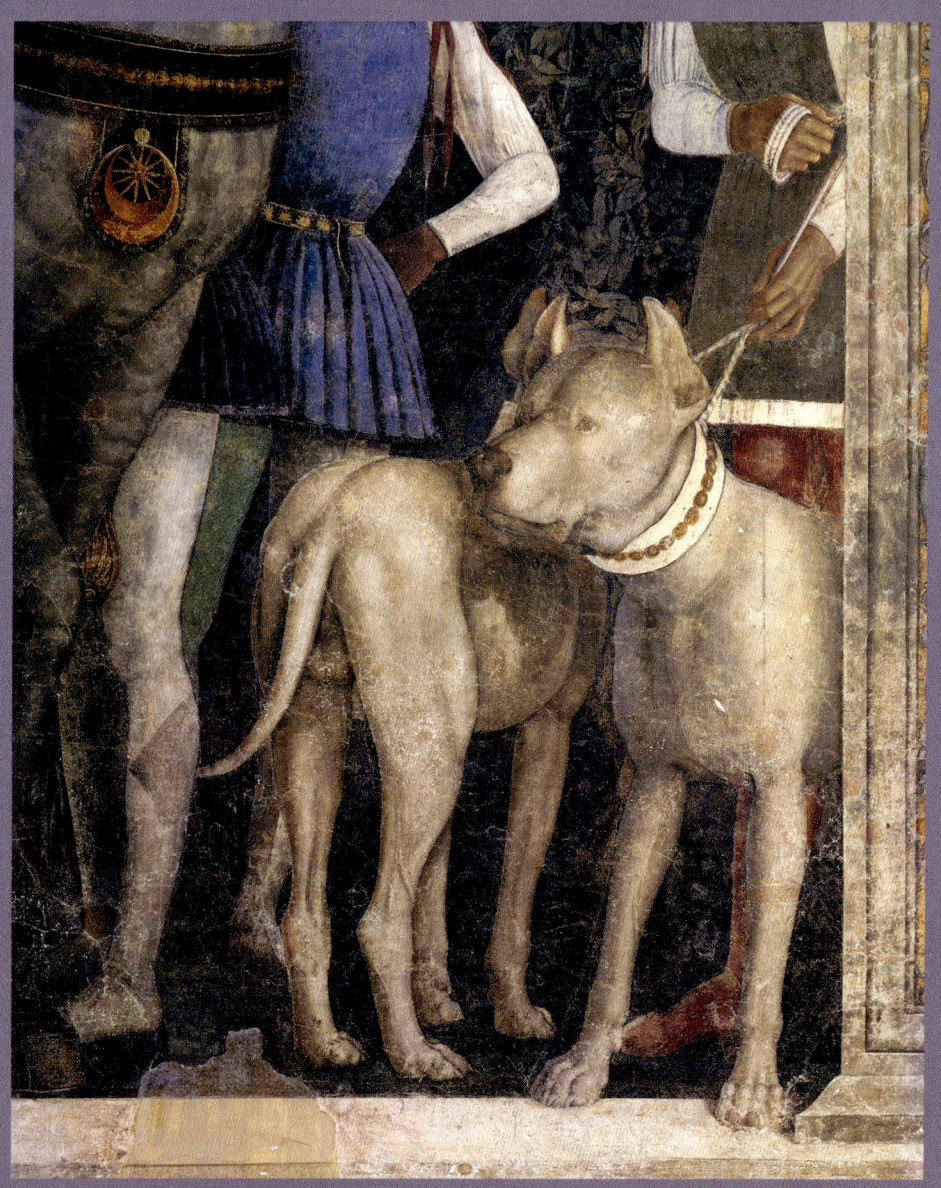

Family portraits

Painted by the Italian artist Andrea Mantegna (c. 1431–1506), these are two of seven dogs depicted in the Camera degli Sposi (Bridal Chamber) or the Camera Picta (Picture Chamber) of the Ducal Palace in Mantua, Italy. Strongly influenced by classical art, Mantegna was a pioneer of spatial illusionism, and his room of frescoes gives the impression of a window opening out into the surrounding landscape. He created a space full of lavish, detailed and colourful portraits of his patrons, the ruling Gonzaga family of Mantua, as well as other significant figures. It was used for several private and semi-private functions, including as a bedchamber for the Marchese Ludovico III Gonzaga (1412–78), as a gathering area for the family and close courtiers, and as a reception room for important guests. Mantegna created detailed, lifelike narratives around the room, including meeting scenes of members of the Gonzaga family and their court, often in front of sweeping, idealized landscapes, plus their pet dogs. The intricate and extensive frescoes took Mantegna seven years to complete. The Gonzagas were known for their horses and dogs, and Mantegna included images of their greyhound, a Spinone, German pointers and two huge, muscular Molossian hounds.

5
ANDREA MANTEGNA
Camera degli Sposi (detail)
1465–74
Fresco
Dimensions unknown
Palazzo Ducale, Mantua, Italy

Overleaf: detail

MOLOSSIAN HOUND

Also known as the Epirus mastiff, this is an extinct breed from ancient Greece. These dogs were kept by the Molossians in the Epirus region and became renowned for their size and ferocity. Frequently mentioned in ancient literature, they are often described as being the breed from which all mastiff-type dogs have descended. One theory has it that the first Molossian hounds arrived in Molossia from Asia, and that the breed was later discovered by the Romans. Another maintains that during his military conquests, Alexander the Great found giant dogs in Asia. He sent some home and they were named in his honour as the son of a Molossian princess.

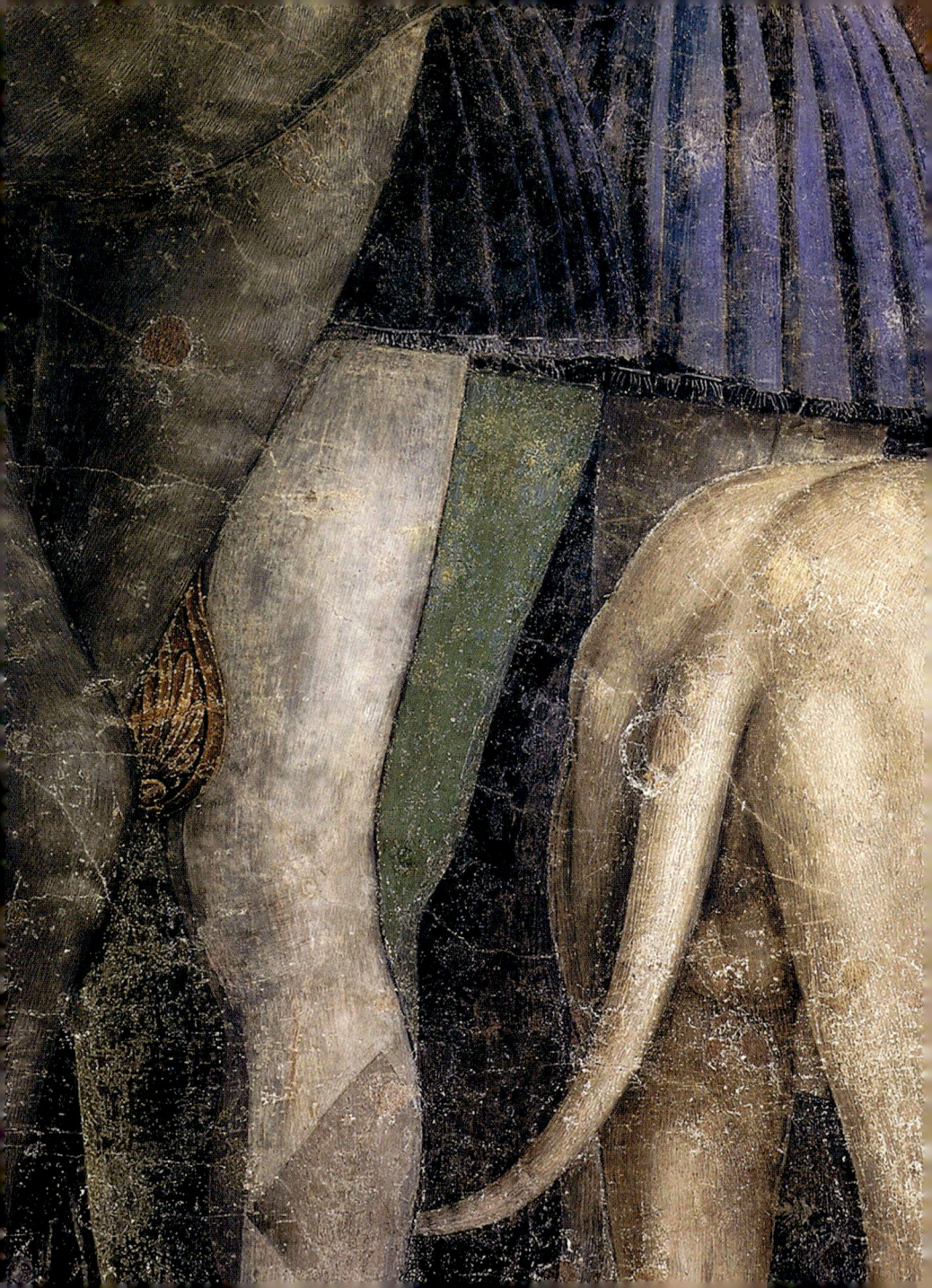

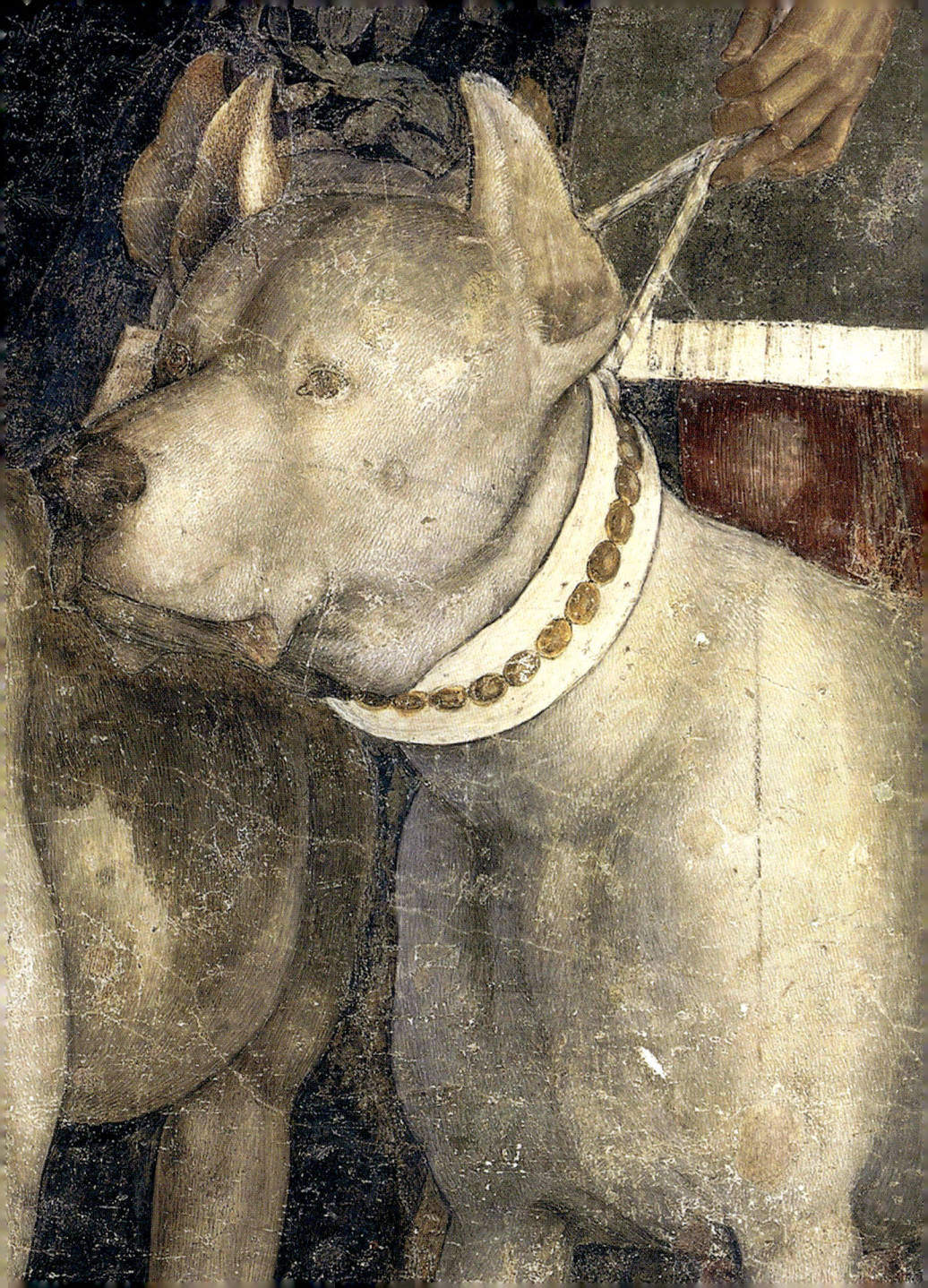

Escape from Egypt

While in Florence from about 1461 or 1462, young Sandro Botticelli (c. 1445–1510) was apprenticed to Fra Filippo Lippi (c. 1406–69), one of the leading painters in the city at the time. Lippi taught Botticelli to create compositions peopled with colourful figures drawn with clear, smooth contours. In 1480 Botticelli and other Florentine artists were summoned to Rome by Pope Sixtus IV (1414–84) to decorate his Sistine Chapel. From the spring of 1481, Botticelli painted a fresco on the chapel walls, conveying parallels between the biblical stories of Moses and Christ, of the Old and the New Testaments. Aided by assistants, Botticelli painted several scenes, and the one shown overleaf depicts many episodes of Moses' youth in one composition. In every scene, Moses can be found through his yellow tunic and green cloak. On the right of the image, he kills an Egyptian who had harassed a Jew. Next, he flees to the desert, and soon afterwards he fights shepherds who were preventing some young women from giving water to their cattle. In the third scene, God tells Moses to return to Egypt and lead his people to freedom. In the queue of people who are following Moses from Egypt there is a blond boy dressed in blue carrying his pet white chihuahua.

6

SANDRO
BOTTICELLI AND
ASSISTANTS
The Trials of Moses
1481–2
Fresco
137¼ × 220 in
(348.5 × 558 cm)
Sistine Chapel,
Vatican City, Italy

Opposite: detail

CHIHUAHUA

The chihuahua's origins are unknown, but some of these dogs were discovered among ruins in the state of chihuahua, Mexico, in the mid-to-late nineteenth century. Some people believe that they are descended from a small dog known as the Techichi, which lived among the Toltec people during the tenth–twelfth centuries. Others suggest that the Chinese Crested Hairless breed is a likely ancestor, which perhaps bred with the Techichi. A further theory is that chihuahuas hail from Malta. This notion is borne out by the white dog in this painting, which was made ten years before Christopher Columbus sailed to the Americas in 1492. chihuahuas are popular miniature dogs with fine short or long coats.

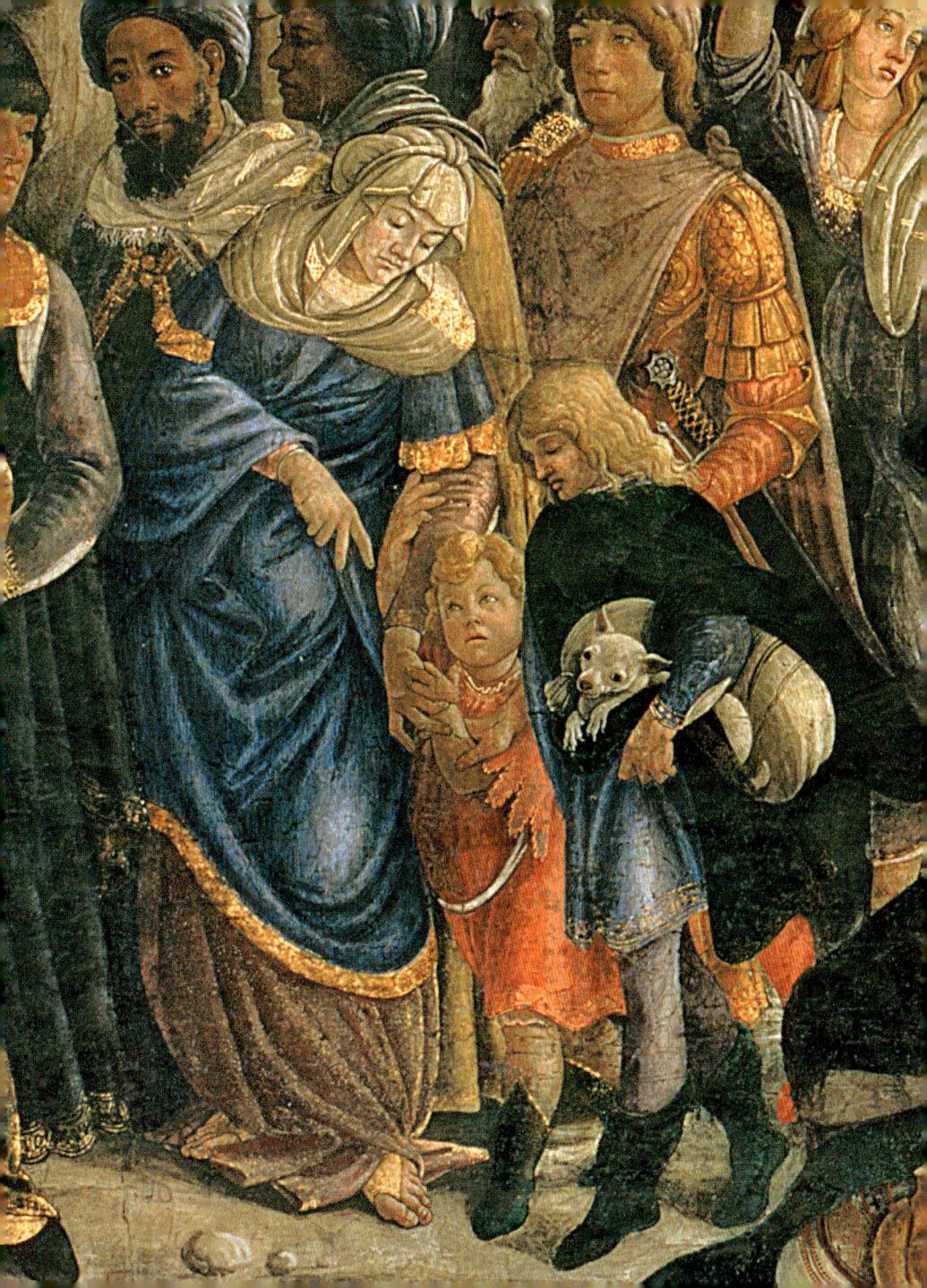

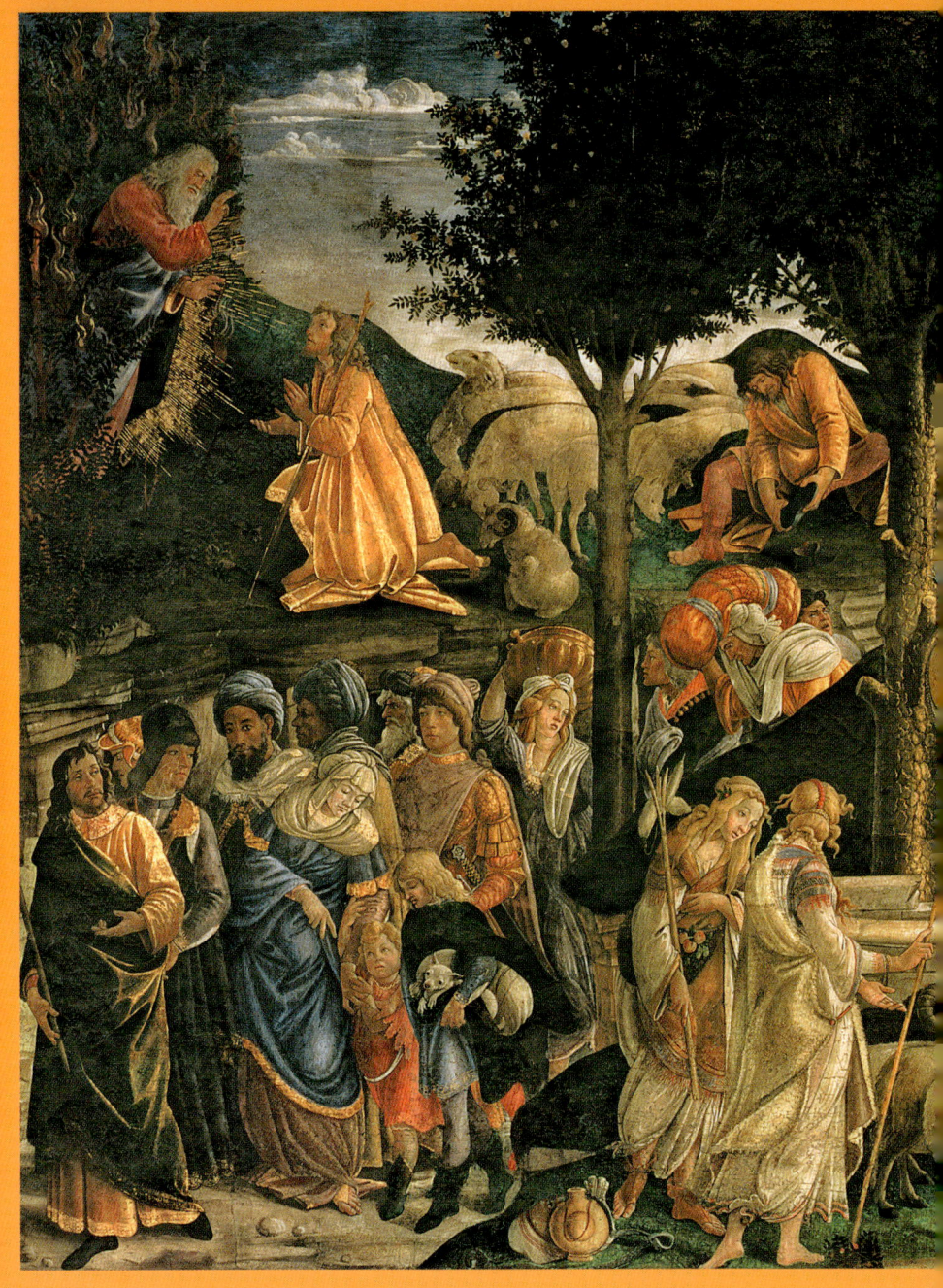

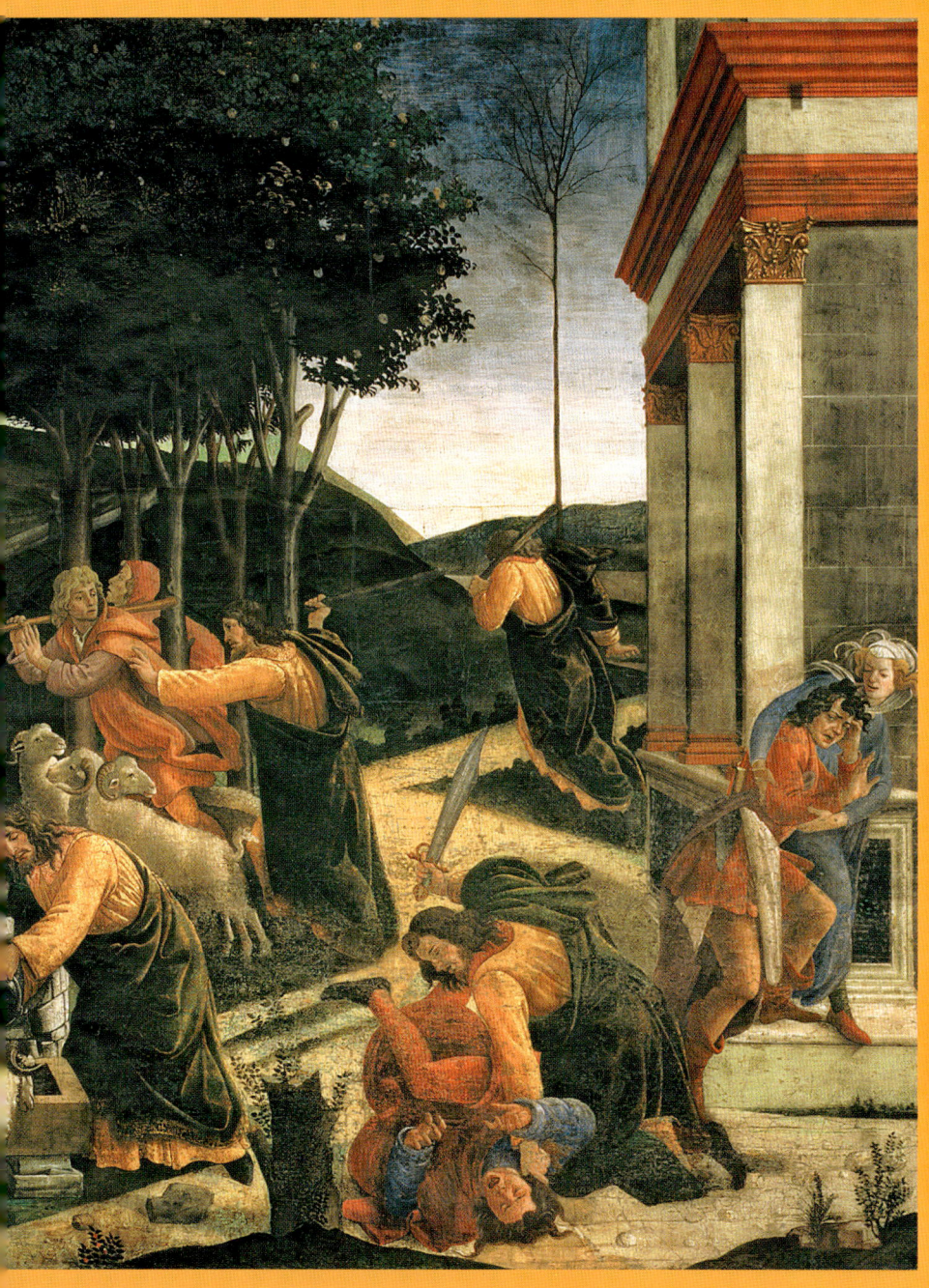

Vanity and lust

The German-Flemish painter Hans Memling (c. 1430–94) lived for a while in the Netherlands and spent time in the Brussels workshop of Rogier van der Weyden (1399/1400–64). In 1465 Memling was made a citizen of Bruges, where he became master of a large and successful workshop. This is a detail of an allegorical painting he created that originally included six panels. A naked woman stands in a northern European landscape looking into a mirror. She is Vanity, and this panel was flanked by two others, representing Death and the Devil. The proximity of a woman embodying earthly pleasure to death and damnation would have impressed upon the viewer the temporality of worldly vanities. She clearly depicts the consequences of pride, conceit and narcissism. With a diadem in her long hair and sandals on her feet, she gazes at her own reflection, flaunting her nakedness. The erotic nature of the image, with her exposed genitals, was rare in fifteenth-century Northern Renaissance art. Also standing for lust, she is the antithesis of the Virgin Mary. To her left is a white griffon, a breed of dog that was often featured in paintings to express the idea of marriage or physical love.

7

HANS MEMLING
Earthly Vanity and Divine Salvation (detail)

c. 1485

Oil on oak panel

7⅞ × 5 in
(20 × 13 cm)

Musée des Beaux-Arts, Strasbourg, France

WIREHAIRED POINTING GRIFFON

The wirehaired pointing griffon, also called the Korthals griffon, has traditionally been used in hunting as a gun dog and has ancestry in northern Europe, probably either Dutch or German. With a large, long head, the medium-sized breed has big eyes, bushy eyebrows, a beard and a brown nose. The neck is long and the body muscular. Its wire-haired coat makes it particularly well adapted for hunting in thick undergrowth and around water. Most dogs of this breed are grey with brown markings, but they can sometimes be chestnut brown, white and brown, white and orange, or all white, as seen here. These dogs are generally intelligent, energetic and loyal.

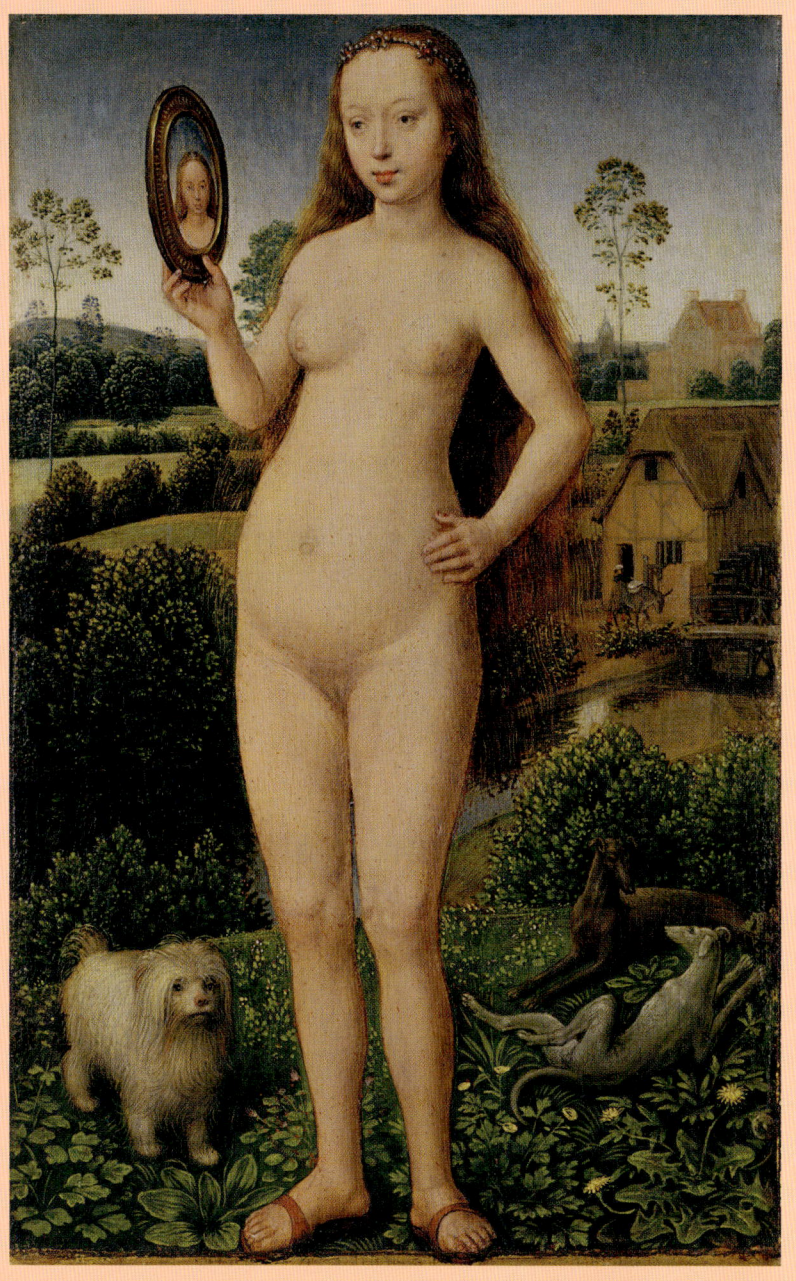

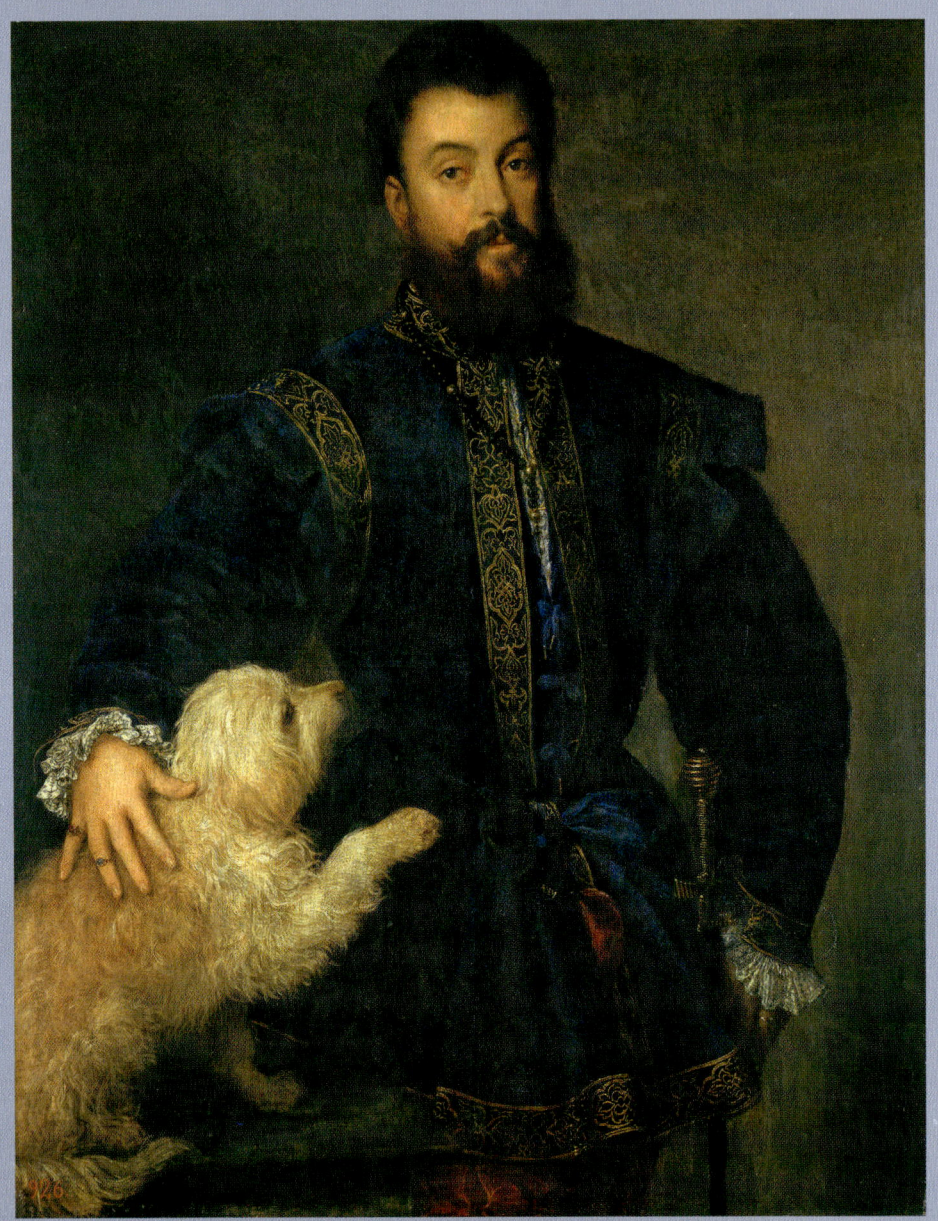

Loyalty
in marriage

In sixteenth-century Venice, images of dogs began appearing in many portraits, usually as symbols of loyalty or status, and from about 1530 they were included increasingly in the paintings of the Venetian artist Titian (1488/90–1576). At that time, owning certain breeds of dog communicated social standing, and this portrait of the Mantuan ruler Federico II Gonzaga (1500–40) shows that prestige, as well as his affection for his Maltese dog. The dog also symbolizes fidelity and loyalty – to the people whom Federico ruled and to the heiress he would soon marry. In red hose and a gold-embroidered doublet of blue velvet, Federico also wears a costly rosary of gold and lapis lazuli. He rests his left hand on his sword, while his right hand, adorned with rings, caresses his pet dog, which leans towards him affectionately. Federico was known for his love of animals, and his family was renowned for breeding Bolognese dogs. This portrait portrays him as affectionate, dignified and aristocratic, while his faithful Maltese suggests loyalty and devotion; overall, the image conveys the enduring bond between humans and their canine companions.

8

TITIAN

Portrait of Federico II Gonzaga

c. 1529

Oil on canvas

49 × 39 in
(125 × 99 cm)

Museo Nacional del Prado, Madrid, Spain

Overleaf: detail

MALTESE

Generally associated with the island of Malta, Maltese dogs might descend from spitz-type canines or from Pomeranians, and are genetically related to the Bichon, Bolognese and Havanese breeds. This ancient breed has been kept as household pets since antiquity, being depicted on Greek amphorae dating from c. 500 BCE and referred to in ancient Greek and Roman literature. Rather than working dogs, these were always family companions, kept for their affectionate, docile characters, their constancy and their endearing personalities. They have drooping ears and curving tails, and their silky white fur does not shed.

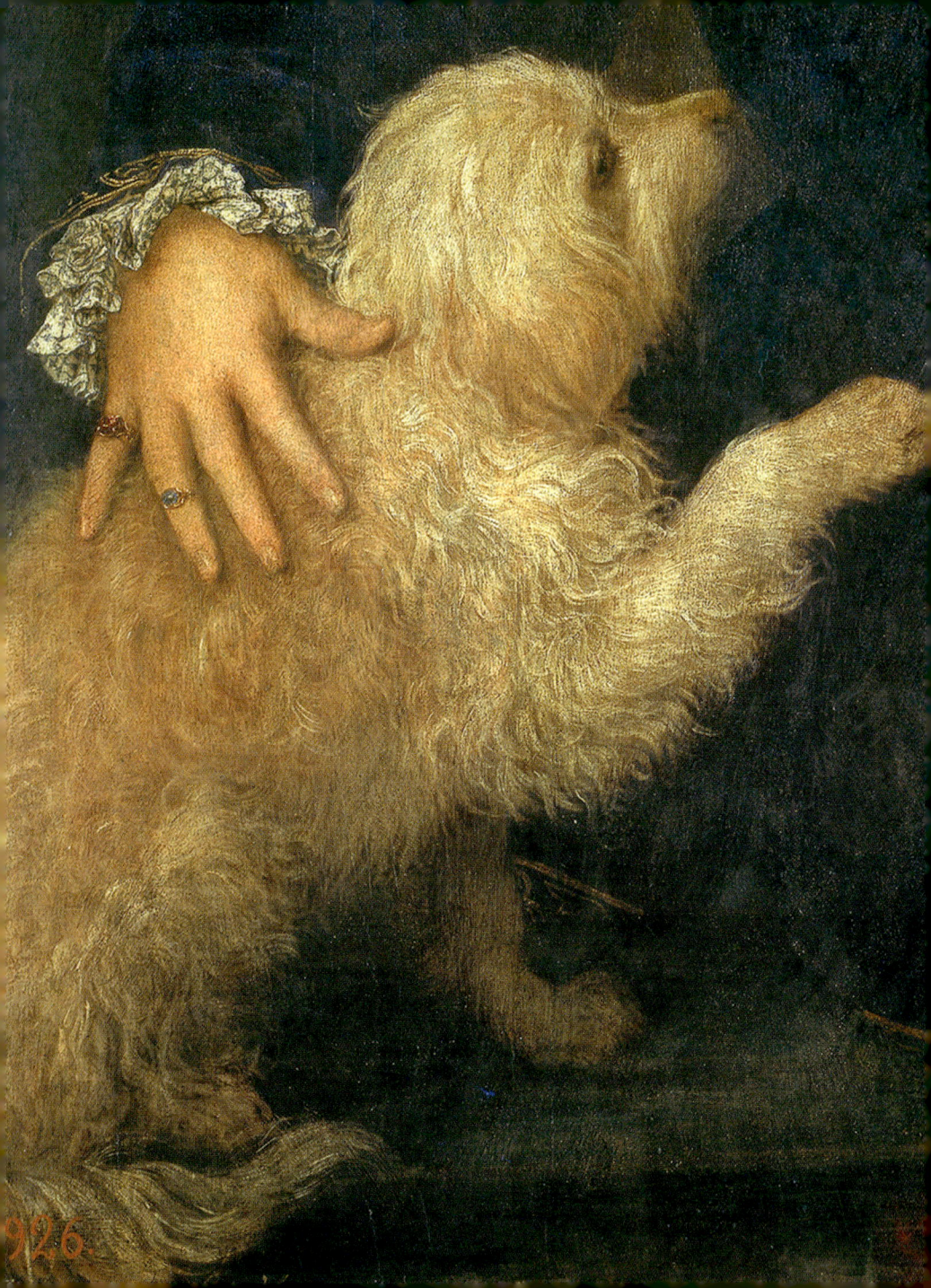

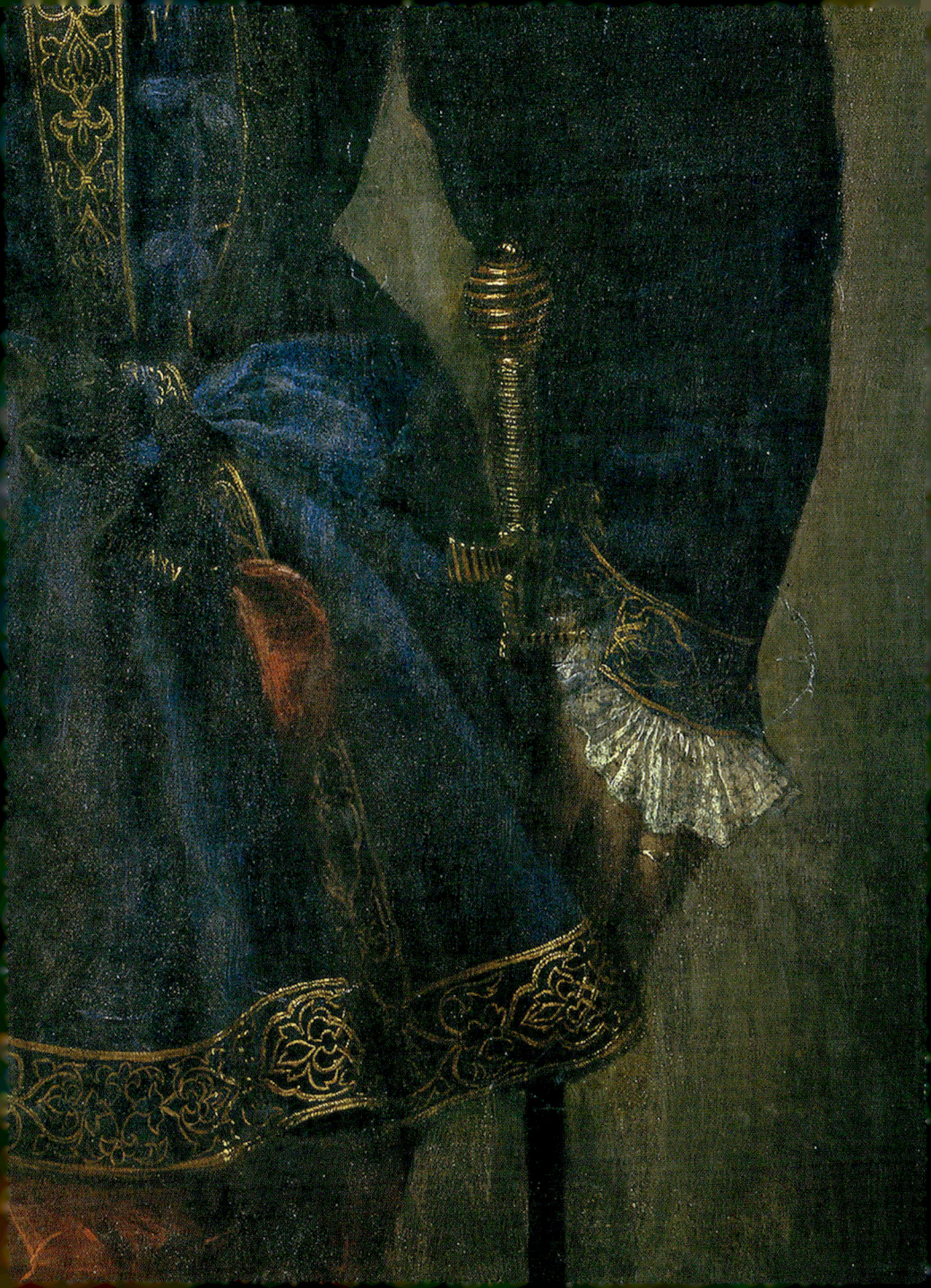

Fidelity and purity

Jacopo Bassano (*c.* 1510–92) was trained by his father, Francesco (*c.* 1475–1539), in his workshop near Venice, then in Venice itself by Bonifacio Veronese (1487–1553). Uniquely, Bassano incorporated influences of several other artists, including Albrecht Dürer (1471–1528), Parmigianino (1503–40), Tintoretto (*c.* 1518–94) and Raphael (1483–1520), having studied some of their art in prints. As a result, he developed a realistic and expressive style, and this was one of the first portraits of dogs in Western art. Paintings of dogs for themselves – not simply as appendages for humans – became popular after it. The two Italian pointers were owned either by Bassano himself or by the patrician, diplomat and philanthropist Antonio Zentani or Zantani (dates unknown), who commissioned the work and whose emblem was a dog tethered to a tree. Soon after Bassano painted this lifelike work, Tintoretto replicated one of the dogs in his huge painting *Christ Washing the Disciples' Feet* (1548–9). Bassano's work, however, focuses solely on the two dogs tied to a tree stump. Using a limited palette, he presents the dogs in lifelike style, capturing their personalities and conveying the animals as symbols of faithfulness and purity. He renders the effect of their soft fur with small, short brushstrokes.

9
JACOPO BASSANO
Two Hunters Tied to a Tree
1548–9
Oil on canvas
24 × 31⅓ in
(61 × 80 cm)
Musée du Louvre, Paris, France

BURGOS POINTER

Also called the Burgalese or Spanish pointer, this breed of dog is native to Spain and originated in Castile, in the province of Burgos, in the sixteenth century. A large and robust dog, it has traditionally been used for hunting small animals, such as rabbits, hares and birds. With its physical endurance and speed, the Burgos pointer can run on almost any terrain. These intelligent, alert dogs learn quickly, and live better in the country than in urban environments. They have long, silky ears, short, smooth fur and two main colour variations: brown with brown patterning, and brown with white spots.

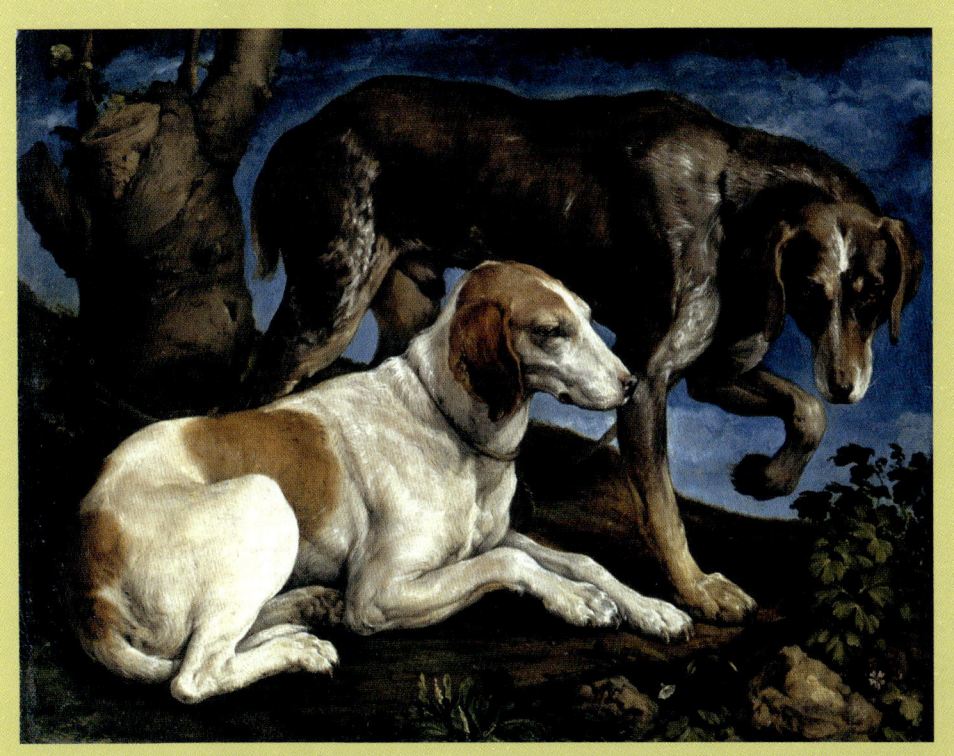

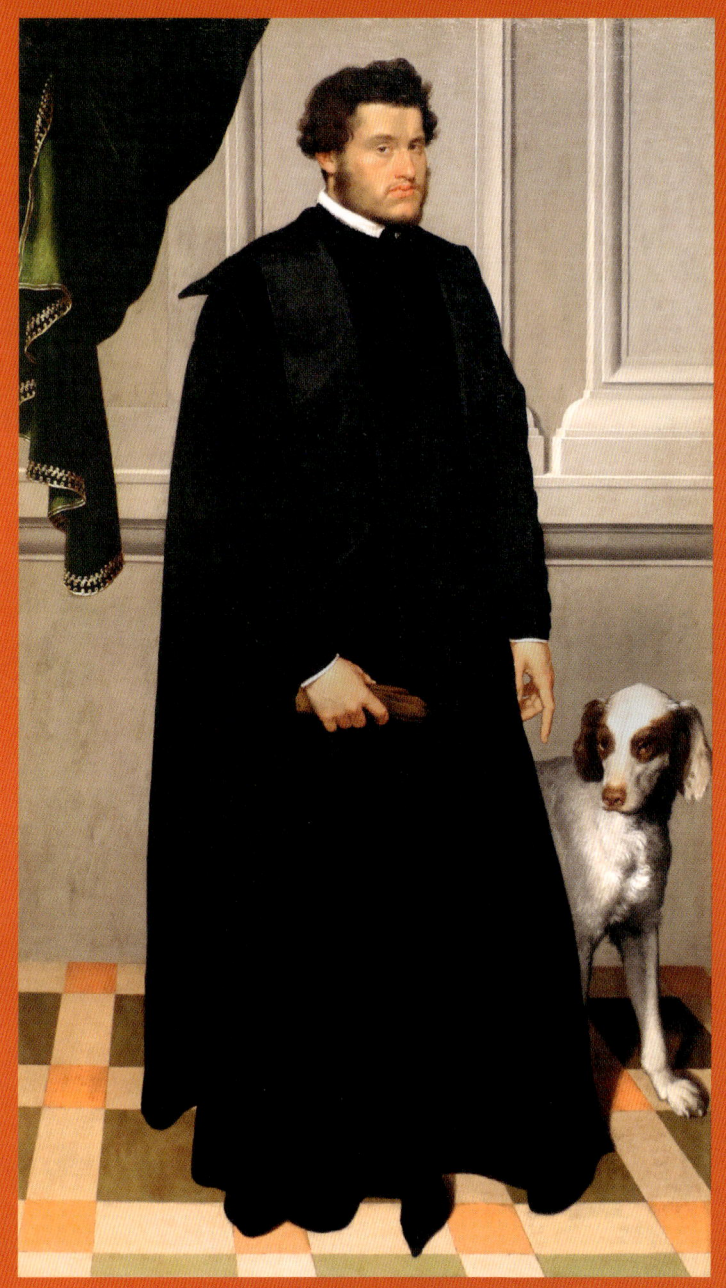

Honourable and compassionate

The son of an architect, Giovanni Battista Moroni (1520/24–78) trained under Alessandro Bonvicino, known as Moretto (c. 1498–1554), in Brescia. Moroni worked in Trento, Bergamo and his home town of Albino in northern Italy. He was in Trento at the same time as the first two sessions of the Council of Trent, 1545–7 and 1551–2, which heralded the Baroque style of art. While there, he painted portraits of the Madruzzo brothers, who were high-ranking Italian-German ecclesiasts. This is Giovanni Ludovico Madruzzo (1532–1600), who succeeded his uncle as prince bishop of Trent and became a cardinal in 1561. In 1559 he performed the funeral oration for Charles V, the Holy Roman Emperor, so this was one of the most prestigious commissions of Moroni's early career. His portraits of the two brothers were created to hang alongside a portrait by Titian of the young men's uncle Cardinal Cristoforo Madruzzo (1512–78). Moroni portrays his sitter with a dignified presence, wearing opulent clothing, including a fur-trimmed robe. The small, caramel-brown-and-white long-haired spaniel with dark eyes sitting near his feet adds a sense of humanity and reality to the stately image. This portrait is a testament to Moroni's skill in capturing both the external appearance and the inner character of his subjects.

10
GIOVANNI
BATTISTA
MORONI
Gian Lodovico Madruzzo
1551–2
Oil on canvas
78⅝ × 45⅝ in
(199.8 × 116 cm)
The Art Institute
of Chicago, USA

SPRINGER SPANIEL

The origins of the English springer spaniel can be traced back to Spain, and the term "spaniel" is believed to be derived from *Español* (Spanish). These dogs were popular in Europe during the sixteenth century, being valued highly for their ability to work closely with hunters, springing game from the brush or retrieving it from water. Springer spaniels are athletic and easy to train, with a keen sense of smell. Of medium size, they have fairly long, silky fur, with feathering on the legs and tail. The particular dog illustrated here has unusual and striking markings, its ears resembling silky wings, its eyes deep and soft, its nose brownish-pink.

A hardy hunter

In a snowy landscape, a small group of hunters return to the village with their pack of dogs. It is deep midwinter, and humans and hounds alike look dejected and weary. A single dead fox dangles from a spear held by one of the men, indicating that their hunt has not been very successful. The painting was originally part of a series depicting seasonal times of the year, commissioned by the wealthy Antwerp banker Niclaes Jonghelinck. These paintings boosted the reputation of Pieter Bruegel the Elder (*c.* 1525–69), who became one of the most significant artists of the Northern Renaissance. In the image, the hunters and their dogs pass a group of villagers. Distant skaters can be seen on frozen lakes. There are possibly three types of dog here, including at the upper right three long-bodied, short-haired dogs that might be greyhounds. The upper left dog with the coarse coat is probably a lurcher. The taller, heavier-built deep brown dog partly hidden behind a tree may also be a lurcher, while the shorter, flop-eared dogs are scent hounds. Overall, this painting – which was created during the Protestant Revolution – conveys the powerlessness of humans against nature.

11
PIETER BRUEGEL THE ELDER
Hunters in the Snow
1565
Oil on wood
46 × 63¾ in
(116.5 × 162 cm)
Kunsthistorisches Museum, Vienna, Austria

Opposite: detail

LURCHER

Slim, athletic and graceful, lurchers are usually short-haired, with long legs and necks, and small ears. They were originally bred in England in the fourteenth or fifteenth century to aid poachers, and are a cross between a sighthound and another kind of breed, either a pastoral guard dog or a terrier. They became known as "poacher dogs", but over the centuries, as well as hunting, they have been used for racing and, more recently, as loyal and affectionate family pets. Lurchers, which can be small or large, have speed, intelligence, stamina and courage.

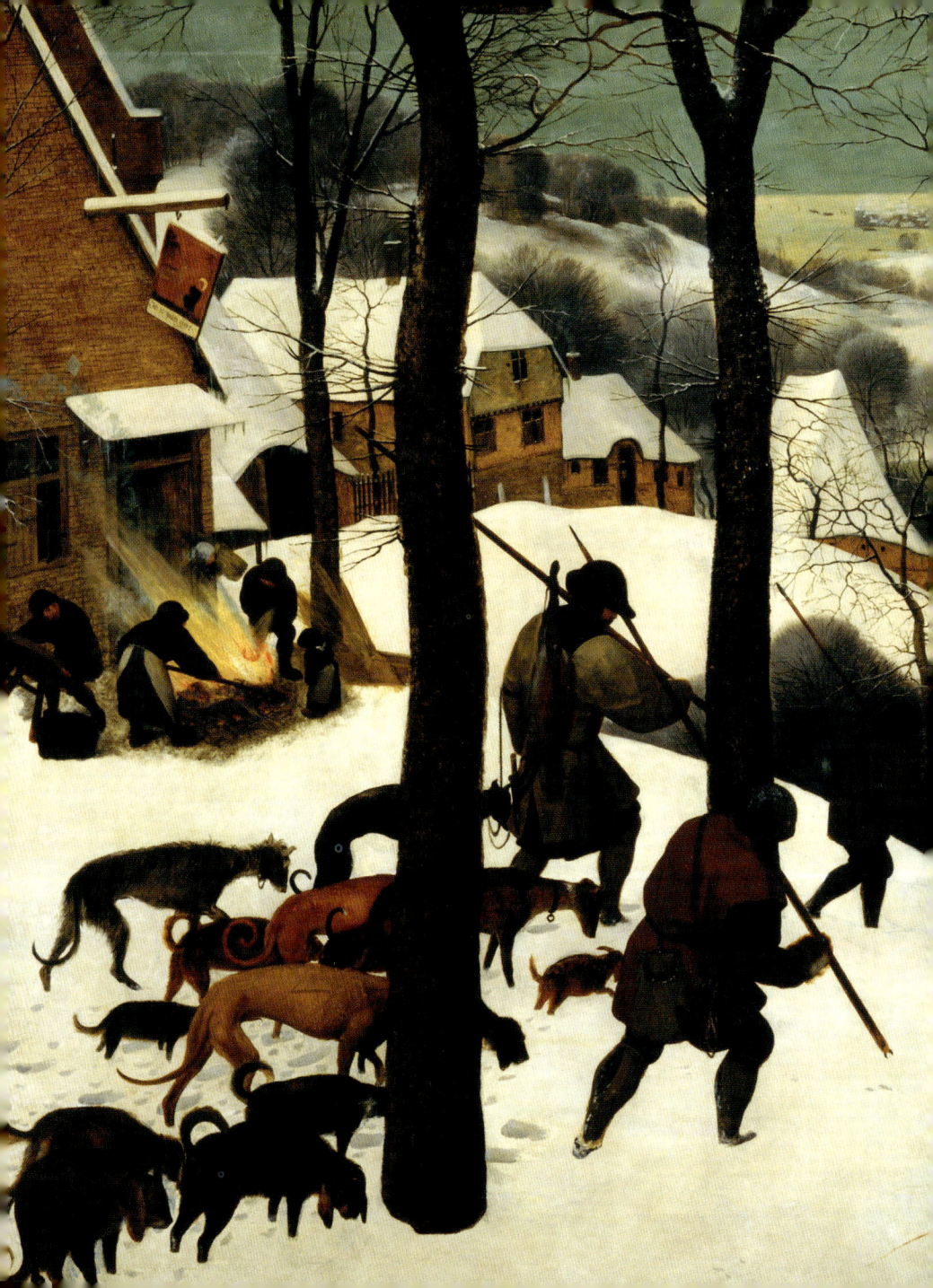

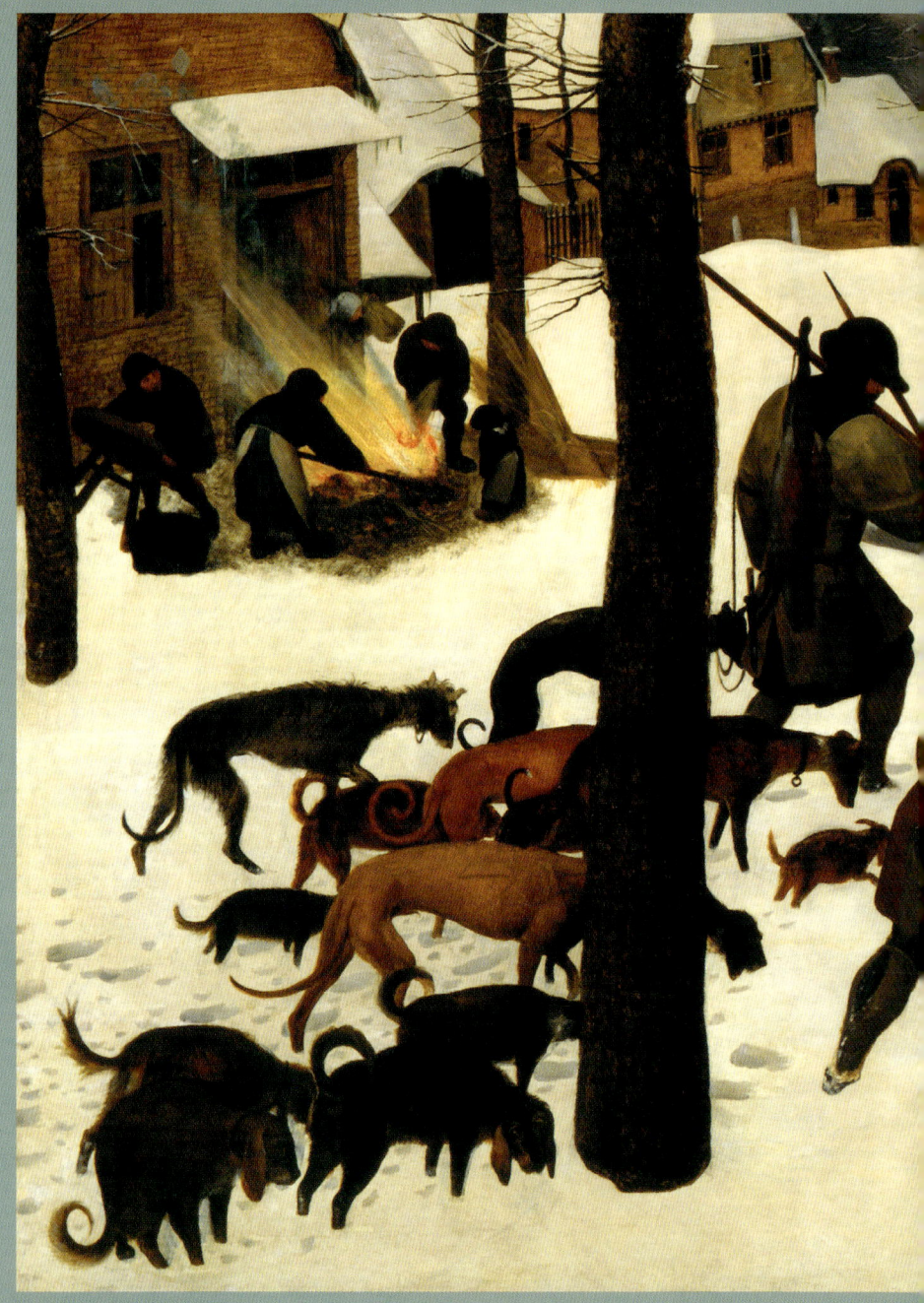

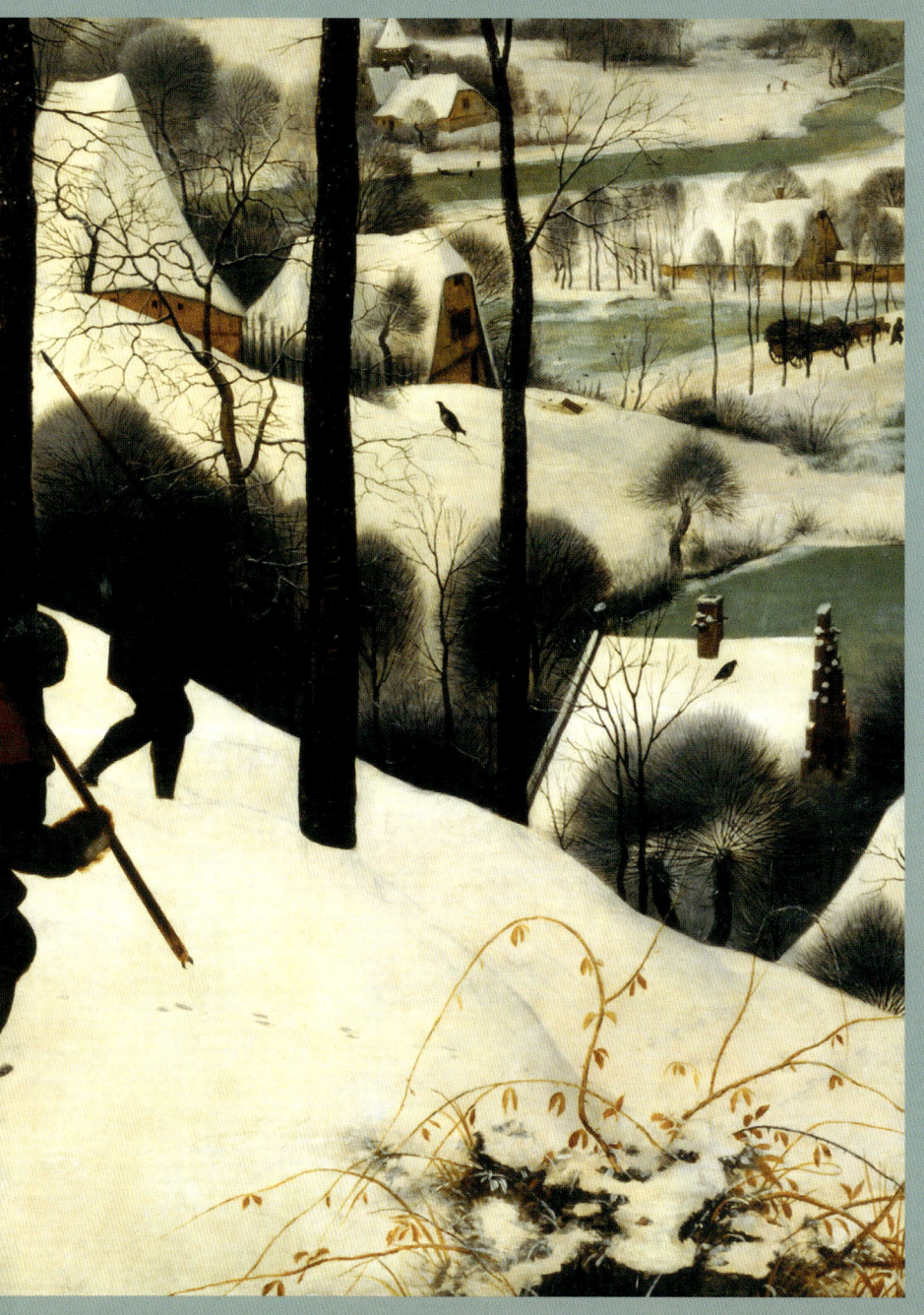

A sense of reality

Achild prodigy, Paolo Veronese (1528–88) became one of the
most famous artists of the late Renaissance. Although he was
born in Verona, he moved to Venice in the early 1550s and stayed
there for the rest of his life, becoming one of the leading painters of
the Venetian School. He became particularly known as a colourist
and painter of lavish scenes, which he expressed with elegance,
drama, unusual lighting effects and vivid colourization. This late
painting is less flamboyant than many of his earlier works, but it still
conveys a lively sense of reality. A small, plump Cupid holds on to
two Italian Spinone dogs, the naked, mischievous-looking god a foil
to the natural-looking hounds. As usual with Veronese's paintings,
this one features an incredible level of visual and psychological
realism, created with fine brushstrokes and emphasized with
a delicate use of chiaroscuro (light and shade). The dogs' markings,
fur and facial expressions are rendered exceptionally sensitively. By
the time Veronese made this work, he was successful, his patrons
were among the most powerful in Europe, and he had established
a large workshop with his sons Gabriele and Carlo (or "Carletto"), and
his brother Benedetto.

12

PAOLO
VERONESE
*Cupid with
Two Dogs*
c. 1581
Oil on canvas
39⅓ × 52¾ in
(100 × 134 cm)
Alte Pinakothek,
Munich, Germany

ITALIAN SPINONE

An Italian breed of hunting dog traditionally used for tracking,
pointing and retrieving game, the Spinone is a strong, solidly built
dog with a square, muscular frame, so it is suitable for hunting
over any kind of ground. These dogs are also good swimmers.
Their slightly wavy coats are rough and thick, and about 1½–2½ in
(4–6 cm) long, marginally shorter on the head, the feet and the front
of the legs. Hair on the eyebrows and around the mouth is longer
and stiffer, creating the appearance of a moustache and beard.
Most Spinone are white, white with orange or brown markings,
or variegated brown or orange.

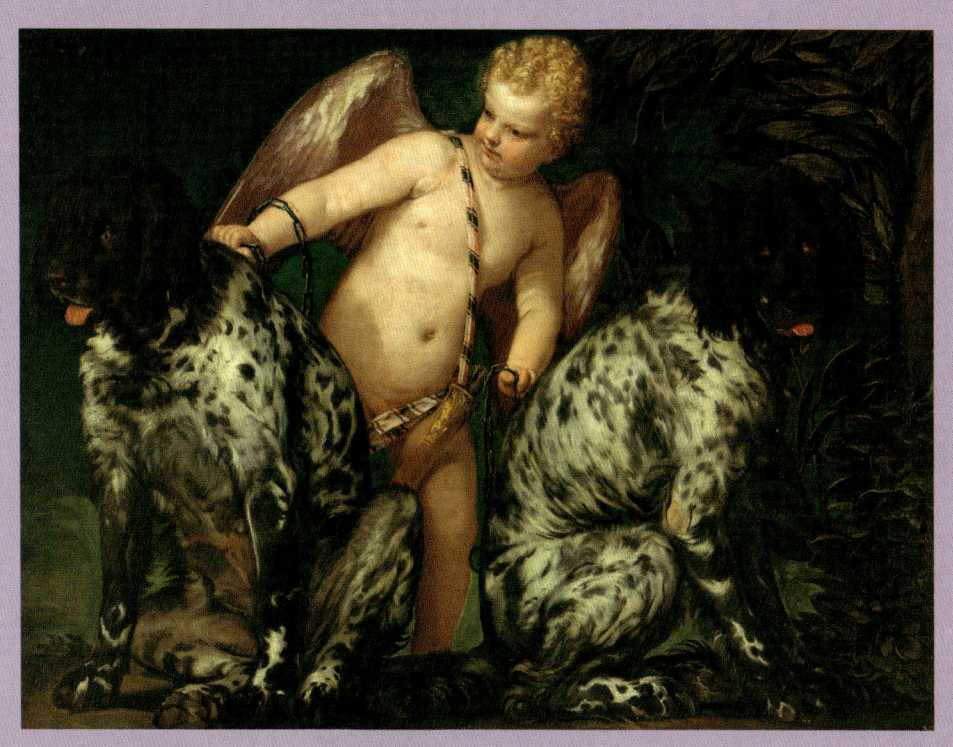

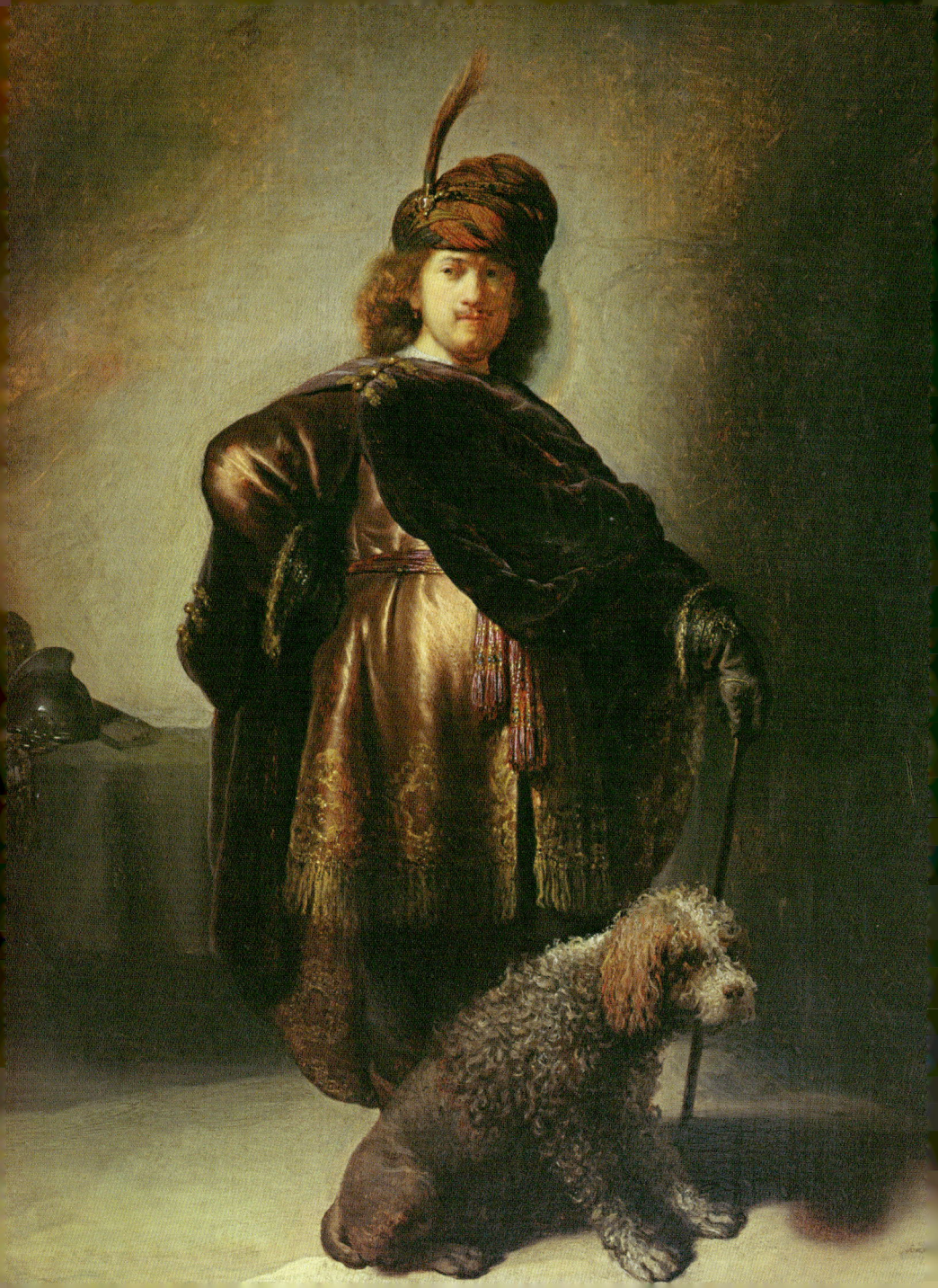

Camouflage

13
REMBRANDT
VAN RIJN
*Self-portrait in
Oriental Attire*
1631
Oil on wooden
panel
24⅞ × 22 in
(63 × 56 cm)
Petit Palais, Paris,
France

Rembrandt van Rijn (1609–69), one of history's most innovative artists, was born in Leiden, the Netherlands, and his talent was nurtured from an early age. He experienced fluctuating fortunes, popularity and obscurity, wealth and poverty over the course of his life, but remained true to his innovative approach, employing a wide range of materials and techniques. Using chiaroscuro and visible brush marks to create powerful and natural-looking effects of light, texture and emotion, he created many portraits, self-portraits, landscapes, and historical, biblical and mythological scenes. He became renowned for his ability to capture lifelike appearances while portraying feelings, imperfections and morality, and he painted an unprecedented number of self-portraits (nearly 80), effectively psychological studies of himself as he aged. This is one of several that he produced in costume. Depicted without vanity, it is the only self-portrait that shows him standing. X-rays have revealed that he altered his hair and shortened his legs as he worked on the painting. Two years later he painted a curly-haired poodle over his feet and legs. His Asian costume, which he used for other works depicting biblical scenes, includes a turban with a feathered aigrette, a velvet cloak buttoned at one shoulder, and a short silk tunic with golden brocade and fringing, tied by a sash at the waist.

POODLE

Their origins are not confirmed, but poodles have been bred across Europe since the Middle Ages and used as water dogs to retrieve game and fowl from rivers and lakes. Indeed, their name is thought to derive from a word of Old German extraction, *pudeln*, which translates roughly as "to splash in water". Poodles soon became desirable pets for the aristocracy, as well. Larger than the miniature and toy versions, the dog depicted here is a standard poodle. With their curly hair and solid colours of brown, white or black, poodles are one of the most intelligent breeds in the world, highly trainable, but requiring physical and mental stimulation.

Children's best friend

One of the most important Flemish painters of the seventeenth century, Anthony van Dyck (1599–1641) was extremely successful as a portraitist and a painter of religious and mythological images in Antwerp and Italy, but is now best remembered for his paintings of the English king Charles I and his court. Van Dyck was particularly accomplished at painting dogs, and his works featuring children and dogs helped to elevate these subjects to the same level of artistic regard as adult sitters. His confident, sympathetic paintings set a new standard for English portraiture, and here he conveys the status of his royal subjects, their youth and the characters of their pets, breaking with earlier, more rigid traditions of portraiture. The five children shown here are, from left to right: Princess Mary (later Princess of Orange and mother of William III); James, Duke of York (later James II); Prince Charles (later Charles II); Princess Elizabeth; and Princess Anne in her sister's lap. Prince Charles rests his hand on the head of an enormous mastiff, which sits comfortably amid the royal children, appearing as their pet and protector at a time of civil unrest. A smaller dog, a King Charles spaniel, curls up on the right.

14
ANTHONY VAN DYCK
The Five Eldest Children of Charles I
1637
Oil on canvas
64¼ × 78¼ in (163.2 × 198.8 cm)
Royal Collection Trust, London, UK

Overleaf: detail

ENGLISH MASTIFF

Often called gentle giants, English mastiffs, with their square heads and broad skulls, are even larger than Spanish mastiffs. These ancient, short-coated dogs were used as guard dogs in the fifteenth century. Typically with a black mask, they are coloured fawn, apricot or brindle, and their wrinkled faces and droopy jowls give them a slightly comic appearance. Known for their immense power and strength, and for their intense devotion to their beloved companions, they are calm and loyal, valued for their gentle, loving, easy-going personality. Thanks to these characteristics, English mastiffs are often used as therapy dogs.

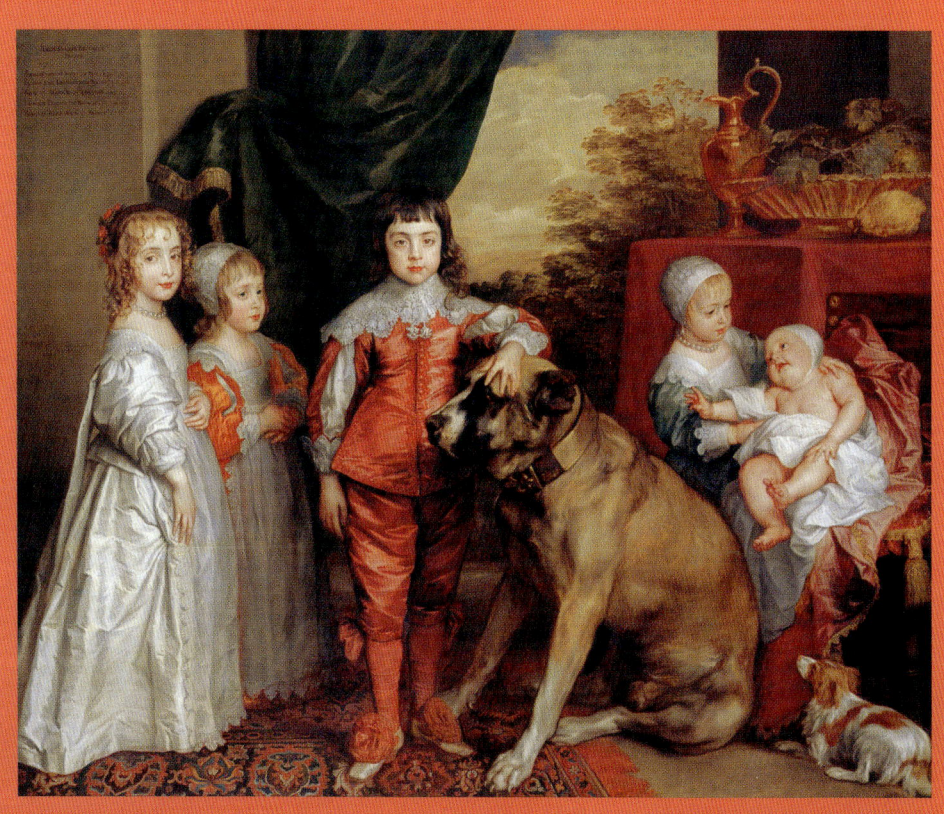

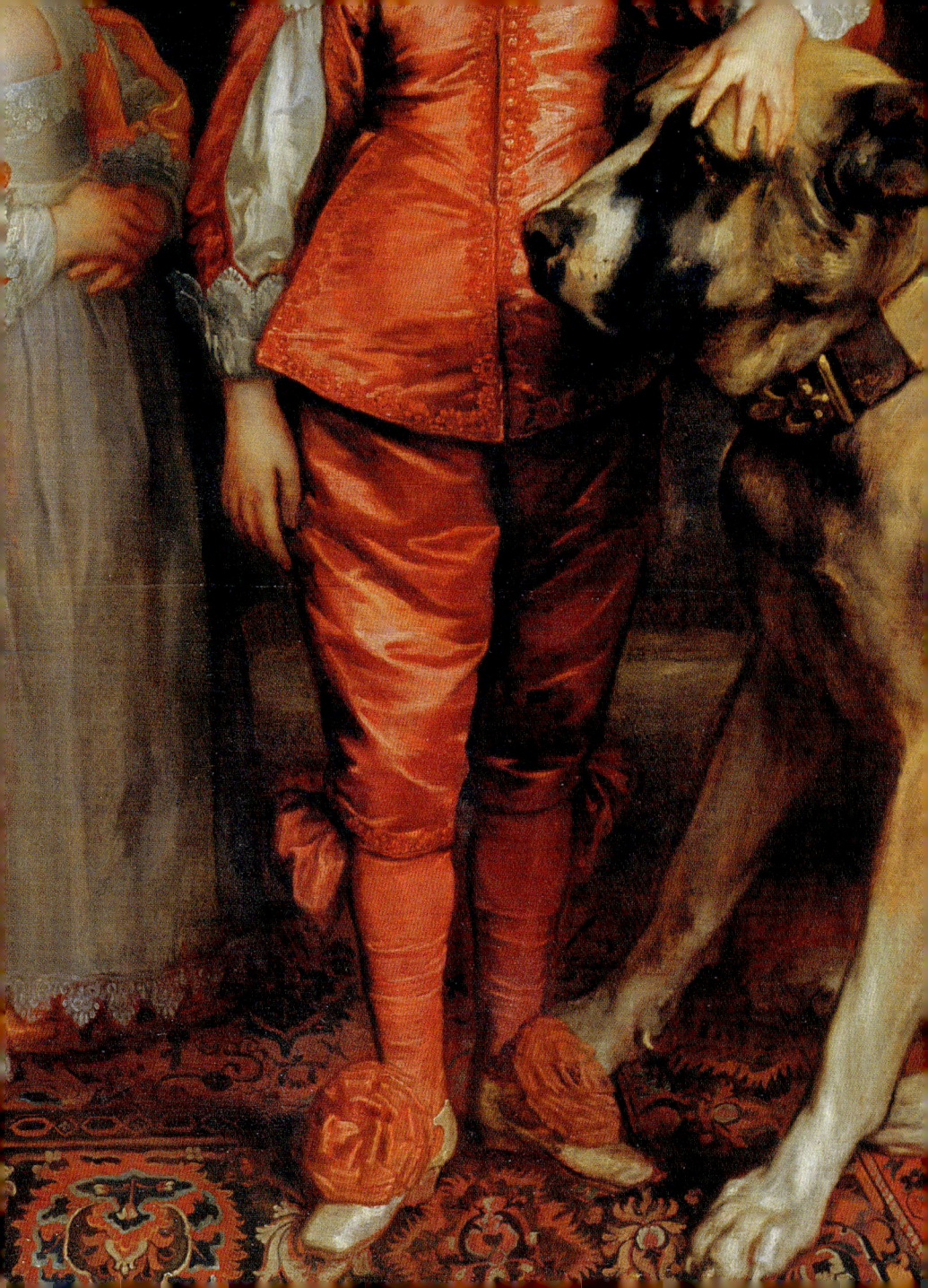

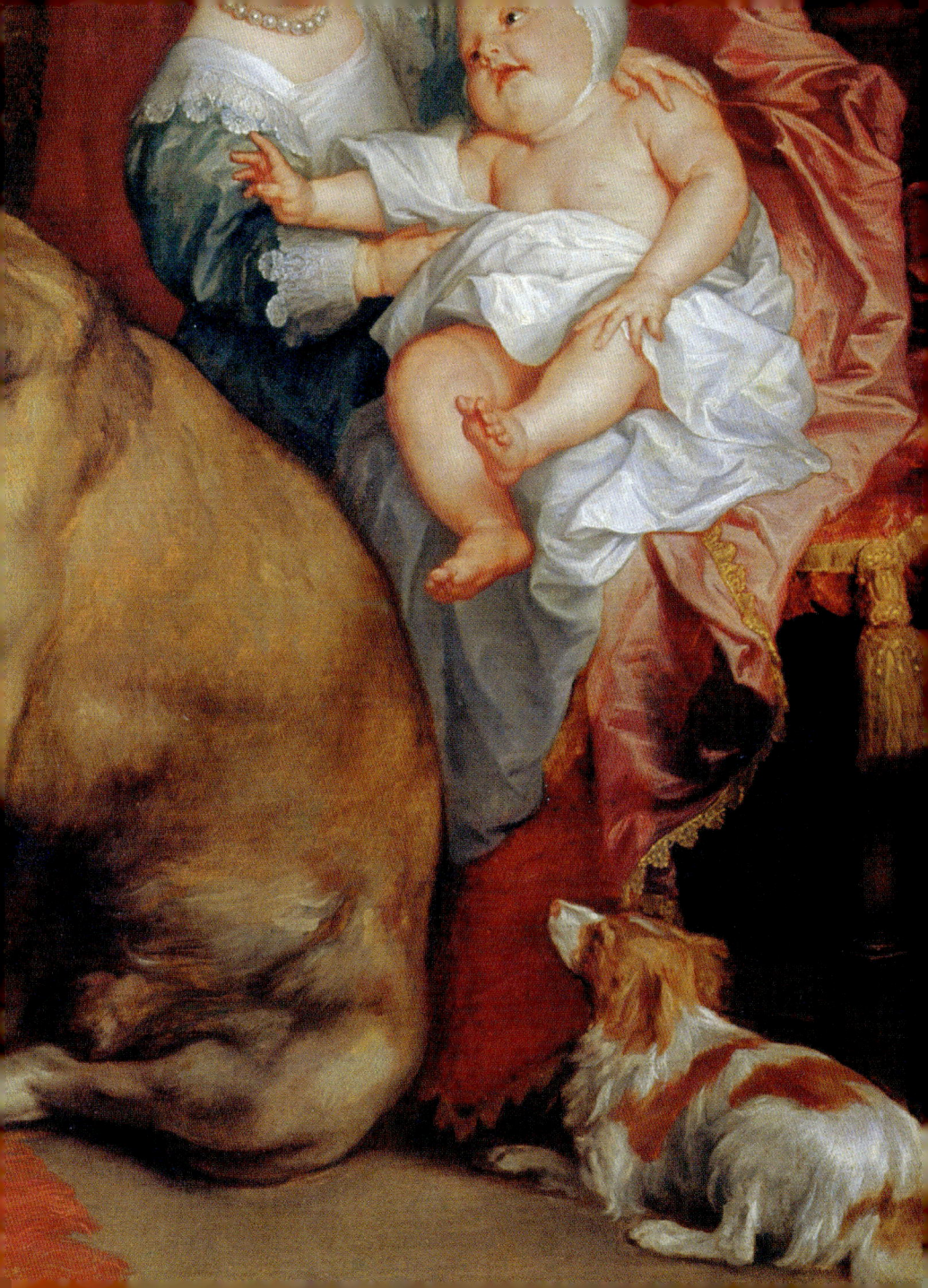

As small as a teacup

A tiny lapdog with large brown eyes sits on a pink tablecloth, close to some Italian biscotti and a Chinese porcelain cup, each of which serves to prove just how small the dog really is. The portrait also emphasizes the dog's docile nature and the way it can evidently be trusted not to eat the biscuits. Two flies have settled on them, displaying the artist's incredible observational skill. The Italian Baroque painter Giovanna Garzoni (1600–70) was admired for her miniatures and paintings of plants, vegetables and animals, religious, mythological and allegorical subjects, and for her portraits. Born in the Marche region of Italy, Garzoni travelled and worked all around the country (in Venice, Naples, Turin, Florence and Rome) and in England and Paris, for various courts and nobles, including King Charles I and the powerful Medici and Rovere families. She painted this miniature for the Grand Duchess of Tuscany, Vittoria della Rovere. At the time, lapdogs were especially prized and often given as diplomatic gifts, although they were associated mainly with women and children. Garzoni's remarkable attention to detail is evident here in the precise rendering of the dog's hair and the realism of the flies and cup.

15
GIOVANNA
GARZONI
*Lapdog with
Biscotti and
a Chinese Cup*
c. 1648
Tempera on
parchment
10⅞ × 15½ in
(27.3 × 39¼ cm)
Gallerie degli
Uffizi, Florence,
Italy

ENGLISH TOY SPANIEL

A small, gentle and affectionate dog breed, with a long, silky coat, large, dark eyes, and long, floppy ears, the English toy spaniel (also called the King Charles spaniel) is quieter and more reclusive than the King Charles Cavalier, although they look similar. Having originated in eastern Asia, toy spaniels were first seen in Europe during the sixteenth century and were made famous by a later association with King Charles II. These dogs have domed heads and flat faces, and were first used as hunting dogs, although they have little stamina – even though they are moderately active – so are best suited as lapdogs.

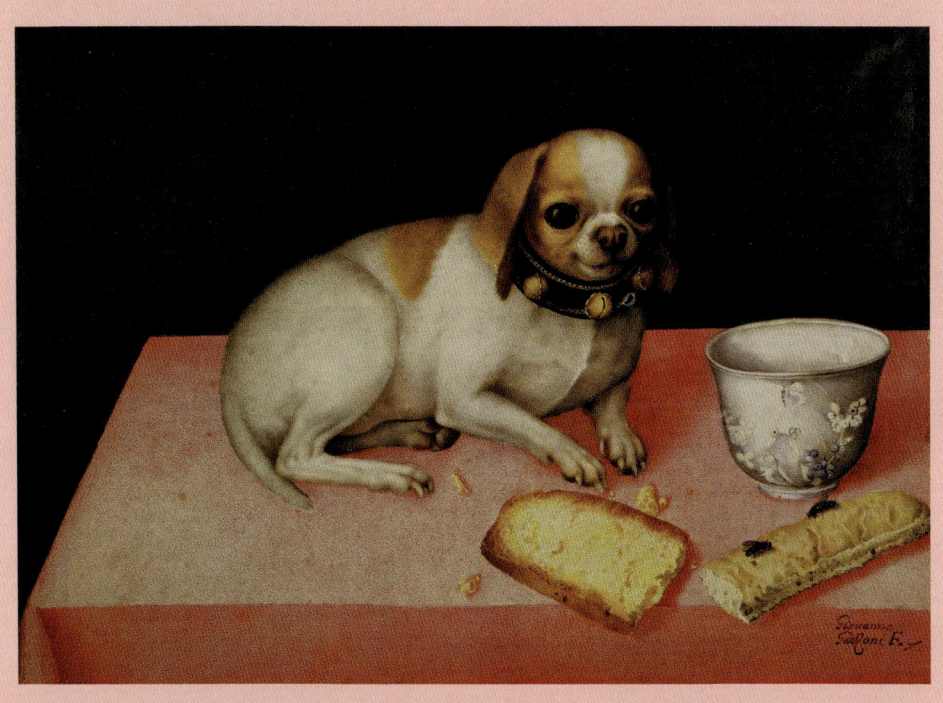

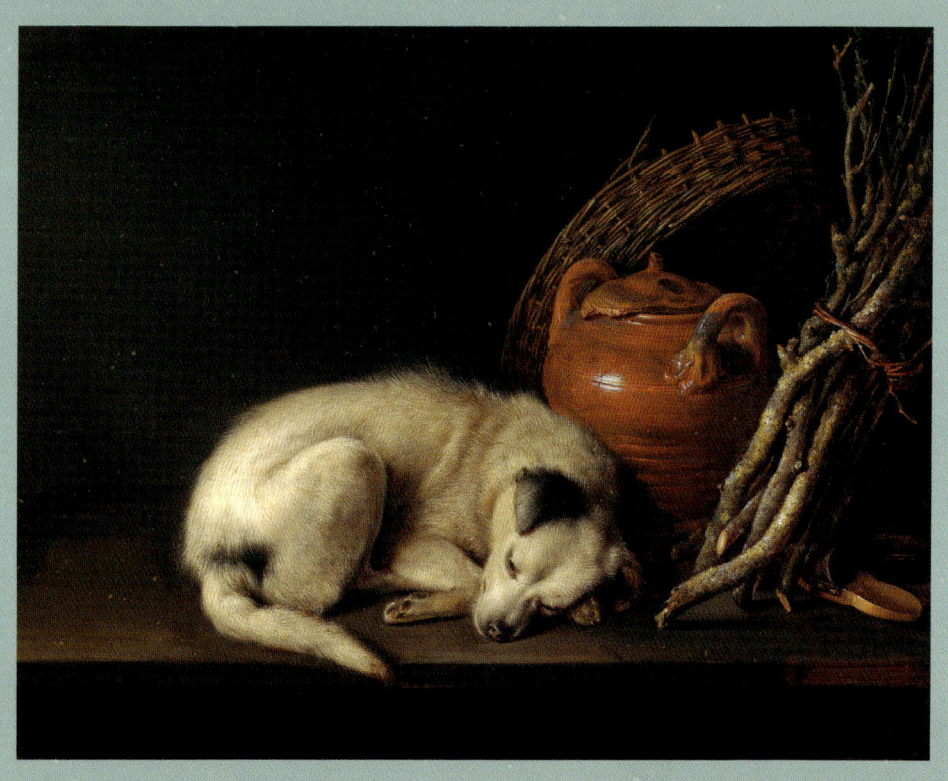

A quiet nap

At the age of 13, Gerrit (or Gerard) Dou (1613–75) studied under 20-year-old Rembrandt van Rijn (see page 51). By the 1660s he had achieved international fame and attention, including from King Charles II of England and Grand Duke Cosimo III de' Medici of Tuscany. Dou developed a reputation as an outstanding artist of small domestic or genre paintings with exceptionally lifelike textures, tonal contrasts and a subtle use of colour. His skill can be seen here in the lifelike fur, shiny nose and soft ears of the small white dog resting against a glossy jar with broken lid, near a bundle of twigs (probably kindling) and a wicker basket. The image represents comfort, cosiness and love. Heavily influenced by Rembrandt, it relies on strong chiaroscuro. Dou included the same dog in an earlier painting, *Spinner's Prayer* of about 1645. To achieve a sense of great depth, radiance and texture, he applied up to 10 or even 15 thin layers of glaze. The objects and the surrounding darkness suggest that this scene is set in a basement or cellar where the little dog has chosen to fall asleep.

16

GERRIT DOU

Dog at Rest

1650

Oil on panel

6½ × 8½ in
(16.5 × 21.6 cm)

Museum of Fine
Arts, Boston,
USA

SMOOTH FOX TERRIER

One of many terrier breeds, the smooth fox terrier is among the earliest types. These dogs are lively, happy, exceptionally energetic and intelligent. Most are predominantly white, usually with black or tan markings. The coat is short and quite wiry but smooth, and the small ears are V-shaped. Dogs of this breed were commonly used for "bolting" after foxes on the hunt and driving them out of their hiding places, or for hunting small prey, such as rabbits. Mostly warm and friendly, they make great companions for humans, although for such diminutive animals they bark extremely loudly, so they can also be excellent household guards.

Gentle giant

The great Baroque painter Diego Velázquez (1599–1660) had an enormous influence on Western art, and this is one of his greatest masterpieces, a painting that broke with the stiff formality of traditional royal portraits. The large canvas shows the Infanta Margarita, the Spanish king Philip IV's five-year-old daughter, surrounded by her staff. By the time Velázquez painted this, he had been working at King Philip's court for more than 30 years. The finished portrait was displayed in the king's private office at his summer palace. Dressed in Habsburg splendour, the Infanta is attended by two ladies-in-waiting, one on either side of her. Two court dwarves, the German Bárbola and Italian Pertusato, stand at the right-hand side of the canvas, and in front of them, stretched out on the floor, is a large Spanish mastiff, apparently dozing comfortably. Pertusato's foot nudges the dog's back, as though he is trying to awaken the animal. Although bred as a royal guard dog, the mastiff seems to be both a beloved pet and a symbol of loyalty and protection. Native to Spain, this breed was understood to protect everyone in its charge. Numerous other characters populate the painting, including the king and queen in a tiny mirror reflection and Velázquez himself, standing painting at his easel.

17
DIEGO VELÁZQUEZ
Las Meninas
1656
Oil on canvas
126 × 108½ in
(320 × 276 cm)
Museo Nacional del Prado, Madrid, Spain

Overleaf: detail

SPANISH MASTIFF

Powerful and strong, the Spanish mastiff has been valued as a guard dog since ancient times. When they moved to the Iberian Peninsula in 218 BCE, the Romans used these dogs to help them fight and to guard their livestock. During the Middle Ages, the dogs continued to guard and herd livestock. Yet although their muscular build and grand size have traditionally singled them out as guard dogs, they can also be loyal companions. They have large, broad heads and short, thick, dense coats in fawn, black and brindle, and they can be independent and reserved, gentle, calm and affectionate.

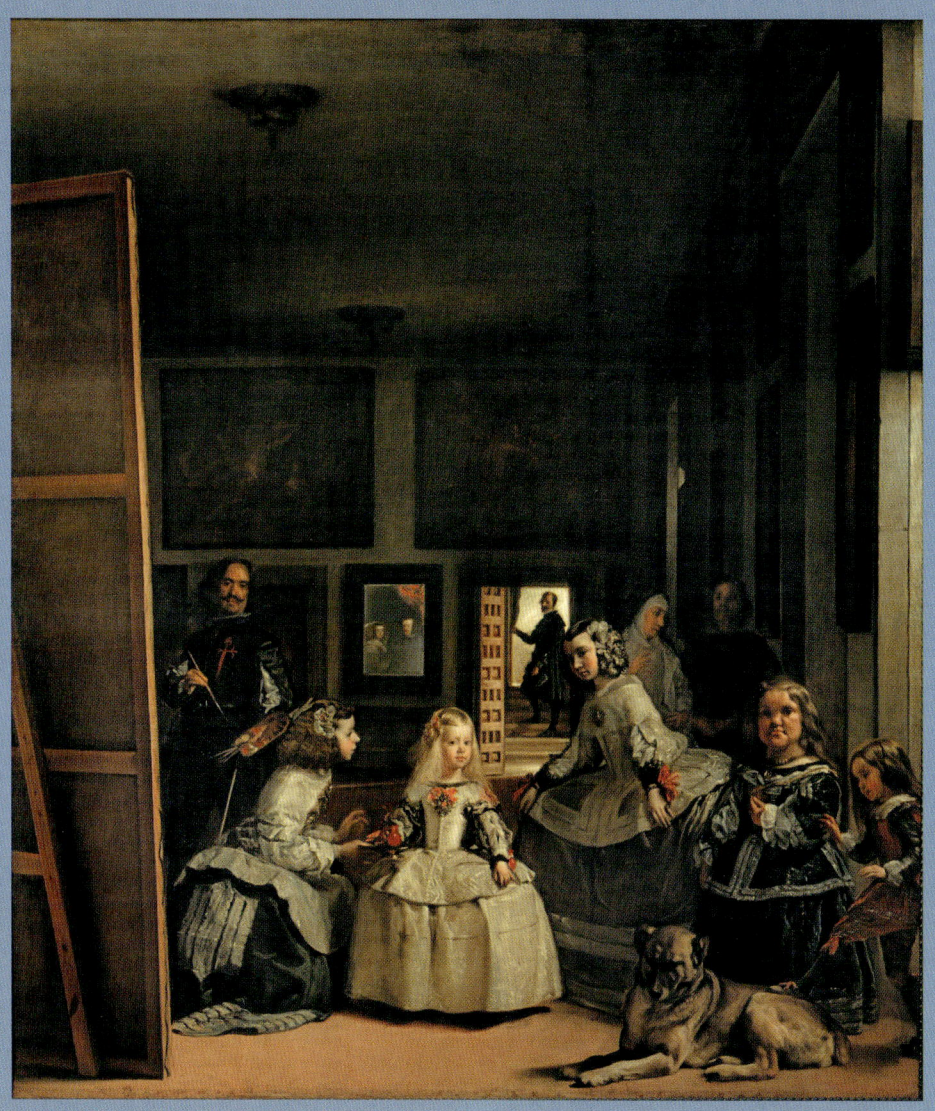

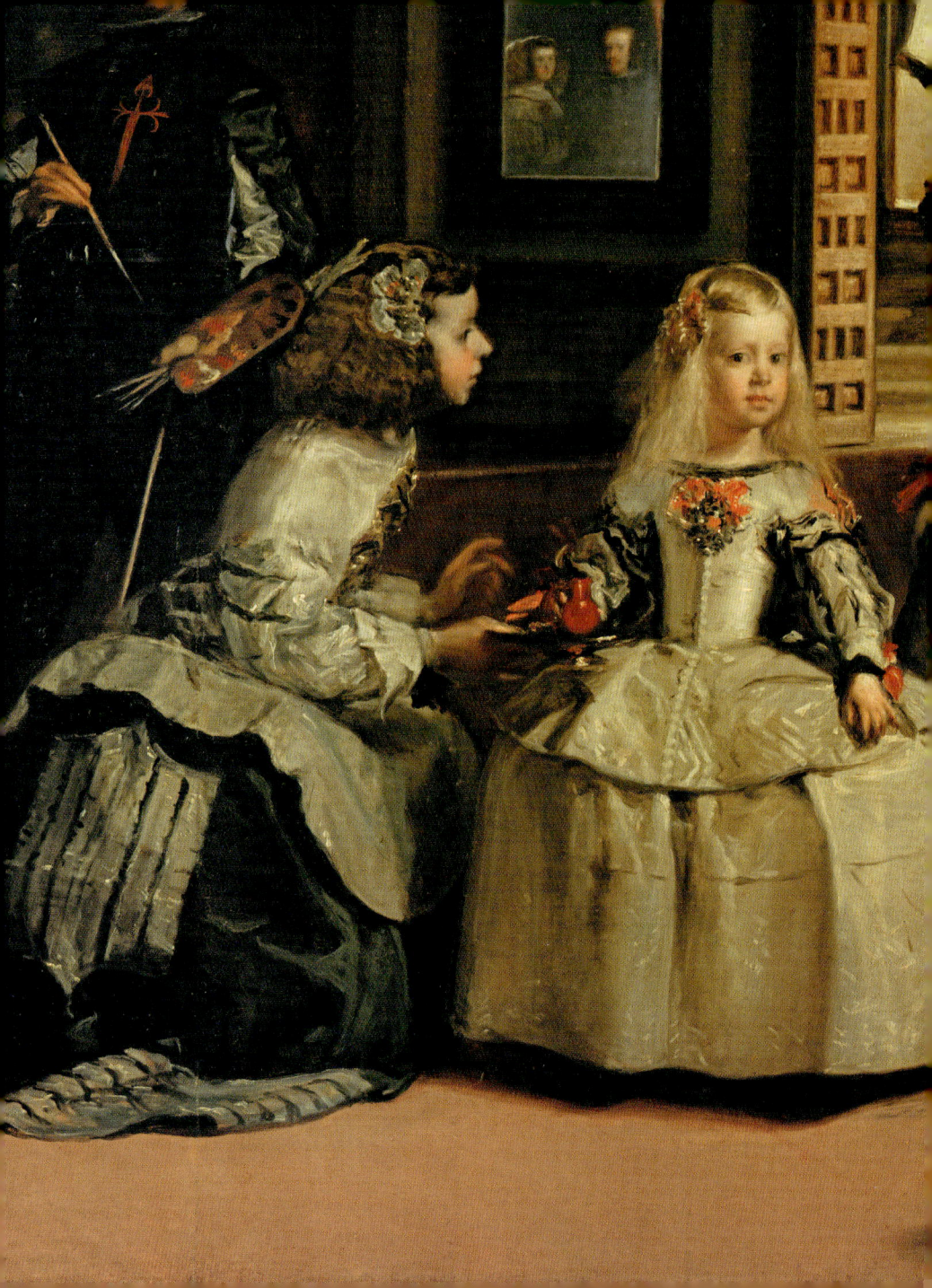

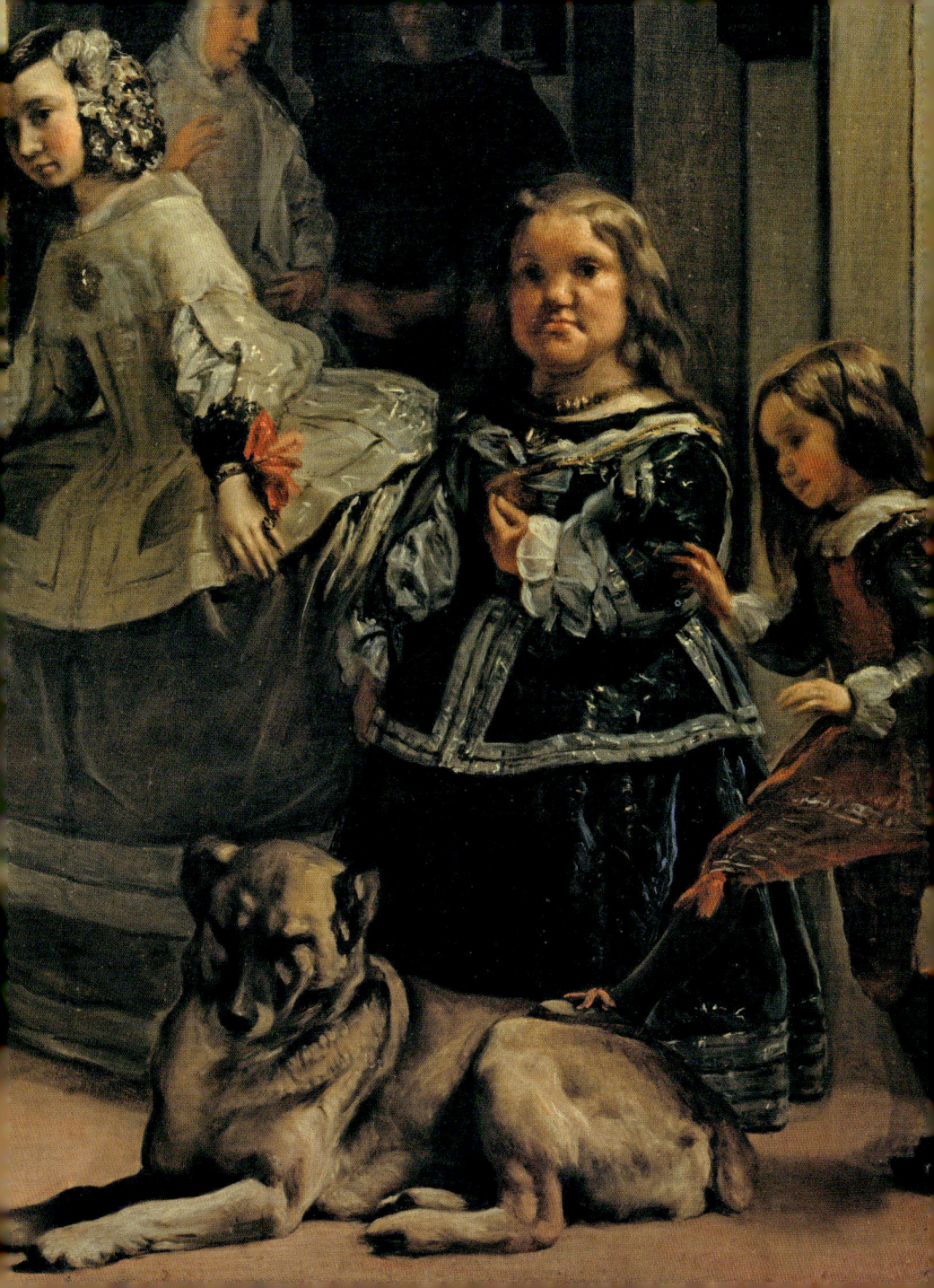

Fit for a future king

Charlotte de La Motte Houdancourt, Duchess of Ventadour (1654–1744), served at the French royal court for more than 70 years. During that time she undertook many important roles, including maid of honour to the queen and governess to the royal children. Here she is depicted as Governess of the Children of France, next to her little charge, who was at the time Duke of Anjou but became King Louis XV. The painting was made to commemorate Madame de Ventadour's saving of the royal line by not allowing doctors to perform what she believed were fatal administrations when the little duke had contracted measles during an epidemic in 1712. As a result, although everyone around him died after "treatment" from the doctors, he survived. Here he is with Madame de Ventadour and his playful little pet dog, surrounded by his deceased ancestors, including Henri IV and Louis XIII (both depicted in busts); Louis XIV sitting in the centre; Louis, the Grand Dauphin, leaning against his father's chair; and the boy's father and Louis XIV's grandson, the Duke of Bourgogne, standing to the right. As was conventional for babies and toddlers at the time, the little duke is dressed in feminine attire and has long hair.

PAPILLON

Little dogs of this breed have long been popular pets at European courts, and they appear in many paintings by Italian, Flemish, Dutch, French and English artists. Probably descended from spaniels, they are named after their large, heavily fringed, upstanding, wing-like ears – *papillon* being French for butterfly. Their coats are long and silky, usually white, with patches of brown or black. Intelligent, confident, energetic and spirited, these dogs make great companions since they are also calm and affectionate, and, being exceptionally alert, they make excellent watchdogs too.

18
FRENCH SCHOOL
Madame de Ventadour with Louis XIV and His Heirs
1715–20
Oil on canvas
50¼ × 63⅓ in (127.6 × 161 cm)
The Wallace Collection, London, UK

Opposite: detail

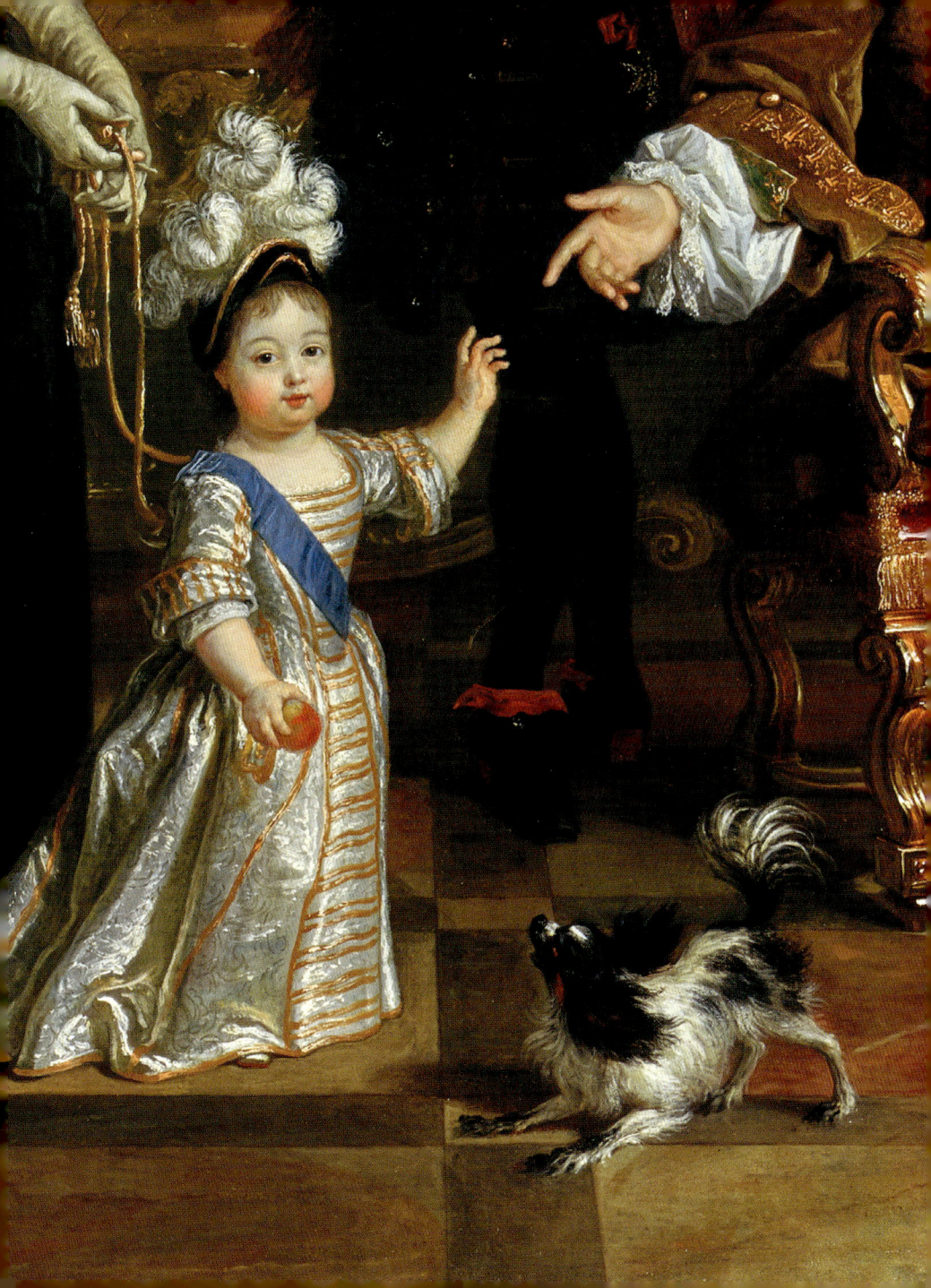

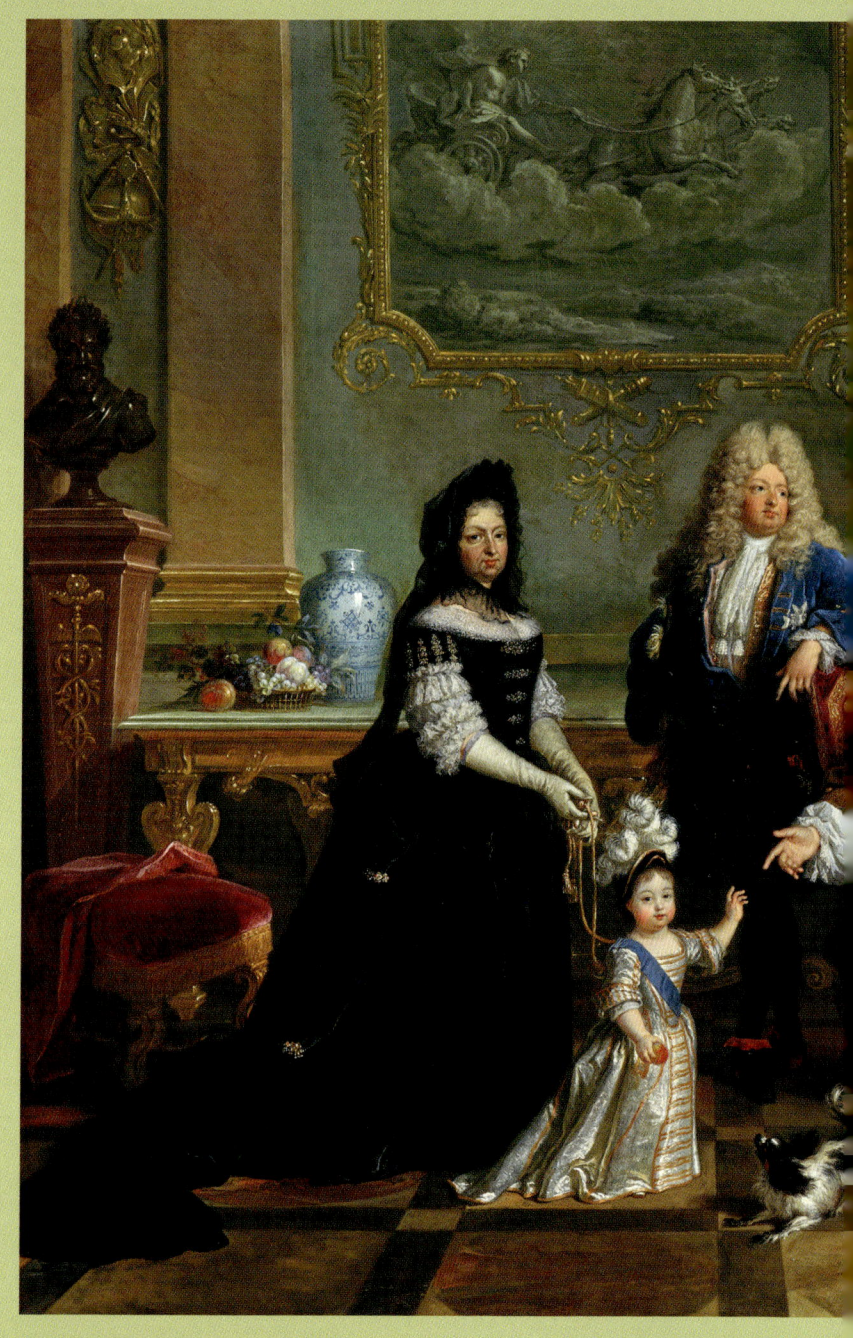

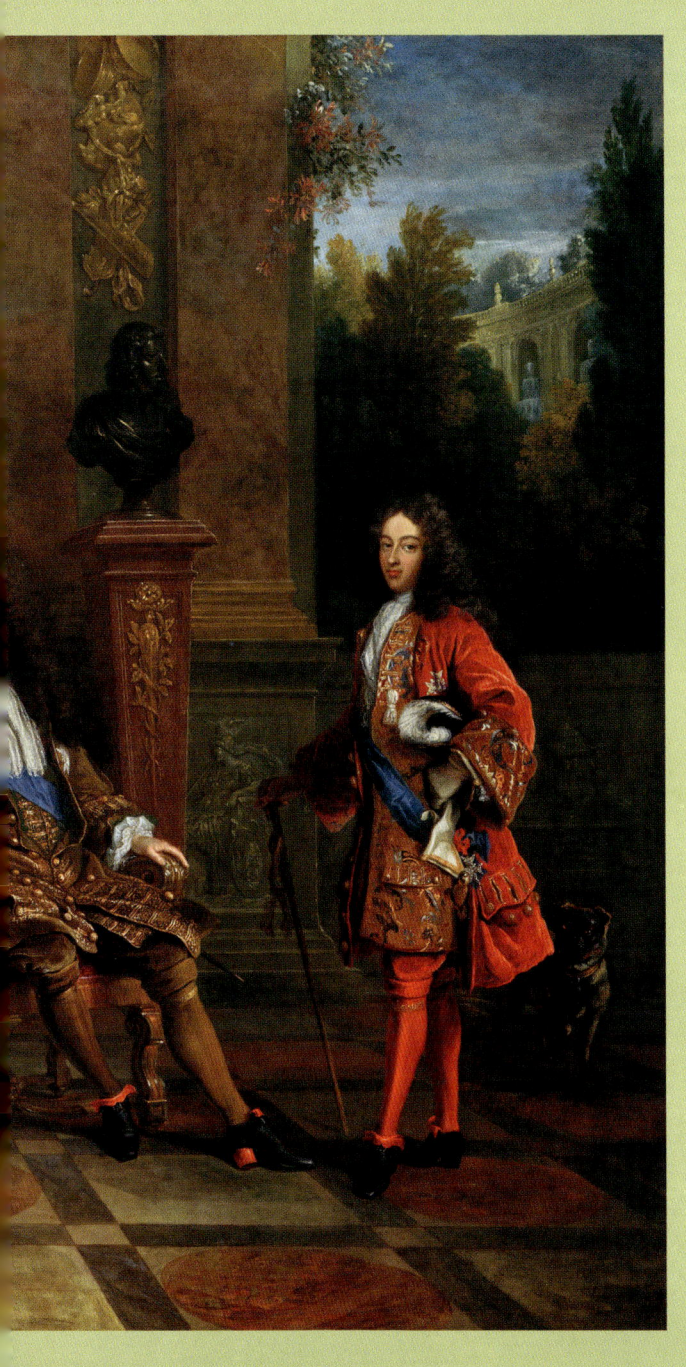

Devoted gun dog

Known for his portraits and landscapes, the painter, draughtsman and printmaker Thomas Gainsborough (1727–88) was born in the eastern English county of Suffolk and studied art in London. Using a light palette and quick brushstrokes, he became one of the most important British artists of the later eighteenth century. This informal portrait of Mr Robert (1725–1806) and Mrs Frances Andrews (c. 1732–80) is set under an oak tree in the grounds of their house, where the park meets their farmland. Behind them, the wide view stretches south over the Stour valley. Robert wears a worn shooting jacket with twisted bags of powder and shot dangling from his pocket, his long-barrelled shotgun under his arm and his devoted gun dog by his side, gazing up at him, seemingly yearning to get back to the shoot. Frances, aged 17 or 18, sits more stiffly in a pale blue skirt and jacket, and a pair of slip-on shoes. The emphasis on the landscape allowed Gainsborough to demonstrate his skill as an innovative – at the time – painter of weather effects and naturalistic scenery. A cloudy sky throws dappled light and shadow over the fields and meadows. The unpainted patch in Frances's lap remains a mystery.

19
THOMAS GAINSBOROUGH
Mr and Mrs Andrews
c. 1750
Oil on canvas
27⅓ × 47 in (69.8 × 119.4 cm)
The National Gallery, London, UK

Opposite: detail

ENGLISH POINTER

The medium-sized dog in this painting seems to be an English pointer, the exact ancestry of which is not known. Named after the characteristic pose these dogs assume when they catch the scent of game, they were bred to locate quarry for hunters on both land and water. They are athletic and muscular, with short, sleek coats and exceptional scenting abilities. They are also lithe and nimble, intelligent, affectionate and gentle, and they thrive on regular exercise and mental stimulation, making them suitable as family pets. With a well-proportioned, balanced frame and boundless energy, English pointers are built for speed and endurance and require plenty of exercise.

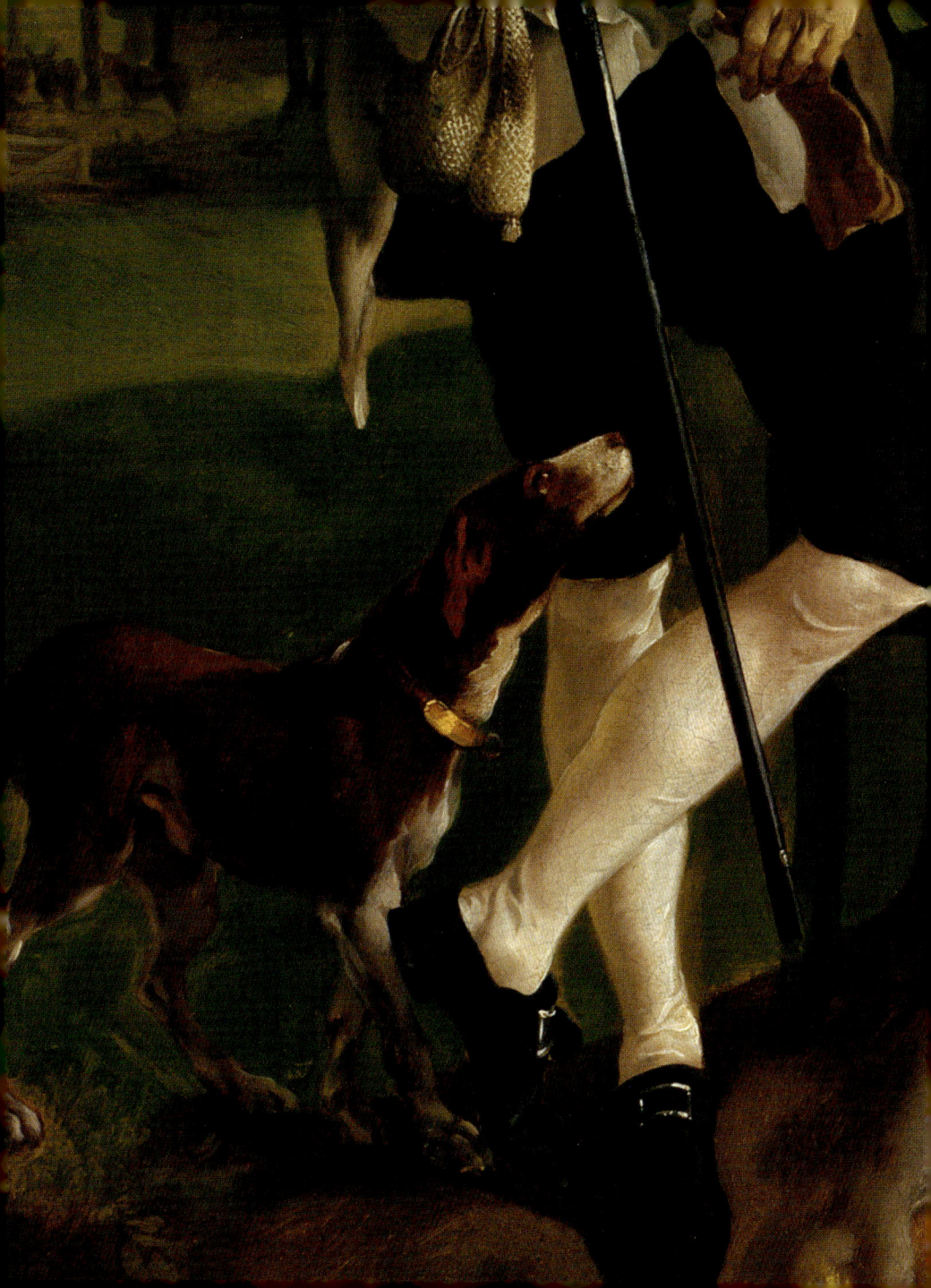

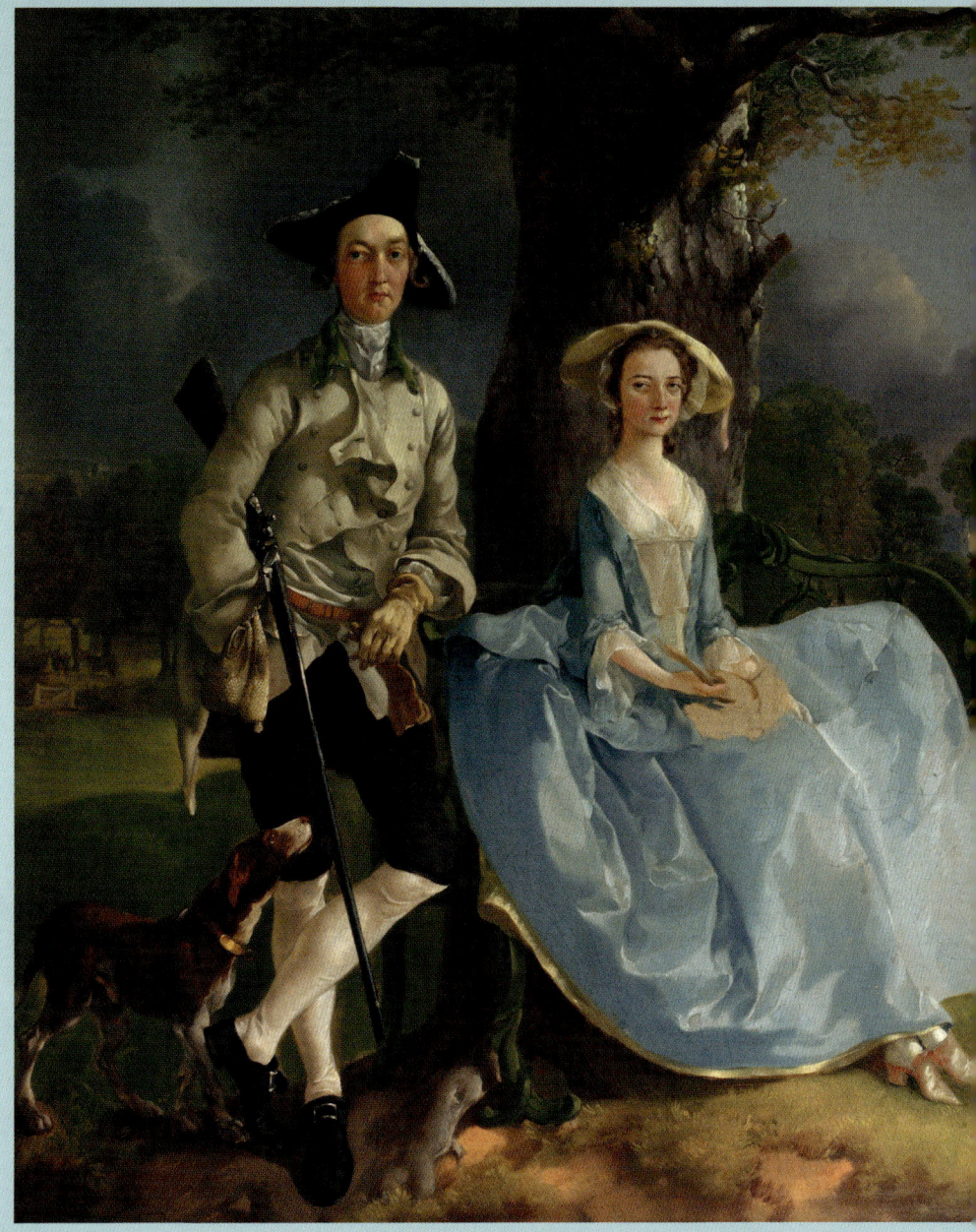

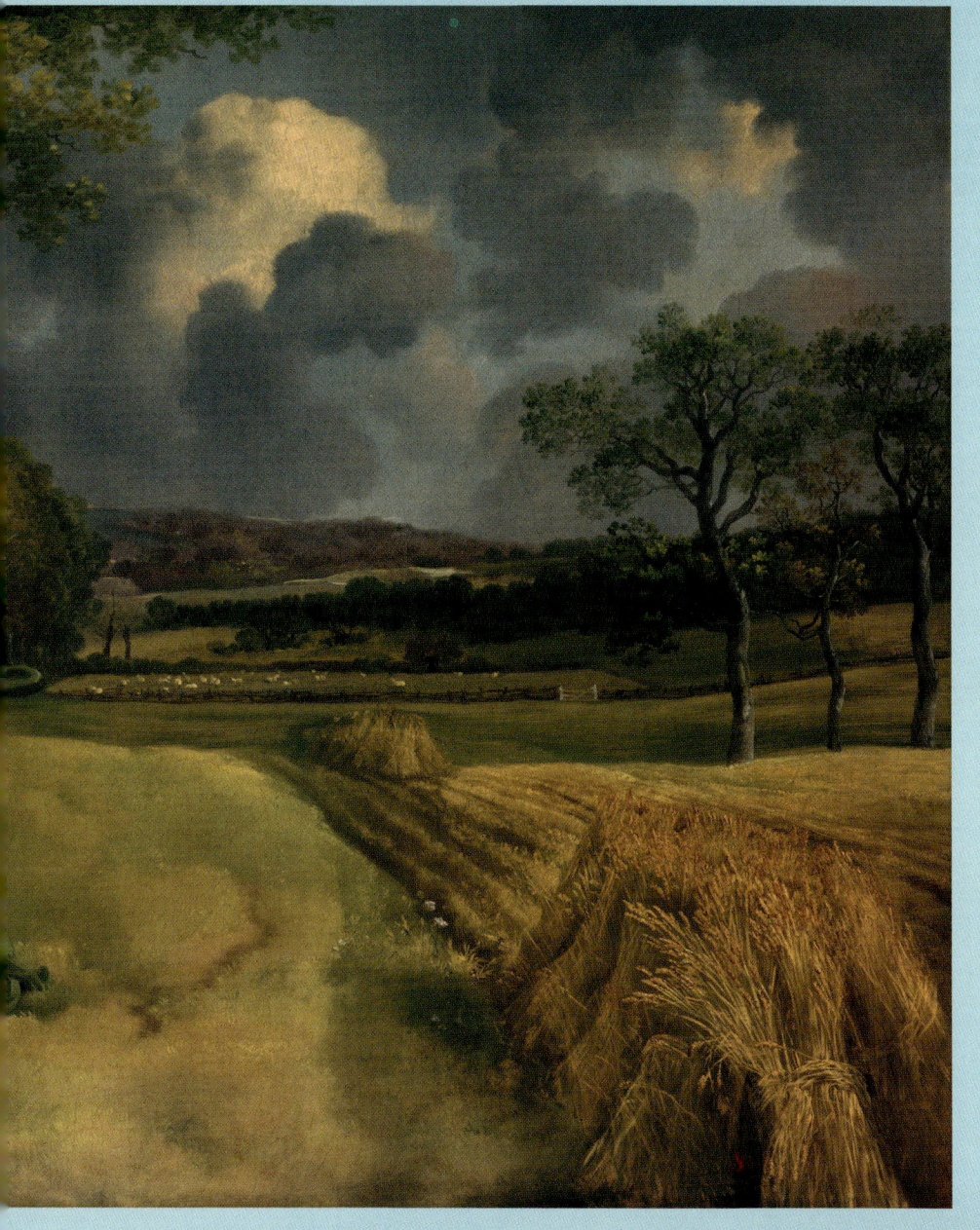

Luxury and confidence

Sir Joshua Reynolds (1723–92) was one of the most prominent and influential portrait painters of the Georgian era in Britain. He served as the first president of the Royal Academy of Arts and is celebrated for his masterful depictions of aristocrats, gentry and other prominent figures of eighteenth-century English society. A renowned intellectual, he mixed with the elite of London, and his innovative approach of depicting his subjects as classical figures made him immensely popular. Miss Beatrix Lister (1749–1807), pictured here, was the sister of the first Lord Ribblesdale, and this portrait would probably have been painted in their family home, Gisburne Park in Lancashire. The 16-year-old young lady is wearing her best clothes, which appear somewhat mature for her, including valuable pearls in a choker, in her hair and on her dress, among them a particularly costly pearl drop. On her lap, Beatrix holds her little Bichon Frisé. It features prominently in this portrait, highlighting the breed's association with luxury and nobility, but also giving the girl confidence as she strokes it while sitting extremely still for the eminent portraitist. Using opaque paint in evenly blended strokes, Reynolds captured the grace, elegance and innocence of his sitter and the composure of her beloved pet.

20

SIR JOSHUA
REYNOLDS
Miss Beatrix Lister
1765
Oil on canvas
29½ × 24½ in
(74.9 × 62.2 cm)
National Gallery of
Art, Washington,
DC, USA

BICHON FRISÉ

The word *bichon* means "white dog", and *frisé* describes the soft corkscrew curls of this breed's coat. Although the breed developed in France, it probably originated on Tenerife in the Canary Islands in the thirteenth century. The dogs were taken by traders to mainland Europe, where they endeared themselves to everyone, especially nobles and royalty, with whom they were often depicted in portraits. These small dogs are gentle, sensitive, playful, affectionate, intelligent, energetic and outgoing; they thrive in company and hate being left on their own. All these qualities make them ideal companion dogs.

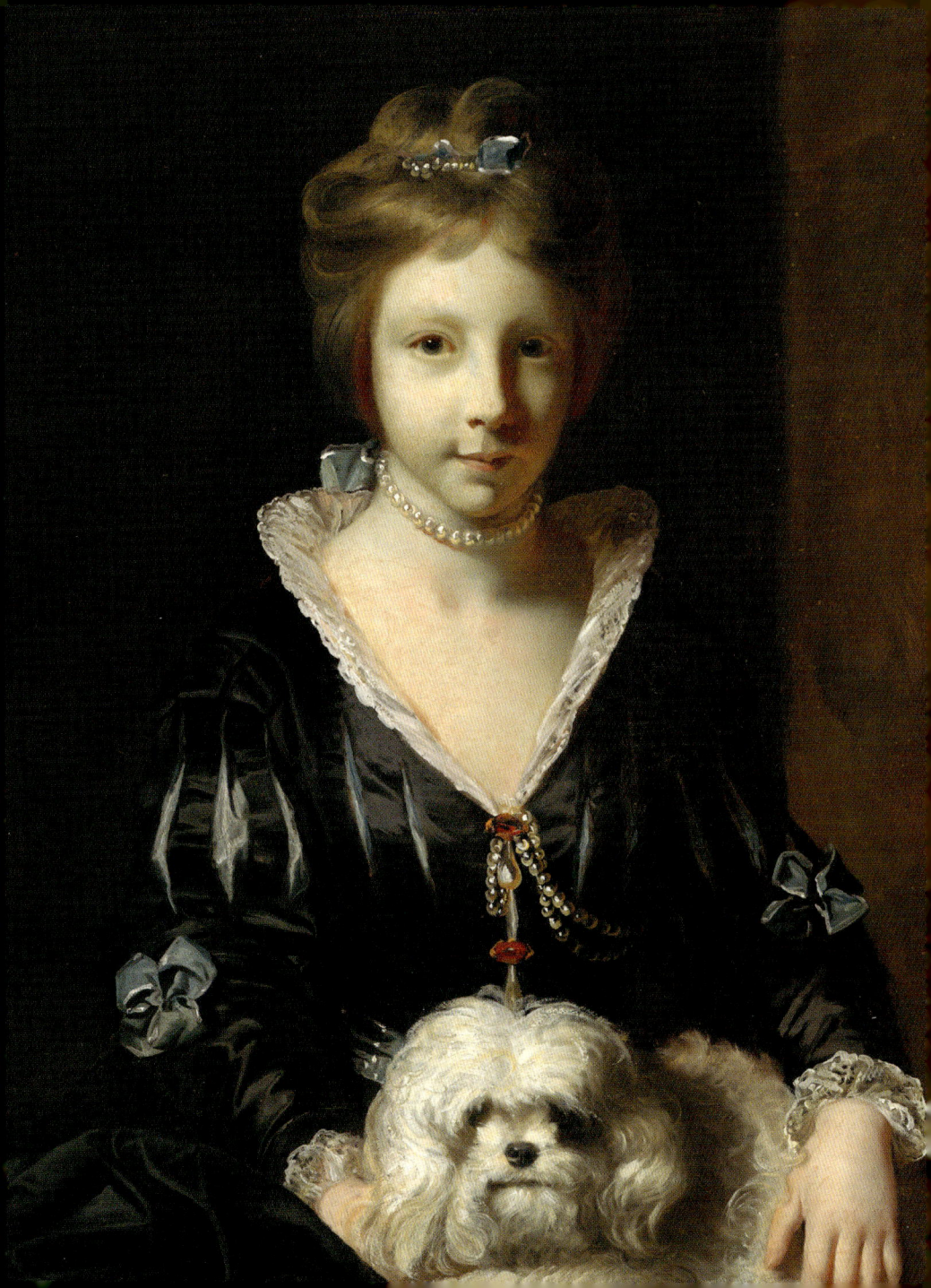

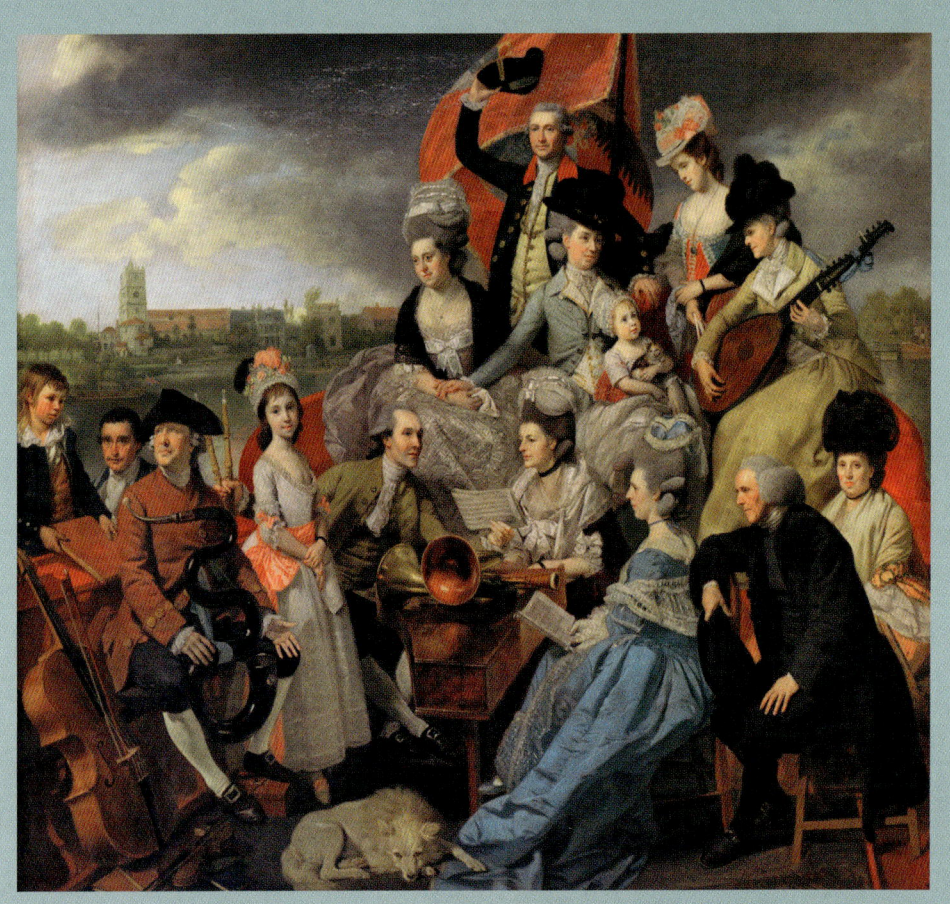

Close family

The German Neoclassical painter Johann Zoffany (1733–1810) was active mainly in England, Italy and India, and a founding member of the Royal Academy. He was extremely popular among the highest echelons of English society for his informal portraits. The one opposite depicts the freethinking Sharp family, consisting of four brothers and three sisters, and their offspring, plus Zoffany's pet dog. Among the lively group is the scholar and musician Granville Sharp, one of the first British campaigners for the abolition of the slave trade. John, a clergyman, constructed a miniature welfare state in Northumbria, while William was surgeon to the King of England and members of the aristocracy, also running a daily free surgery for the poor. James became a pioneer of the industrial and agricultural revolutions. The brothers and sisters were exceptionally close. Judith, an artist, turned down two marriage proposals, and Frances spent her later years with Elizabeth, who helped the rural poor. The family held many parties, including several on their barge, *Apollo*, on the River Thames. Here they are at one of these gatherings, seated around a harpsichord, each holding a musical instrument. Local dignitaries and even royalty often joined these lavish musical boating parties, during which they cruised along the Thames.

21
JOHANN
ZOFFANY
The Sharp Family
1779–81
Oil on canvas
45½ × 49½ in
(115.6 × 125.7 cm)
On loan to the
National Gallery,
London, UK,
from a private
collection

Overleaf: detail

POMERANIAN

The Pomeranian is a breed of the spitz type that originated in the region of Pomerania, in northwestern Poland and northeastern Germany. The breed may also have a kinship with such Arctic breeds as the Samoyed, elkhound and Finnish spitz, and with the Italian Volpino. When they were introduced into European royal courts in the eighteenth century, these dogs were fairly large, as seen here, but they have gradually become smaller and are now classed as a toy breed. The earliest Pomeranians were usually white, occasionally brown or black. They have a soft fur ruff around their neck, and a lavishly plumed tail.

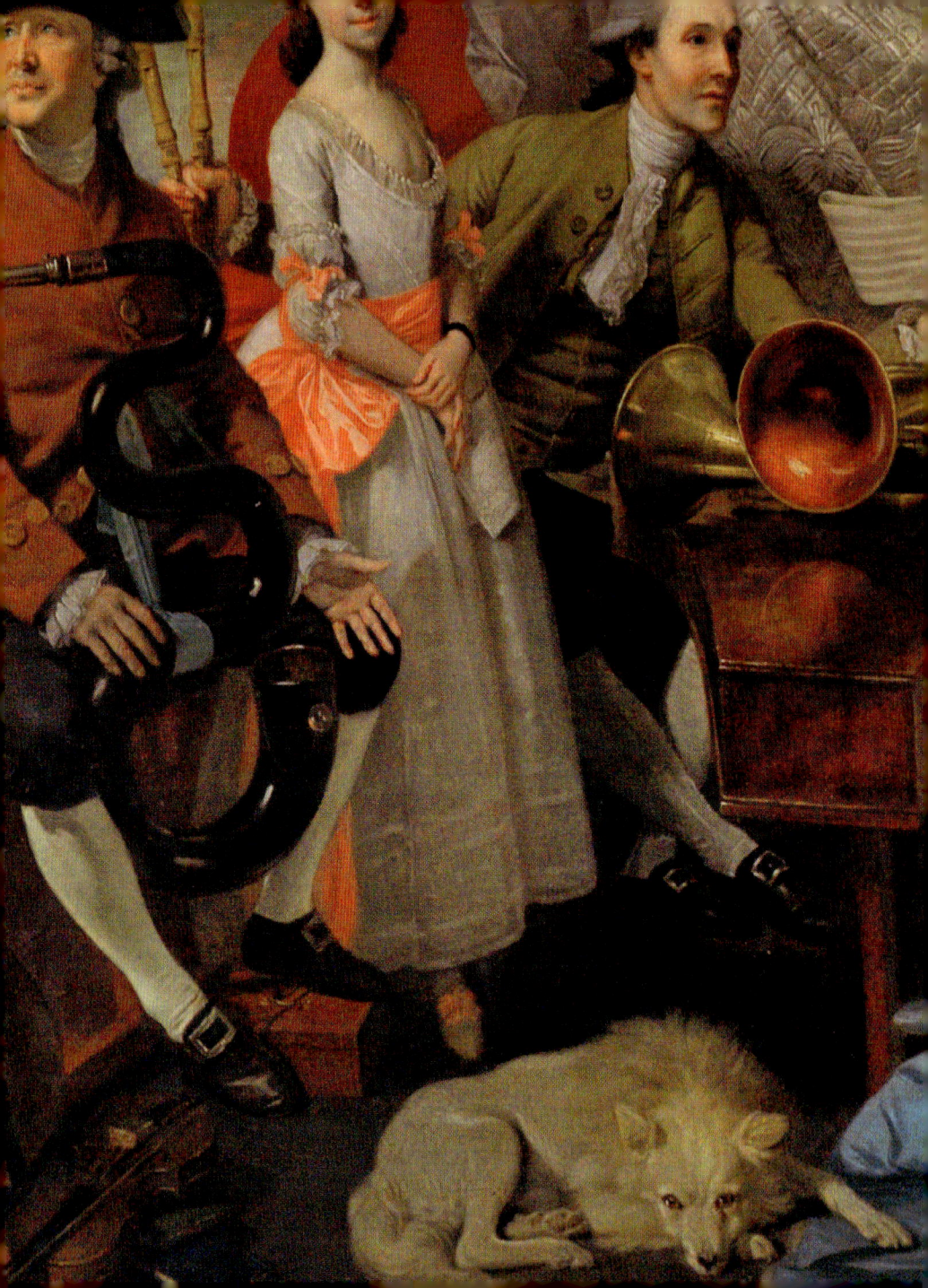

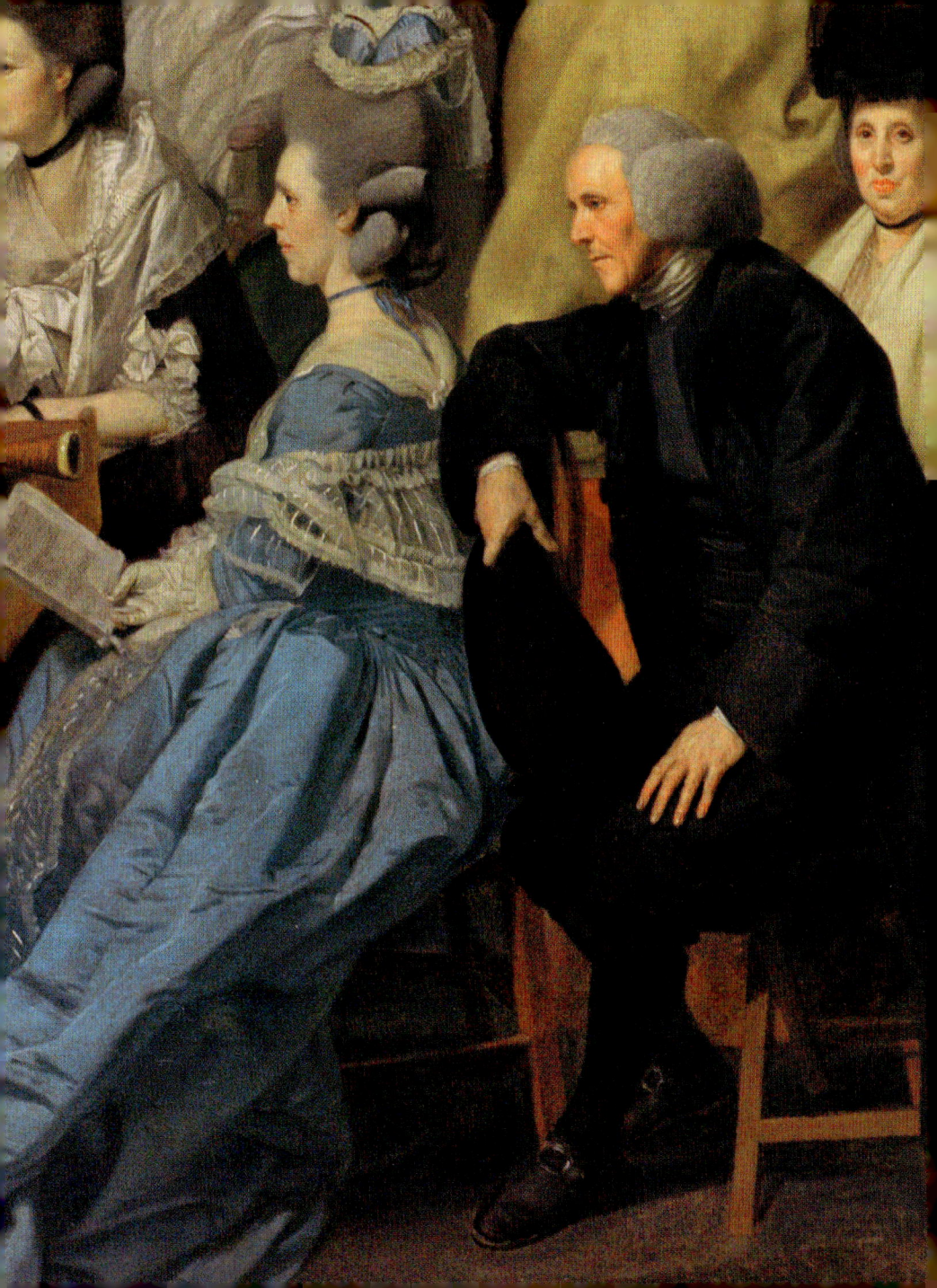

In costume

The Spanish artist Francisco Goya (1746–1828) is often described as both an Old Master and the first truly modern artist. His art also fits in with Romanticism's emphasis on subjectivity, imagination and emotion. An astute observer of the world around him, Goya responded visually to the turbulent events in Spain at the time, which included the dominance of the Inquisition and the invasion of Napoleon's army. In the year he made this painting, he became court painter to King Charles III of Spain, and his work had a significant impact on later artists. Set against a lush landscape, this softly coloured image is a full-length portrait of the tiny-waisted figure of María Ana de Pontejos y Sandoval, Marquesa de Pontejos (1762–1834). Painted soon after her wedding to Spain's ambassador to Portugal, the marchioness wears clothes that emulate the style of Queen Marie Antoinette of France, who was known to dress as a shepherdess. It includes an elaborate hairstyle, a straw sun hat and a flower-trimmed gown that emphasizes the marchioness's fashionably tight-corseted waist. In her right hand, she holds a pink carnation as a symbol of love, and by her feet is her beloved pet pug, adorned with ribbons and bells at his neck.

22
FRANCISCO GOYA
The Marquesa de Pontejos
c. 1786
Oil on canvas
82¾ × 50 in (210.3 × 127 cm)
National Gallery of Art, Washington, DC, USA

PUG

An ancient breed that may date back to 400 BCE, pugs are tiny dogs with short, fine coats, well-developed muscles and compact, squat bodies. They arrived in Europe in the sixteenth century from China, where the Lo-Sze (the ancestors of contemporary pugs) were companions to imperial families. In Europe, similarly, they immediately became the pets of royalty and the aristocracy. Usually fawn or black, they have curly tails, large round eyes, flattish muzzles and small ears. Their lower teeth usually protrude more than their upper teeth, so this breed can suffer breathing problems. Sensitive and affectionate, these little dogs love human companionship.

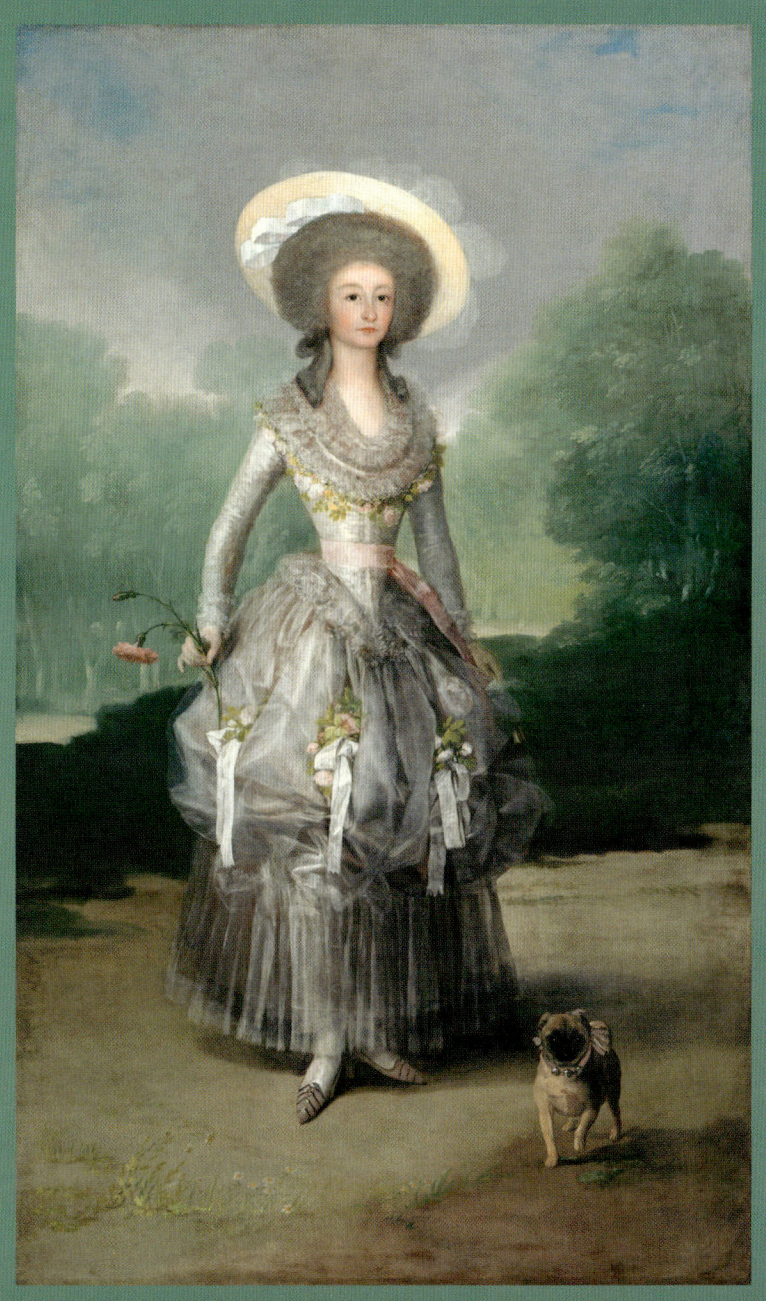

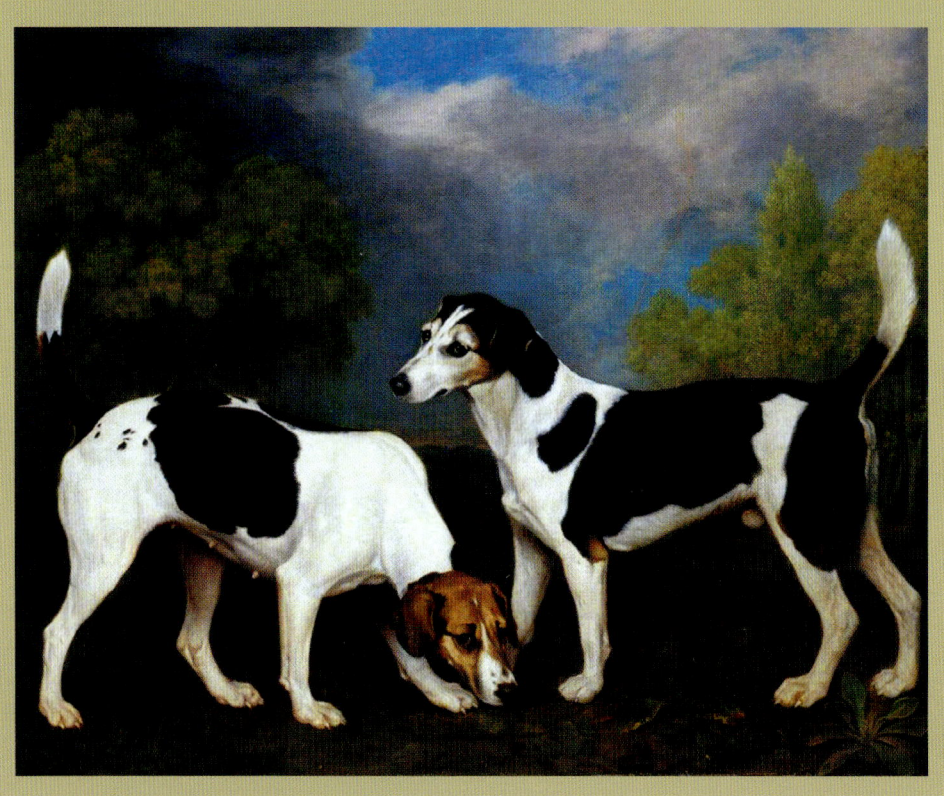

Sport and companionship

Although the title of this painting describes the two dogs pictured as foxhounds, it is often speculated that they might be the slightly smaller breed of hare-hound or harriers. The painting was probably commissioned by the dogs' owner, Revd Thomas Vyner of Lincolnshire, who was an enthusiastic hunter and an expert at breeding hounds. It is likely that the two dogs were bred from a famed pack of hounds belonging to Vyner's friend the 1st Earl of Yarborough. Largely self-taught, the British artist George Stubbs (1724–1806) worked for the Vyner family in 1776 and 1792. He experimented with a variety of media and became a skilled painter and engraver, celebrated for his animal images. Using tiny brush marks, he painted the animals in his compositions first, making them as accurate as possible, then added the background and sky. This detailed, precise painting of the two dogs also conveys their characters. Both tails are up, alert and happy, and the ears are relaxed. The bitch, with light brown markings on her head, sniffs the ground, while the dog, with black markings around his eyes, looks up. Both animals seem happy to be close to each other, and both are calm but shrewdly watchful.

23
GEORGE STUBBS
A Couple of Foxhounds
1792
Oil on canvas
40 × 50 in
(101.6 × 127 cm)
Tate Britain, London, UK

HARRIER

Closely resembling foxhounds, harriers or hare-hounds were bred specifically to hunt hare. As with foxhounds, the history of this breed can be traced back to the thirteenth century at least. These animals are active, strong and determined, as well as affectionate and intelligent. They have relatively large bones and short coats that can feature a variety of colour patterns, although they are usually white with black and brown. Despite their historic role as ruthless hunters of small animals, harriers are lively, gentle and usually relaxed in the company of humans and other dogs.

Inseparable

In 1808 the publisher of the Scots novelist, poet and historian Sir Walter Scott (1771–1832) commissioned a portrait from the artist Sir Henry Raeburn (1756–1823). Unlike earlier portraits of Scott, this one was created to be reproduced and circulated in prints, to publicize the writer's image. Although Scott and his friends said that he looked too solemn – a contrast with his naturally buoyant personality – the painting was hugely influential, both in making Scott famous and in setting an example for Romantic portraiture. Raeburn was a very successful artist who served as portrait painter to King George IV in Scotland. His painting shows Scott sitting on a stone, deep in thought, a notebook in one hand and a pen in the other, flanked by his two favourite dogs. Maida, on his right, appears to be trying to gain his attention. This deerhound, a crossbreed between a Pyrenean wolfdog and a Highland deerhound, was named after a battle that took place in 1806 as part of the Napoleonic Wars. Camp, at Scott's feet on his left, was a cross between a black-and-tan English terrier and a thoroughbred English brindle-coated bull terrier. Both dogs were remarkably intelligent, fun and devoted to their owner.

24
SIR HENRY
RAEBURN
*Portrait of Sir
Walter Scott*
1808
Oil on canvas
30 × 25 in
(76.2 × 63.5 cm)
Private collection

DEERHOUND

One of the oldest breeds in the British Isles, the Scottish deerhound, or simply the deerhound, is a large sighthound, originally bred to hunt red deer. Its use as such continued until the end of the nineteenth century, after which slower tracking dogs became preferred in smaller deer forests. Similar in appearance to the greyhound, but larger and heavier-boned, the deerhound is closely related to the Irish wolfhound. With their long, slim heads and tapering muzzles, usually shaggy coats and long tails that curve in an elegant arc, these dogs are fast and can run silently on many different terrains.

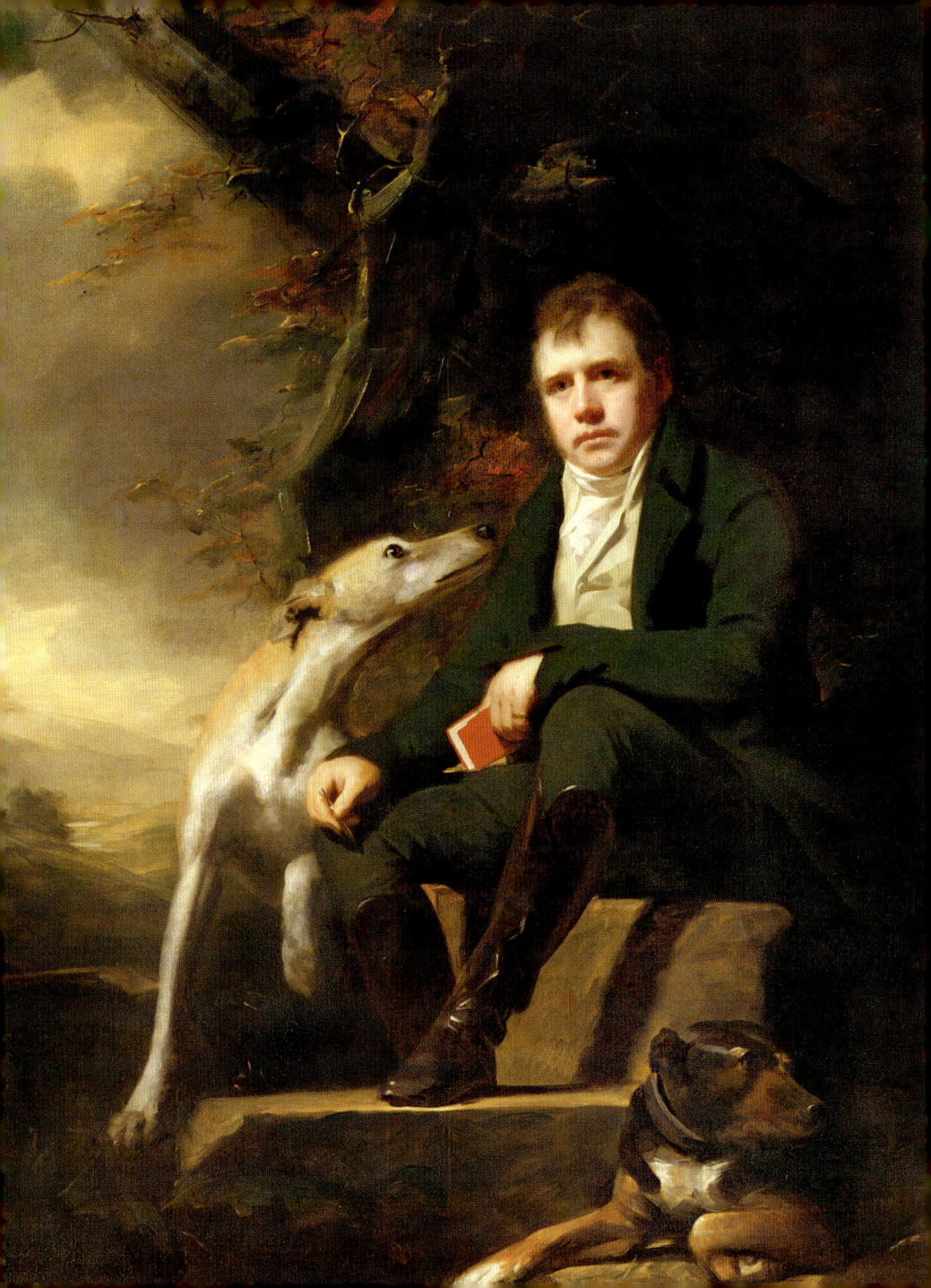

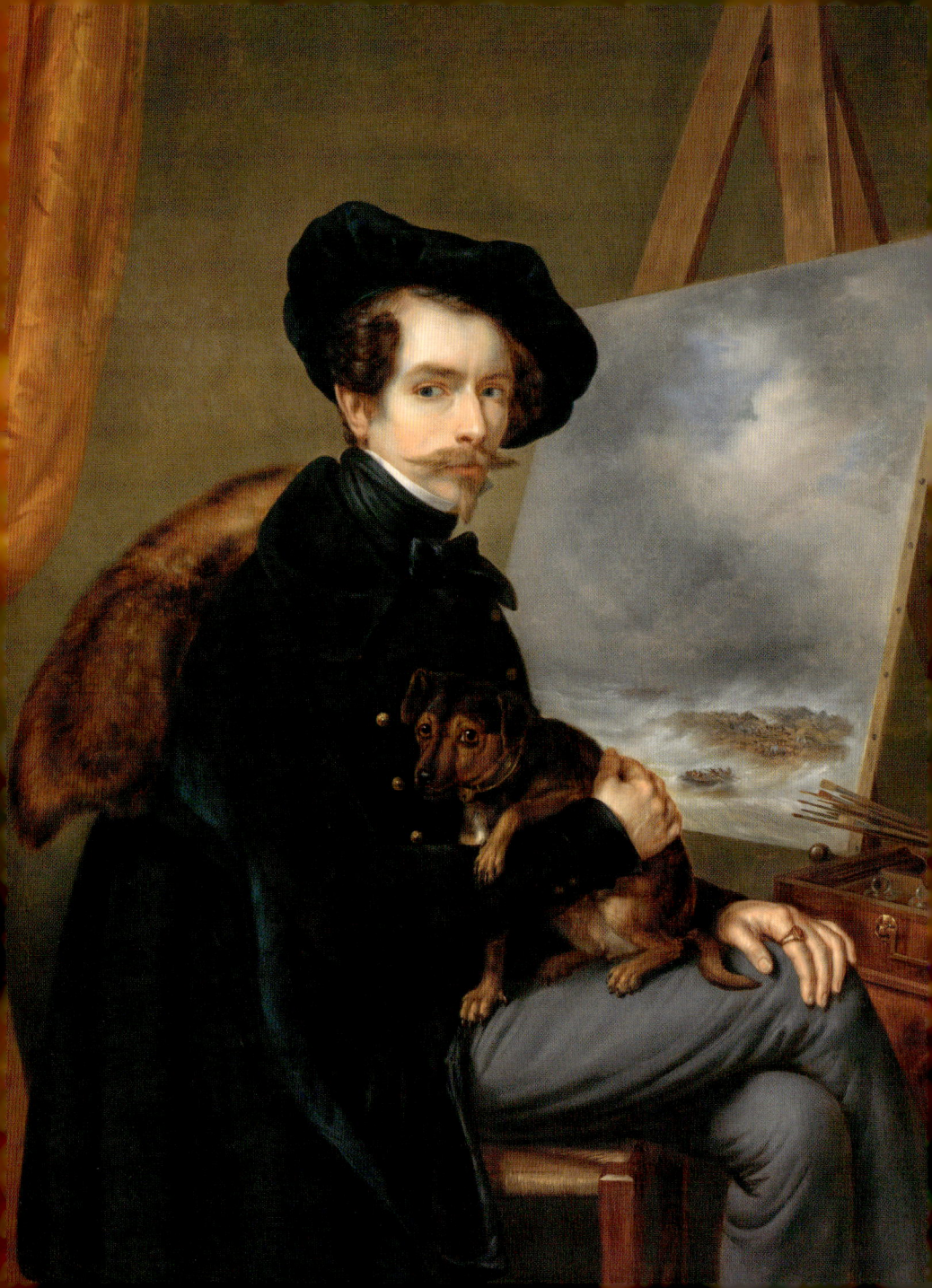

Relaxed yet ready

Louis Meijer (1809–66) was a painter, etcher, lithographer and draughtsman from the Netherlands who worked in the Romantic tradition. Born in Amsterdam, he became famed for his seascapes, captured with sensitive, expressive brushwork and conveying a sense of atmosphere as well as reality. His touch with a brush is light and soft, and although he was sought after for these seascapes, this self-portrait is one of his best-known works. He painted himself in his studio wearing a black beret, double-breasted velvet jacket and silk tie, turning away from his easel, while holding his pet dog on his lap, close to his body. On his easel is a seascape that he is working on, and a table by his knee holds his paints, brushes and palette. A coat with a fur collar is flung over the back of his chair and a gold-coloured curtain is pulled to one side to frame the tableau. The palette is limited, serving to keep the viewer's eye contained as it moves around the image. Meijer has painted himself as if noticing that someone has walked into his studio – an approach that is emphasized by the startled look of his little dog, which leans into its owner.

25
LOUIS MEIJER
Self-Portrait
1838
Oil on canvas
53½ × 47¼ in
(136 × 120 cm)
Rijksmuseum,
Amsterdam,
The Netherlands

ENGLISH TOY TERRIER

The English toy terrier (also known as Black & Tan) is closely related to the larger Manchester terrier, with the same build, colourings and coat. Fast and agile, animals of this breed were bred to chase and kill rats as a sport, probably from the sixteenth century onwards, and they became particularly popular in nineteenth-century London. They are tiny creatures, usually weighing between 3 lb (1.36 kg) and 8 lb (3.62 kg). Their silky coats are black with rich mahogany tan on the muzzle, throat and forelegs, inside the hind legs and under the tail. Gentle and affectionate but often nervous, they can make great pets.

High and low life

Sir Edwin Landseer RA (1802–73) was an English painter and sculptor, well known for his paintings of animals – particularly horses, dogs and stags. His best-known works are the lion sculptures at the base of Nelson's Column in Trafalgar Square, London. From the age of 13, Landseer exhibited drawings of animals at the Royal Academy, and he soon became one of the most popular painters in Victorian England. This work shows how he imbued the animals he depicted with human attributes. Here he has contrasted the large, dignified, soulful-looking bloodhound with the tiny terrier that looks eagerly out of the portrait. The two dogs, Grafton and Scratch, were owned by Landseer's friend Jacob Bell, who commissioned the painting. The composition parodies the Dutch portrait tradition, with a window framing the subject and, rather than an arm or hand extending over the edge, the bloodhound's large paw hanging over the threshold of the kennel. While drawing attention to the dogs' personalities in their looks and poses, Landseer also painted the larger dog in smooth, dappled textures, and the smaller in quicker, shorter and more expressive brushstrokes. The painting also suggests the contrasts of high and low life.

26

SIR EDWIN
LANDSEER
*Dignity and
Impudence*
1839
Oil on canvas
35 × 27 in
(88.9 × 69.2 cm)
Tate Britain,
London, UK

WEST HIGHLAND WHITE TERRIER

The West Highland white terrier or Westie is named after the area of Scotland in which it originated. The earliest mention of them was in the early seventeenth century, when they were called the dogs of Argyleshire. It is likely that the Scottish, Cairn and West Highland white terriers all came from common stock. As with all terrier breeds, the Westie was bred as a vermin hunter, to pursue any animals that were considered by humans to be pests, from rats to foxes. Nowadays, most Westies are family pets. With their rough white coats, these little dogs are extremely active and sociable.

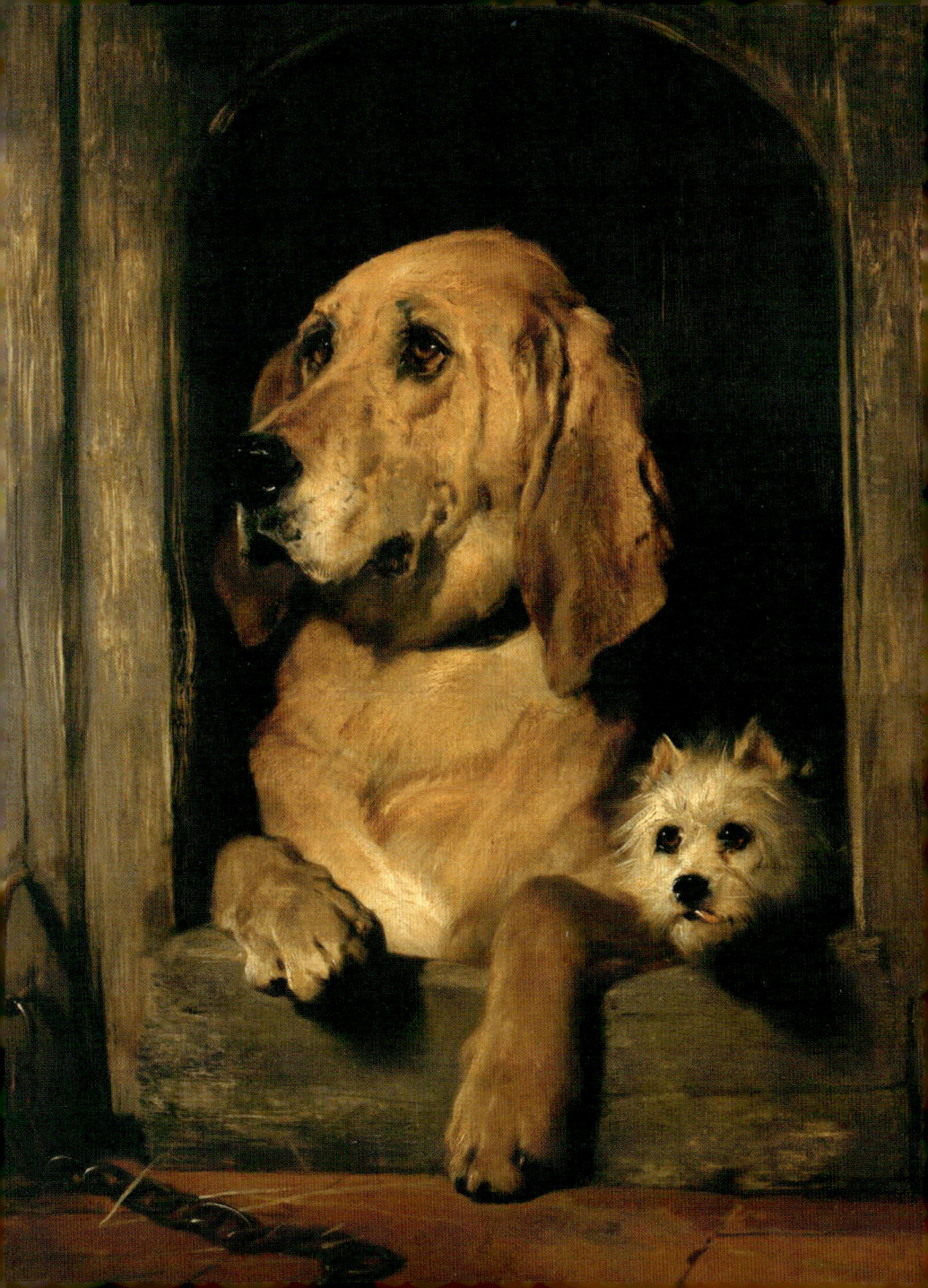

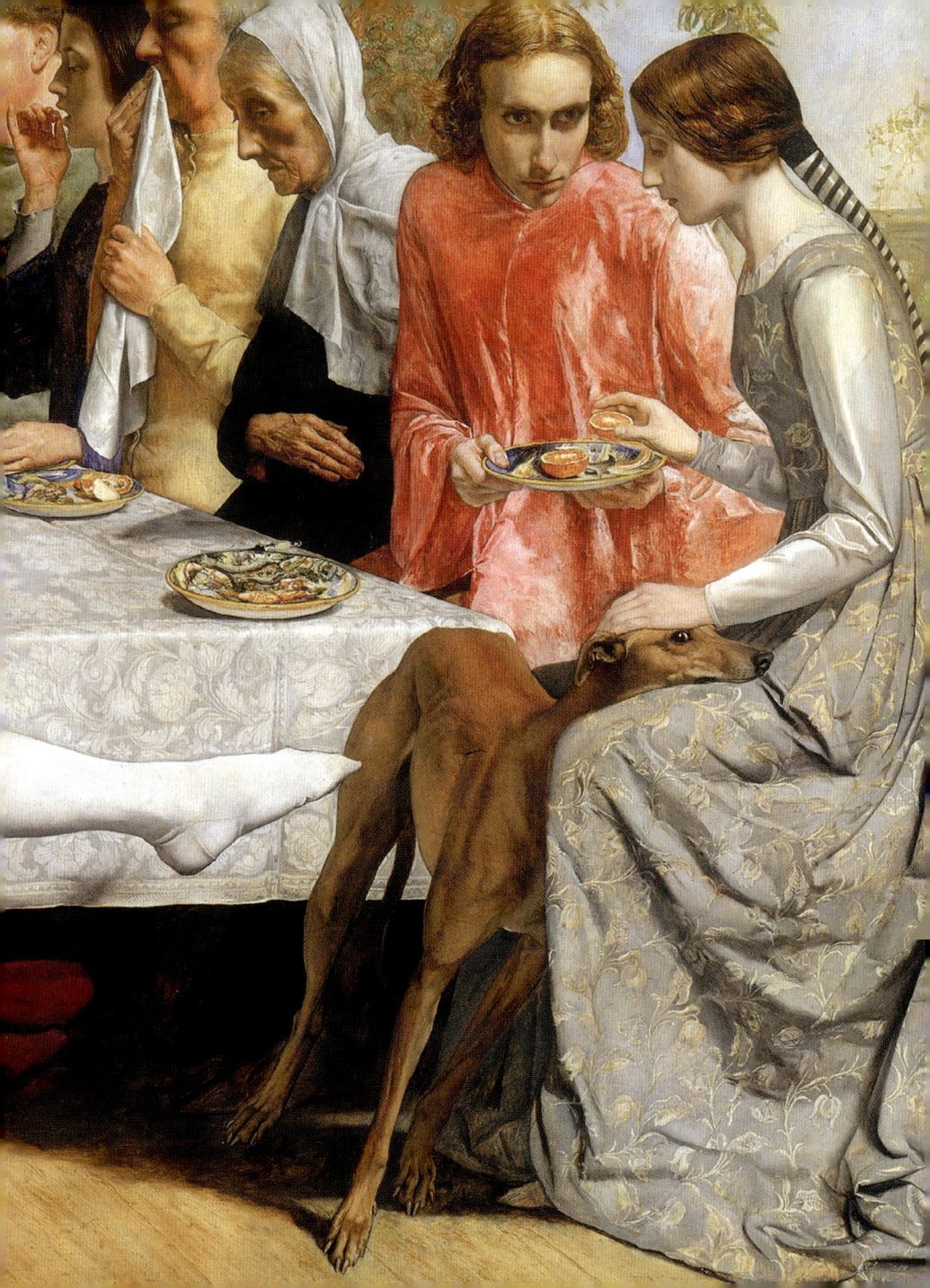

Gentle and quiet

One of the first paintings in the Pre-Raphaelite style created by a founder of the movement, the English artist John Everett Millais (1829–96), this illustrates a scene from a poem by John Keats (1795–1821), "Isabella, or the Pot of Basil", which was in turn adapted from a tale in *The Decameron*, a famous collection of stories by Giovanni Boccaccio (1313–75). The approach used by the artists of the Pre-Raphaelite Brotherhood (PRB) conflicted with traditional art of the time, so they kept their identities secret from the rest of the world. The letters "PRB" can be seen carved on a wooden seat at the lower right of this painting. In shimmering grey dress, Isabella, the sister of wealthy Florentine merchants, is being offered an orange by Lorenzo, her brothers' apprentice. Isabella and Lorenzo have fallen in love, but her three brothers intend to marry her to a wealthy nobleman. Noticing the evolving relationship, the brothers plot to murder Lorenzo, and – unaware of their plan – he offers Isabella a blood orange, symbolizing the blood he will shed. Two of the brothers watch the pair slyly, and the other vindictively tries to kick one of the family whippets. Another pet whippet lies asleep beneath that brother's chair. In this painting, 19-year-old Millais adhered to the Pre-Raphaelite approach through the use of soft tonal contrasts and clear patterns and colours.

27
JOHN EVERETT MILLAIS
Isabella
1848–9
Oil on canvas
41 × 56¼ in
(103 × 142.8 cm)
Walker Art Gallery, Liverpool, UK

Opposite: detail

WHIPPET

A medium-sized British breed, the whippet is a sighthound related to the greyhound. The breed is sleek, gentle and quiet, and its name derives from an early seventeenth-century word, now disused, meaning "to move briskly". In medieval England, a small greyhound-type breed became popular for use as a ratting dog and was gradually adopted by royalty and the wealthy for its elegance, short and silky coat, affectionate nature, intelligence and lack of aggression. Traditionally, whippets were most commonly kept as companion dogs, or used for amateur racing and coursing or catching rabbits. They are the fastest runners of any breed of similar weight and size.

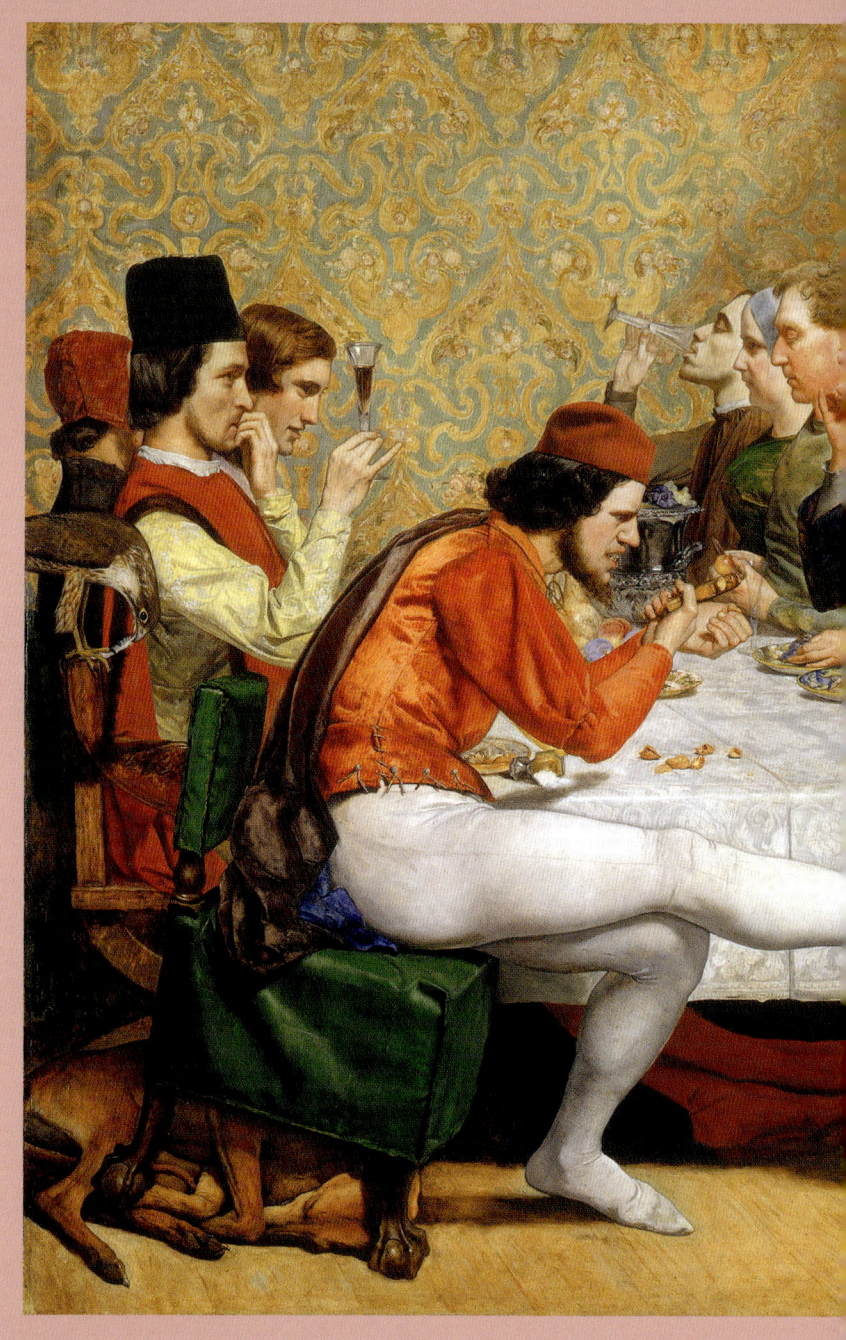

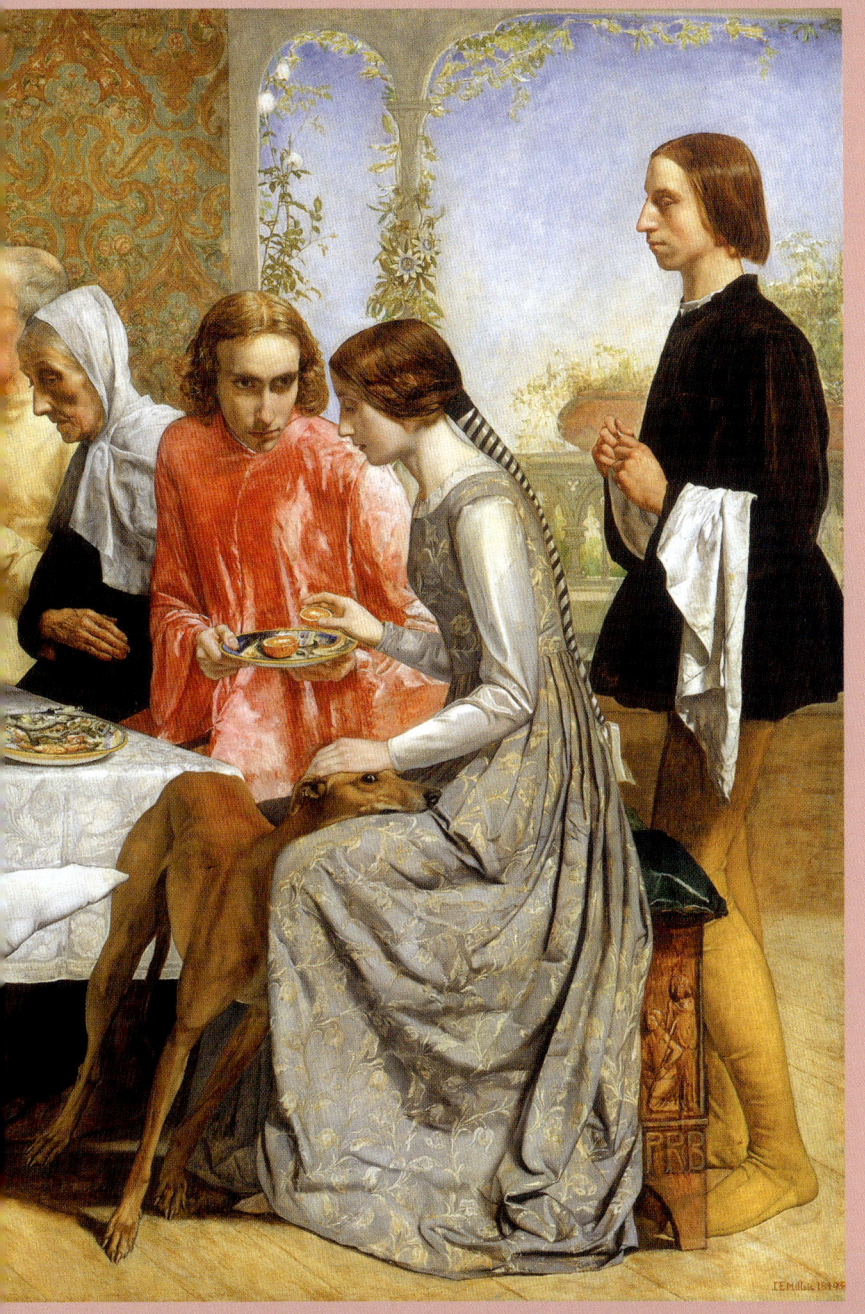

A country walk

This painting, sometimes called *Bonjour, Monsieur Courbet*, depicts the artist, Gustave Courbet (1819–77), who was walking to the city of Montpellier, meeting his patron – and the commissioner of this work – the art collector and industrialist Alfred Bruyas (1821–77), who is accompanied by his servant Calas and his dog. In the background is a carriage with horses. Courbet stands with all he needs to paint directly from nature; on his back is a folding easel containing paints, canvas, palette, oil, turpentine and rags. At that time Courbet was the most influential proponent of French Realism, but when the painting was exhibited in Paris at the Exposition Universelle of 1855, it was ridiculed. It is a large work, which was unusual for such a mundane subject, and it expresses Bruyas's appreciation of Courbet's skill. Bruyas has removed his glove to shake Courbet's hand, but the gesture is not returned. Calas also makes a respectful gesture towards Courbet. Yet Courbet's head tilts back slightly, conveying a sense of self-importance. Even his walking stick is larger than the one held by Bruyas. The meeting seems to contrast the vitality and ease of the countryside with the more complex and restricted style of the city.

28
GUSTAVE COURBET
The Meeting of 1854
1854
Oil on canvas
51 × 59 in
(129 × 149 cm)
Musée Fabre, Montpellier, France

Overleaf: detail

POITEVIN AND GASCON SAINTONGEOIS

It is not clear whether the dog in this painting is a Poitevin (also known as Chien de Haut-Poitou) or a Gascon Saintongeois. Resembling each other, these two refined and elegant breeds of scent hound originated in France, and both were used for hunting in packs. They are similar in appearance to the foxhound and the greyhound, with gently sloping skulls and narrow, tapering muzzles, and both have lean, muscular bodies and long legs, excellent scenting abilities, and exceptional speed, stamina and vitality. The Poitevin originated in the province of Poitou, while the Gascon Saintongeois – of which there are two varieties, Grand (large) and Petit (only slightly smaller) – is descended from an older type of large hunting dog called the Hound of Saintonge.

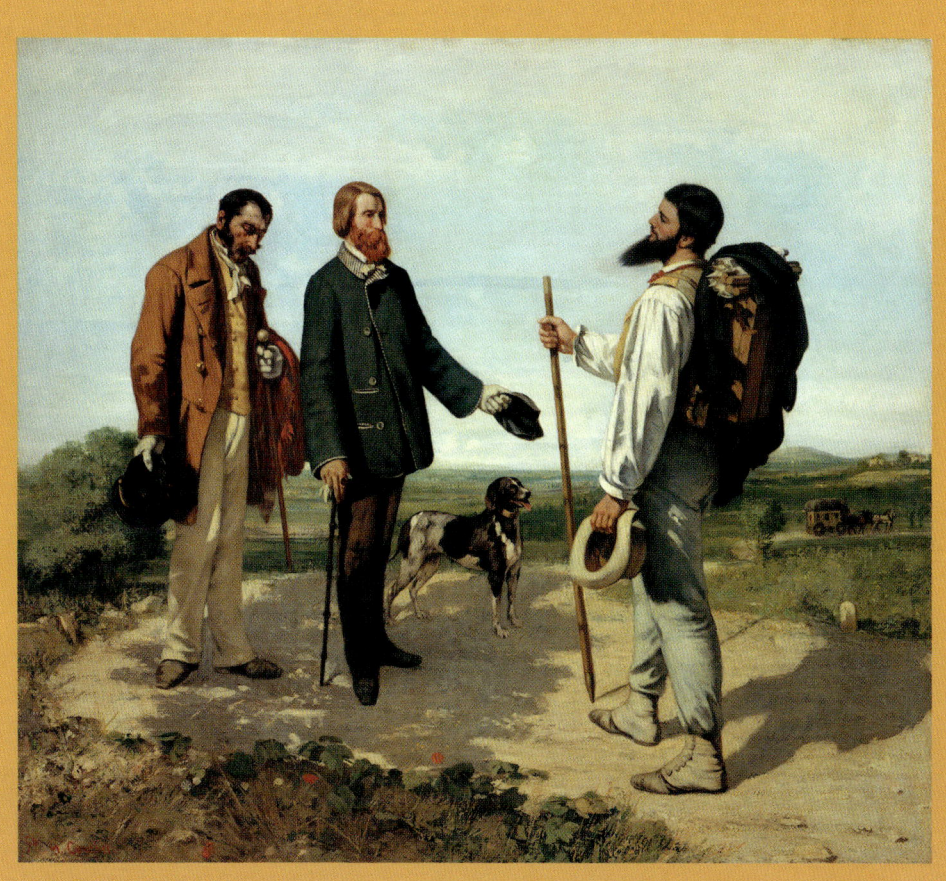

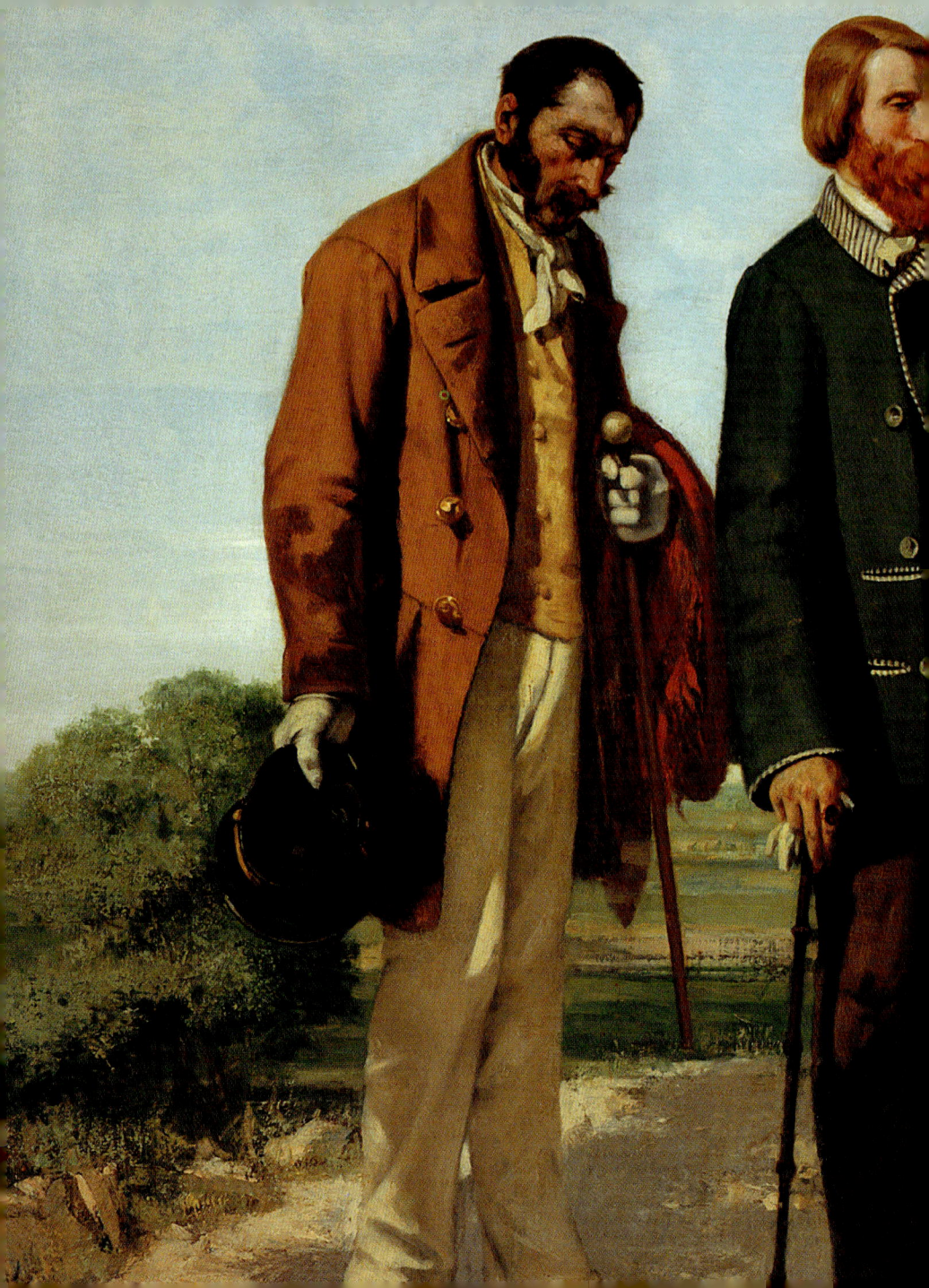

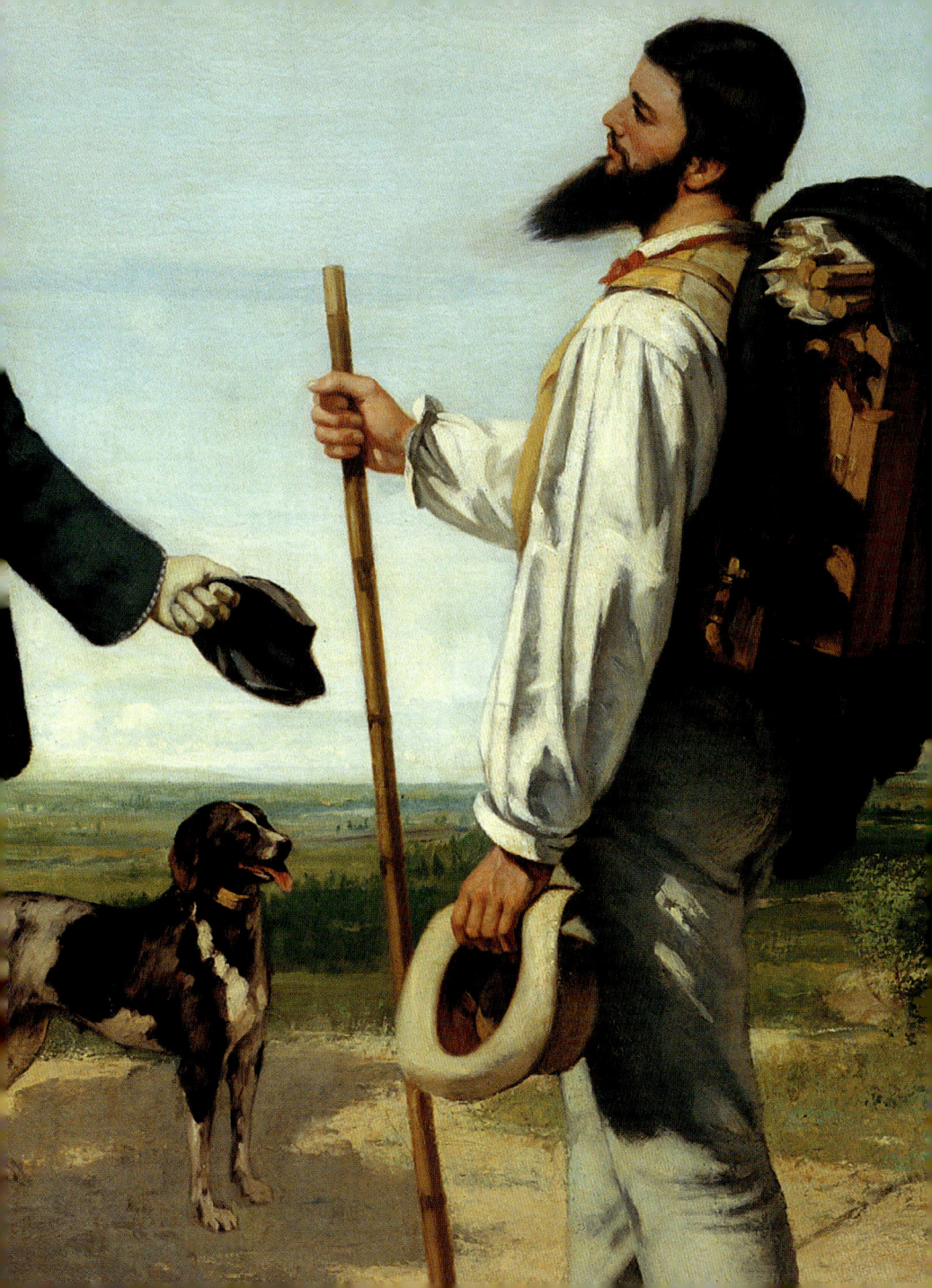

Domestic life

The most successful student of Utagawa (or Andō) Hiroshige (1797–1858), Hiroshige II (1826–69) was another Japanese *ukiyo-e* artist who inherited his master's name. He shared the approach of the elder Hiroshige, and much of his work has been confused with that of the earlier artist, since they are close in style, subject and signature, with influences of Chinese scroll painting, the *kanō, nanga* and *shijō* schools (see page 144), and Western techniques of linear perspective. The word *ukiyo* refers to the human world, and *e* means "picture", so *ukiyo-e* described depictions of the lives of people in the cities of Kyoto and Edo (now Tokyo) during what came to be called the Edo Period (1603–1867). *Ukiyo-e* artists produced paintings and woodblock prints of beautiful women, kabuki actors and sumo wrestlers, and of folk tales, travel scenes and landscapes. Benefiting from Edo's rapid economic growth, their art was bought by the newly wealthy merchants who could afford to enjoy the entertainments of Edo and to decorate their homes. Printed or painted *ukiyo-e* works were popular, and this print depicts a French woman in a rather unusual dress, accompanied by her child and their pet dog. The child sits on the dog, holding its ears as handles. With its bright red tongue, green eyes and sharp white teeth, it is very different from the Labrador that Hiroshige was trying to depict.

29
UTAGAWA HIROSHIGE II
French Woman, Her Child and Pet Dog
1860
Woodblock print, ink and colour on paper
14¾ × 10¼ in (37.5 × 26 cm)
The Metropolitan Museum, New York, USA

LABRADOR RETRIEVER

Originally bred to retrieve nets for fishermen, then game and fowl for hunters, Labrador retrievers are medium-size dogs that are suited to work both on land and in or around water, being alert, good swimmers, sure-footed and instinctive retrievers. They later came to be used as guide and assistant dogs, but most of all, they are beloved throughout the world as companions and family pets for their affectionate personalities and intelligence. Labrador retrievers were bred in the United Kingdom, probably from St John's Water Dogs imported from the colony of Newfoundland (now a province of Canada), and were named after the Labrador region of that colony.

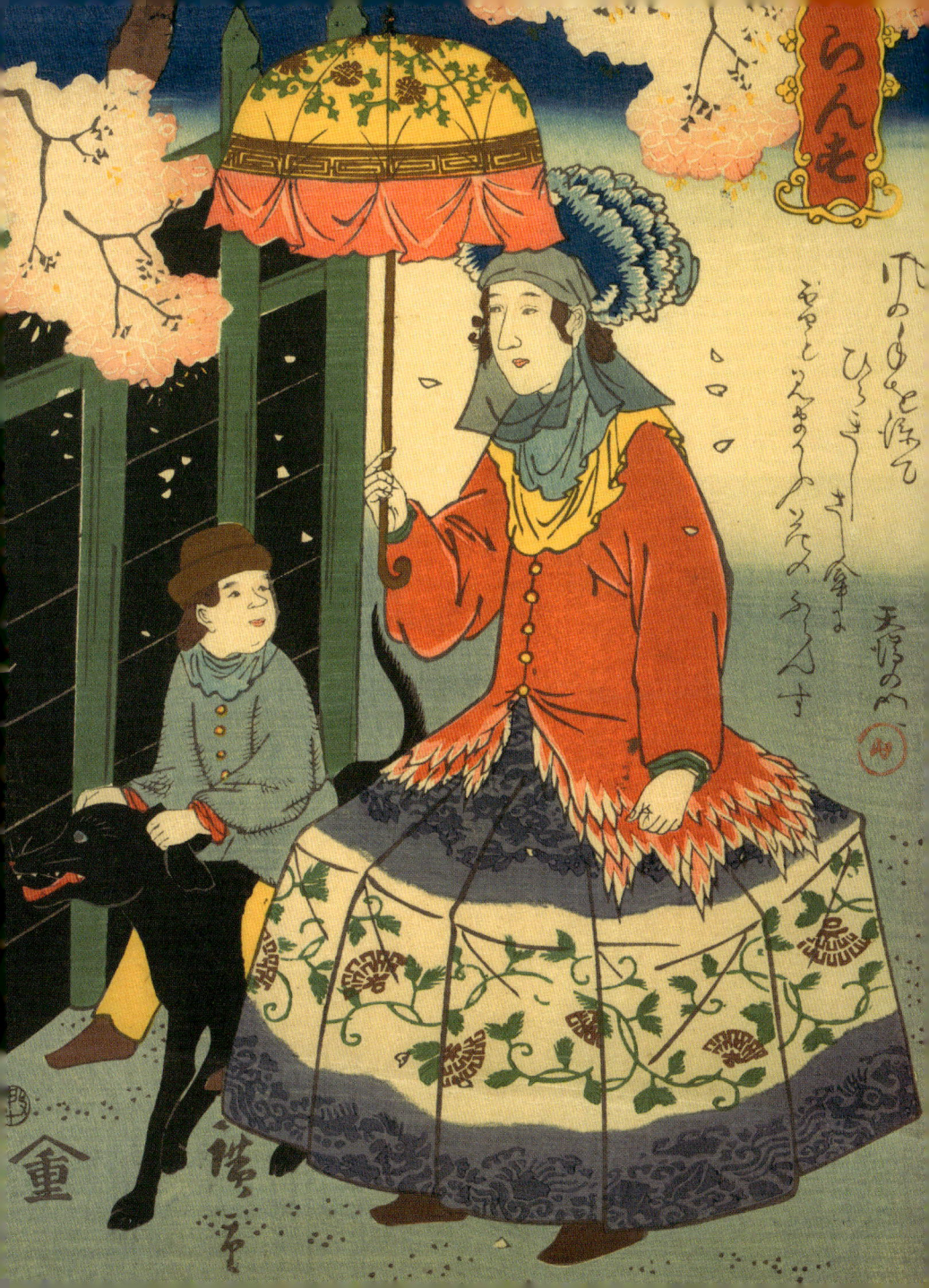

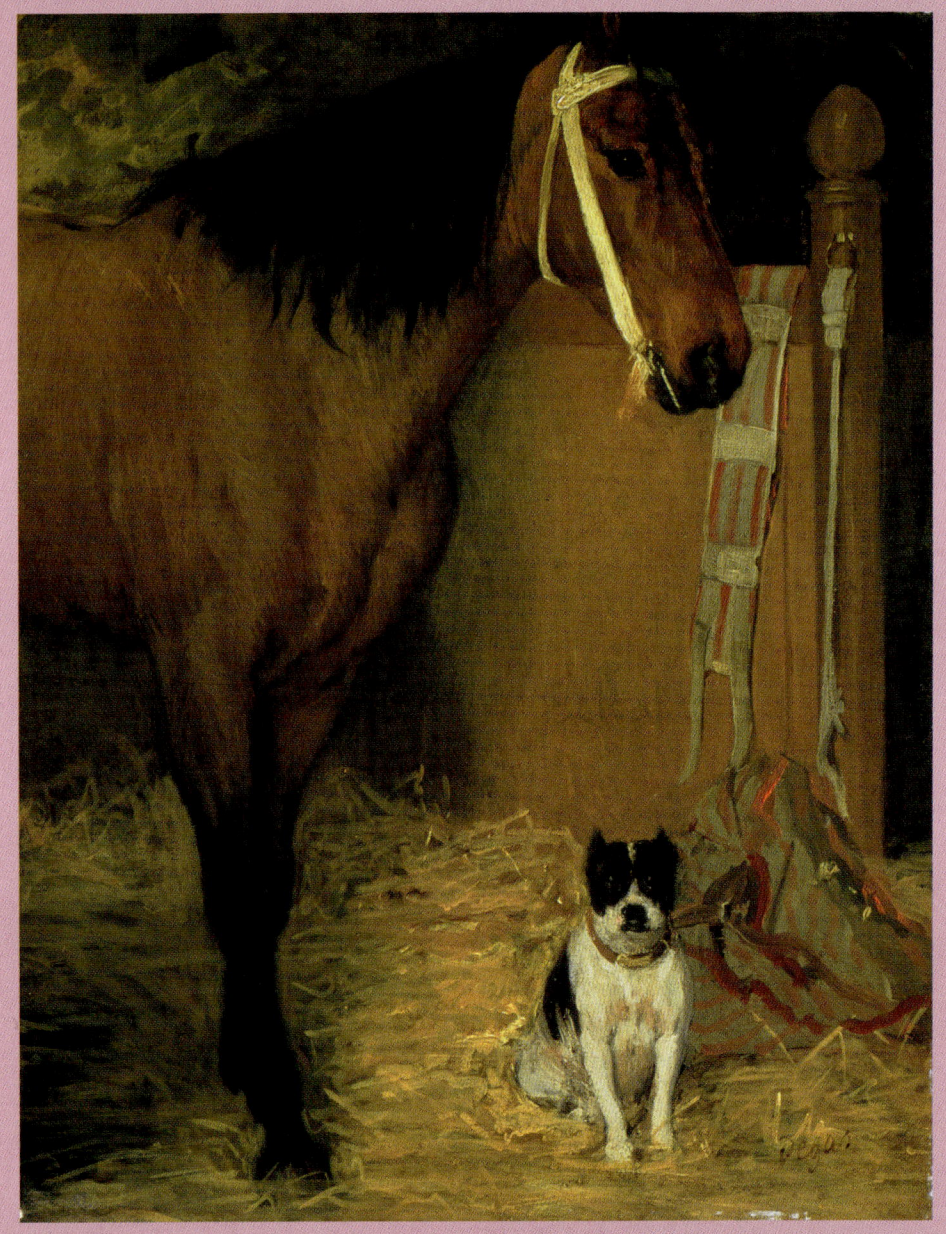

A peaceful moment

30

EDGAR DEGAS

*At the Stables,
Horse and Dog*

c. 1861

Oil on canvas

15¾ × 12½ in
(40 × 32 cm)

Private collection

Overleaf: detail

Painted a few years before the start of the Impressionist movement, *At the Stables, Horse and Dog* shows Edgar Degas (1834–1917) already moving towards some of the latest ideas in art. Although he is categorized as an Impressionist, his work differed from that of most in that group of painters. This is an intimate scene inside a stable, with a horse standing to the left. The cut-off edges show the influence of photography, while the nuances of warm colour and tone give the image a unified appearance. To the right, some red-and-white tack is draped over a wooden partition, creating a contrast with the otherwise muted colour palette. But an even greater contrast is created by a small black-and-white French bulldog, which looks out of the composition, directly at the viewer. The background is dark and shadowy, bringing the animals clearly into focus. The dog's fur is painted with quick textural brushstrokes, while the straw on the ground is built up with short, hatched marks that create an overall impression of the shapes and textures of the rough surface, rather than a detailed rendering. The work is a double portrait of a horse and a dog, but also captures a peaceful, unstudied moment in time.

FRENCH BULLDOG

With its large, bat-like ears, the French bulldog is usually a companion dog and is the result of cross-breeding. It first appeared in Paris in the mid-nineteenth century. Earlier in that century, bulldogs were bred in the United Kingdom, but the French breed is quite distinct in appearance from these. It was created when, having been displaced by the Industrial Revolution, laceworkers from the UK moved to France, taking their small dogs with them. These included toy bulldogs, and English breeders began sending over any small bulldogs that they believed had faults, such as upstanding ears, which were popular with the French people.

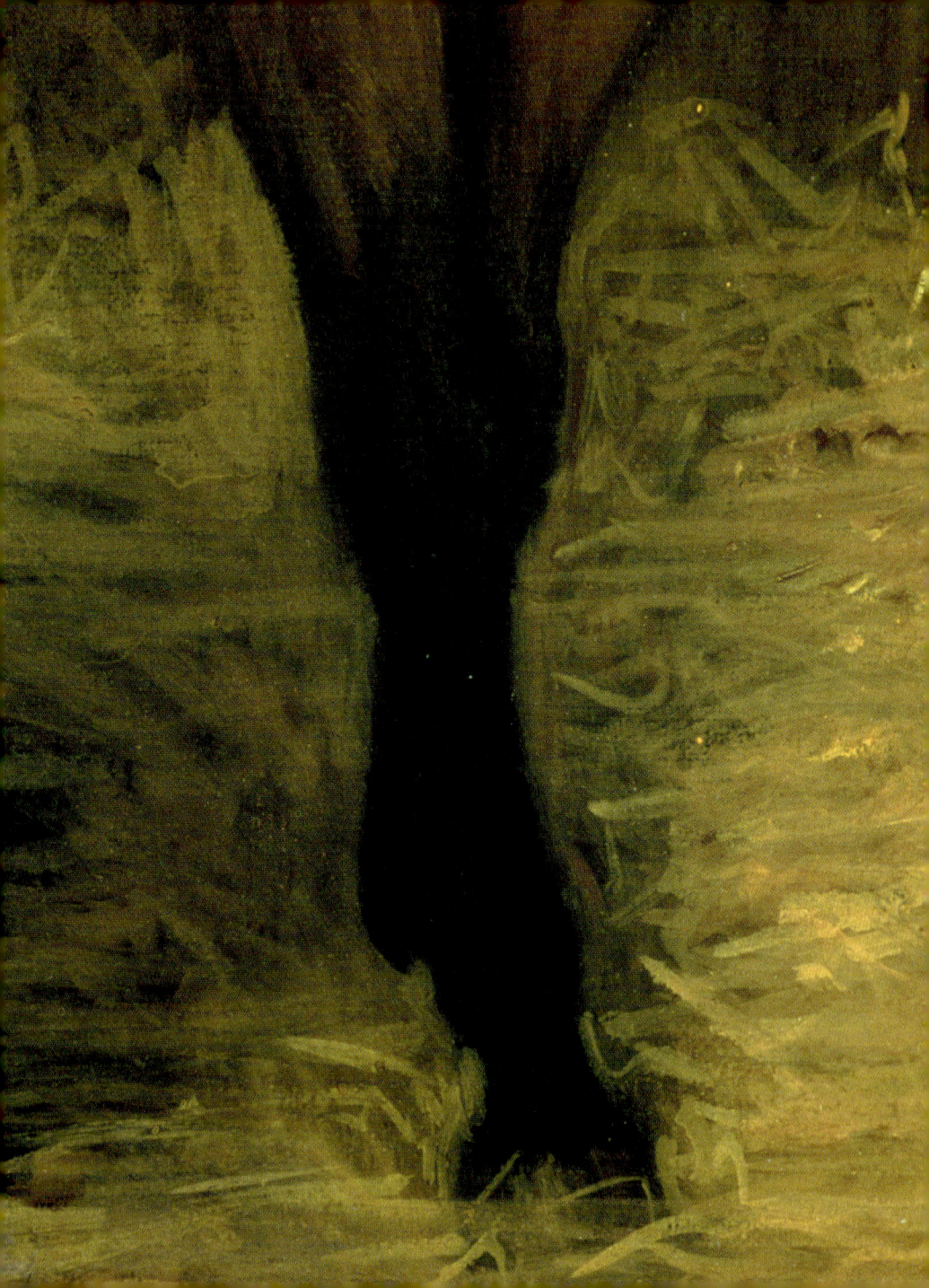

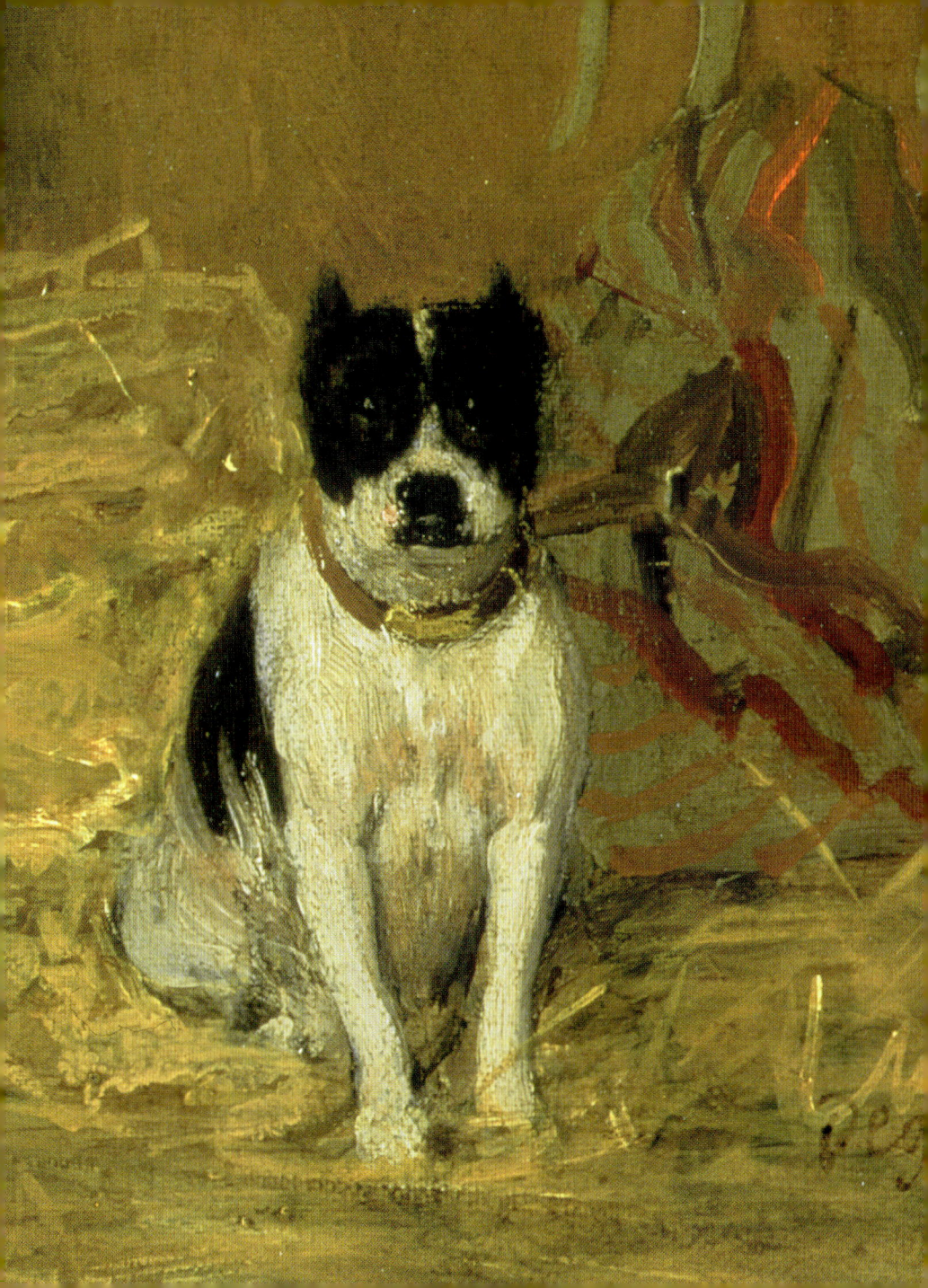

From one palace to another

Looty, a Pekingese Lion dog, is sitting on a red cushion in front of a pale blue Kakiemon-style Japanese vase. Next to her are a bunch of flowers and a blue collar adorned with two little bells. The painting was created with small brush marks and meticulous details, especially conveying the soft, bright-eyed little dog. Looty had been found in China and taken by Captain John Hart Dunne of the 99th Regiment after the looting of the Summer Palace near Beijing (then Peking) in October 1860, during the Second Opium War. In England, Dunne gave the little dog to Queen Victoria, who named her Looty. One of the first Pekingese dogs in Britain, Looty was described in the *Illustrated London News* in 1861 as "the smallest and by far the most beautiful little animal that has appeared in this country". When the German artist Friedrich Wilhelm Keyl (1823–71) was commissioned to paint the dog's portrait, he was told to show her size, so he added the vase and flowers. The name Looty reflects the arrogance of British imperialism at that time. Nonetheless, despite the appalling way she was taken, Looty was treated well. She lived in a palace and was cared for by courtiers for the rest of her life.

31
FRIEDRICH
WILHELM KEYL
Looty
1861
Oil on canvas
13⅛ × 15 in
(33.4 × 38 cm)
Royal Collection,
London, UK

PEKINGESE

The tiny Pekingese, also known as Lion Dog because of its resemblance to Chinese guardian lions, originated in China and was kept by royalty as a companion dog. Named after Peking (now Beijing), the breed could be owned only by members of the Chinese Imperial Palace. Pekingese have coats in various colours – from light reds and golds to black and grey – that are longer around the neck and shoulder, giving the appearance of a lion's mane. Now popular pets around the world, these friendly dogs have bright, inquisitive eyes, short, wrinkled muzzles and plumed tails. They are loved for their sociability, intelligence and placidity.

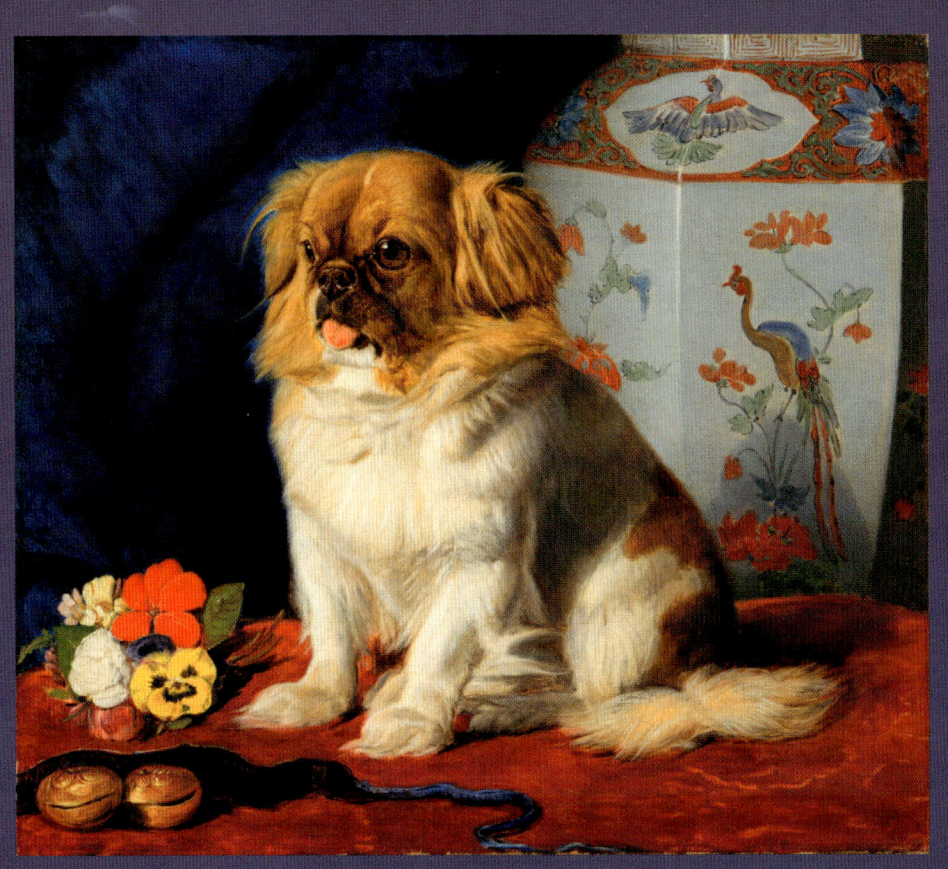

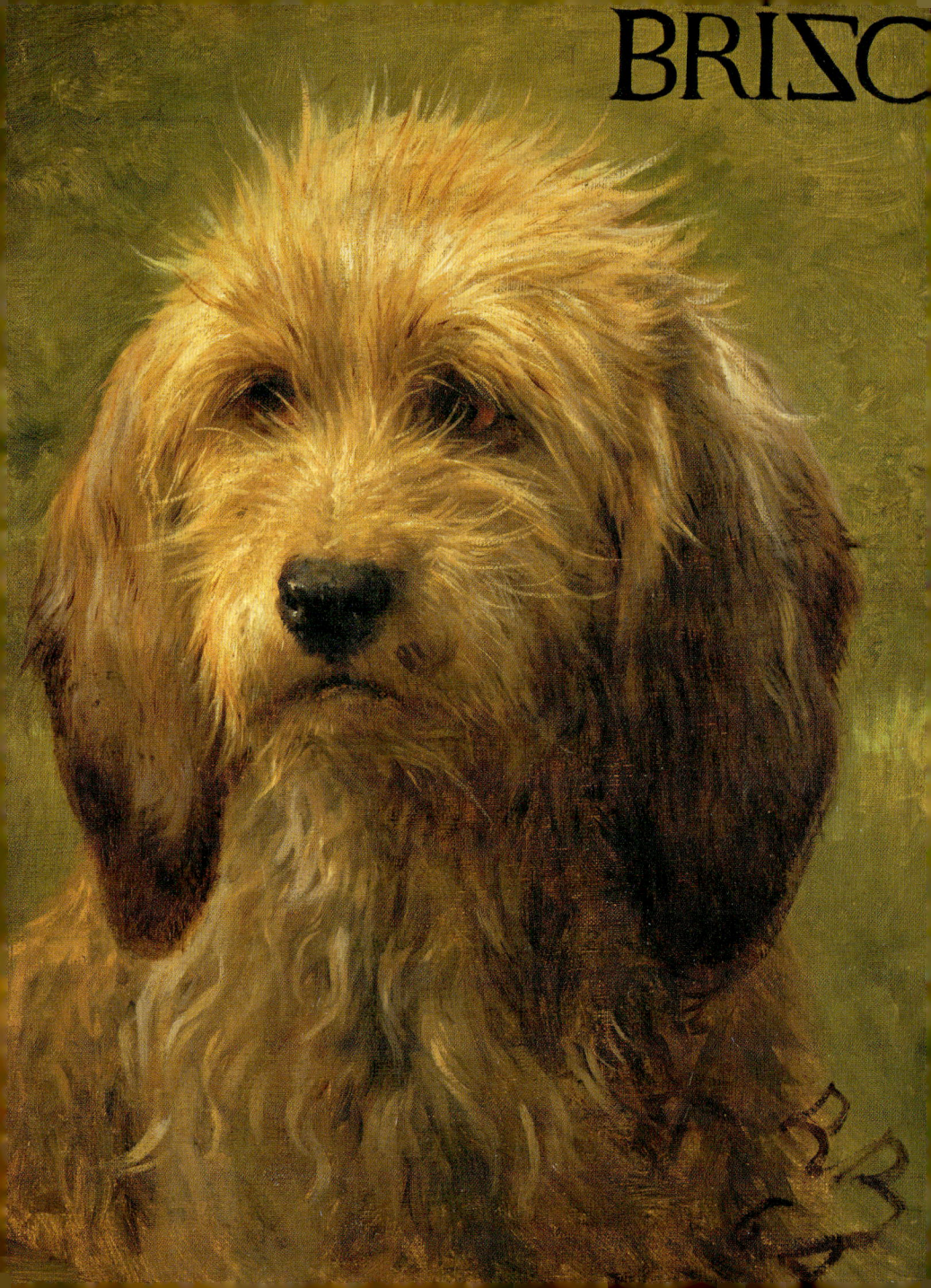

BRISC

Strong females

Rosa Bonheur (1822–99) was a celebrated Realist *animalière* (painter and sculptor of animals). Unconventional and independent, she earned her living from her art, and even obtained police permission to wear trousers so that she could visit animal markets and abattoirs to study animal anatomy. Dedicated to understanding and reproducing exactly how animals look and move, she confounded social norms, yet through dedication, perseverance and skill, she had earned enough from her art by the age of 30 to buy her own chateau, where she kept many animals. This expressive, natural-looking dog is a female otterhound, and it is clear from the painting just how sensitive Bonheur was to canine emotions. The dog's position and expression imbue the work with the dignity of a human portrait. The reference to a shepherd's dog in the title of the work, and the rather crudely written inscription "Brizo" with the back-to-front Z, were probably added later, not by Bonheur. Brizo was an ancient Greek goddess, the protector of sailors and fishermen, and this Brizo was one of Bonheur's many pets that lived with her at her chateau on the edge of the Forest of Fontainebleau.

32
ROSA BONHEUR
Brizo,
a Shepherd's Dog
1864
Oil on canvas
18 × 15 in
(46.1 × 38.4 cm)
The Wallace
Collection,
London, UK

OTTERHOUND

Bred originally in England and probably related to wolves, griffons and bloodhounds, otterhounds are scent hounds, known to be sensitive, strong and good swimmers. Intelligent, patient and even-tempered, they are very much pack animals. There are only about 600 of these dogs known in the world. The first recorded otterhounds were bred in northwestern England in the early nineteenth century, but, since otter hunting dates back to the early medieval period and is what they were bred for, it is likely that a form of this breed was around far earlier. These large dogs have rough coats, wide noses, deep-set eyes and long, drooping ears.

Status symbol

During the 1840s, owing to rising political tension in his home town of Hesse, the German artist Charles Christian Nahl (1818–78) moved to Paris before emigrating to America. Settling in California in 1849, he lived first in Sacramento, then in San Francisco. By 1867 he was recognized as California's foremost portraitist, and the politician Milton S. Latham commissioned him to paint one of his coachmen, a Nisenan Maidu man. Wearing a black suit, white shirt and bow tie, the man sits between two Dalmatians. In the foreground are a cock and a hen, and behind a river and mountain. The liver-spotted dog watches the man, and the black-spotted dog watches the other dog. Yet while the image suggests a peaceful assimilation of Indigenous people, in reality the US government used violent methods to "Americanize" them. In northern California, this violence is evidenced by accounts of Native children being kidnapped and forcibly "civilized" through Indian boarding schools. Seen in this context, the painting illustrates the way in which visual representation can support a larger campaign of cultural oppression.

33
CHARLES
CHRISTIAN NAHL
Portrait of a Man
1867
Oil on canvas
42 × 49¼ in
(106.8 × 125.1 cm)
Fine Arts Museums
of San Francisco,
USA

DALMATIAN

Instantly recognizable with their dark-spotted white coats, Dalmatians are energetic, outgoing and extremely loyal. They are an ancient breed, appearing in images on Greek friezes from about 2000 BCE. Records have also been found of these dogs in Dalmatia, the southernmost part of Croatia, and this might be how they obtained their name, although it is not conclusive. Originally bred as hunting dogs, they were also used as carriage dogs, and in the eighteenth and nineteenth centuries they became a status symbol trotting alongside carriages. Some also guarded stables at night or cleared the route for horse-drawn fire engines by running ahead.

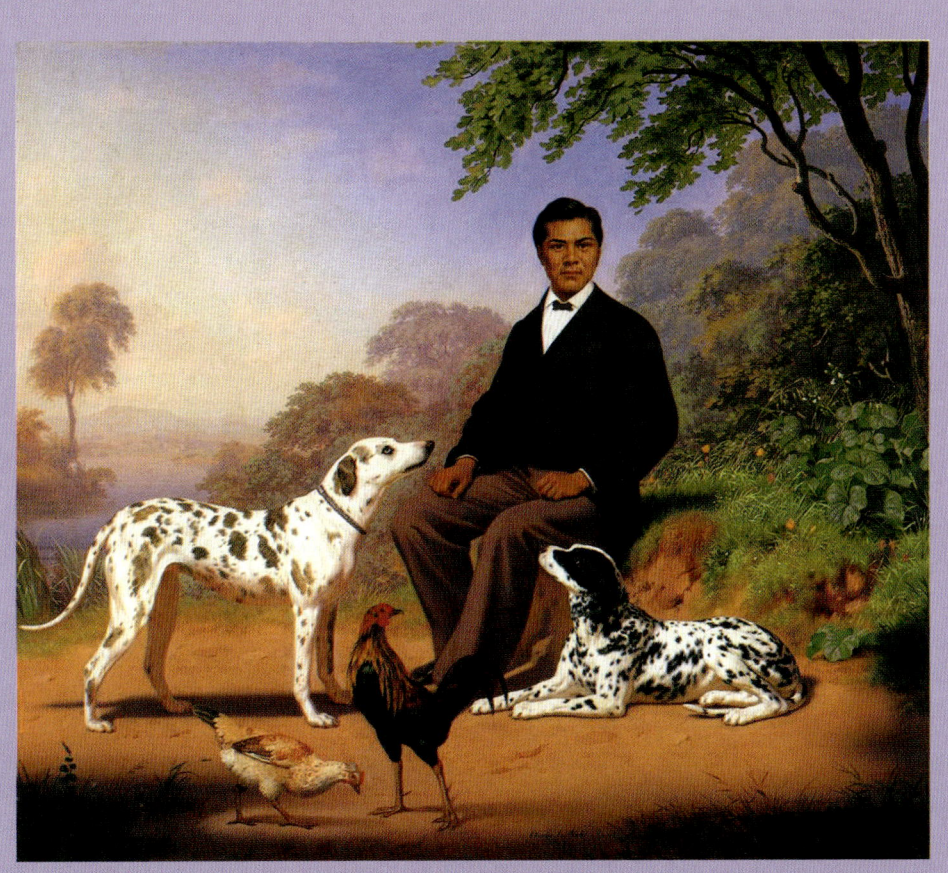

Ready to play

A pivotal figure in the transition from Realism to Impressionism, Édouard Manet (1832–83) was born into an upper-class family, but he rejected the future envisioned for him and became an artist. Although some of his early works caused great controversy, they are now recognized as being crucial to the development of modern art. His style was a unique blend of Realism with the influence of the Dutch painter Frans Hals (1582/3–1666) and the Spanish artists Diego Velázquez (page 60) and Francisco Goya (page 78). He was friends with and admired by the artists who later became known as the Impressionists, but he chose not to exhibit with them. Some time around 1875 he painted this long-haired, small black-and-white dog with loose, visible brushstrokes. Standing in a wood-panelled room, the little animal looks happily at the painter with bright, golden-brown eyes, her pink tongue out, a broken stuffed doll at her feet. We can imagine the dog's long, feathery fur moving slightly as she wags her curling, bushy tail, waiting for the toy to be thrown again. Leaning on the panelling behind the dog is a walking stick made of light wood. The dog's name, Tama (Japanese for "jewel, whole, perfect"), appears in tan block letters at upper left.

34
ÉDOUARD MANET
Tama, the Japanese Dog
c. 1875
Oil on canvas
24 × 19⅞ in (61 × 50 cm)
National Gallery of Art, Washington, DC, USA

JAPANESE CHIN

A dainty little dog with a big personality, the Japanese Chin is distantly related to the Pekingese and the pug. Unusually, these dogs wash their faces using their paws, as cats do. Although they are an ancient breed, their origins are not clear. It is likely that they were first bred in China and entered Japan when the Empress of China gave a puppy to the Empress of Japan. With their long coats, curly tails and feathered fur on their legs, these friendly, bold and intelligent little dogs are mainly white, with black or brownish-red patches, and they are extremely popular companion dogs.

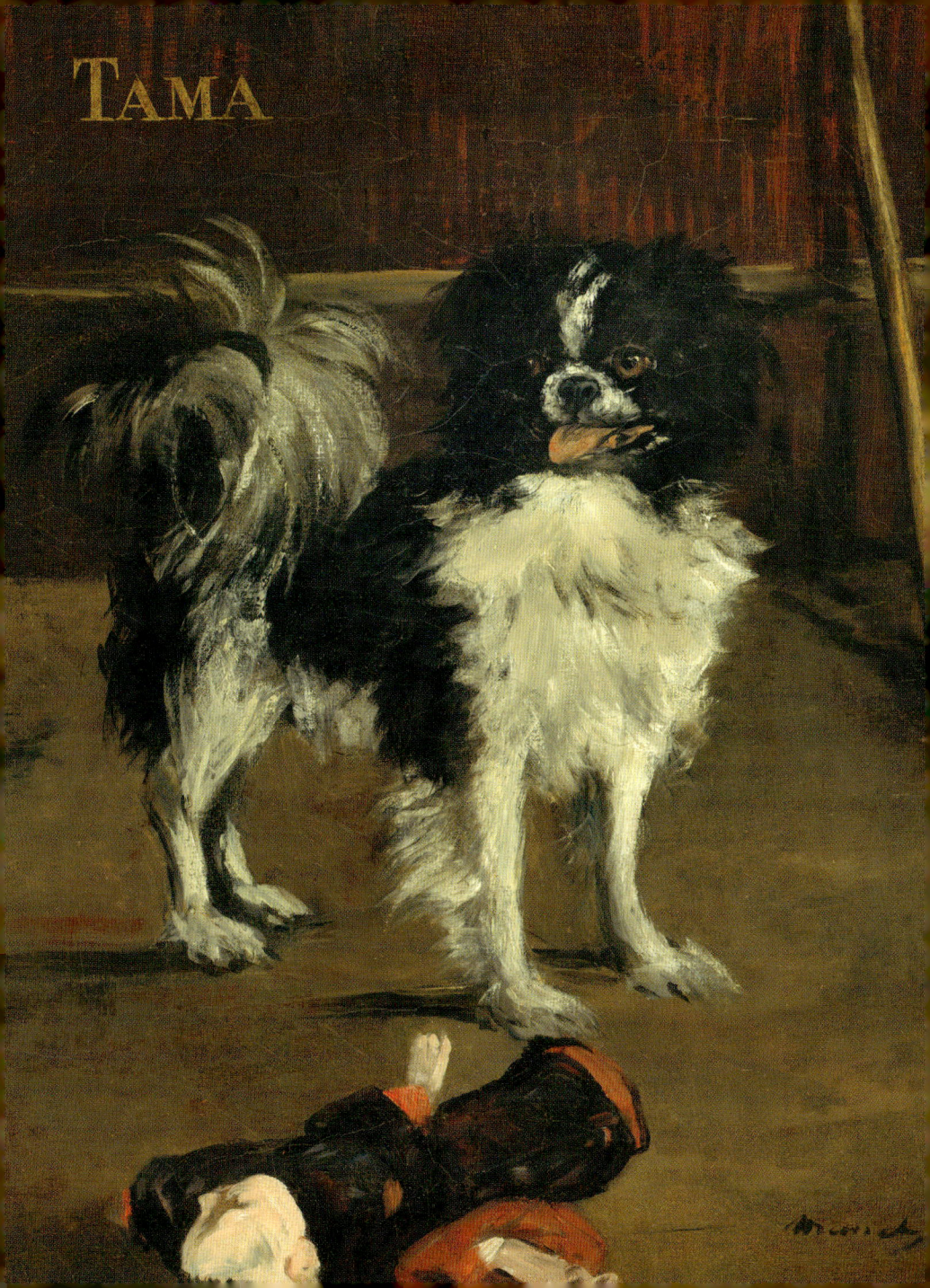

TAMA

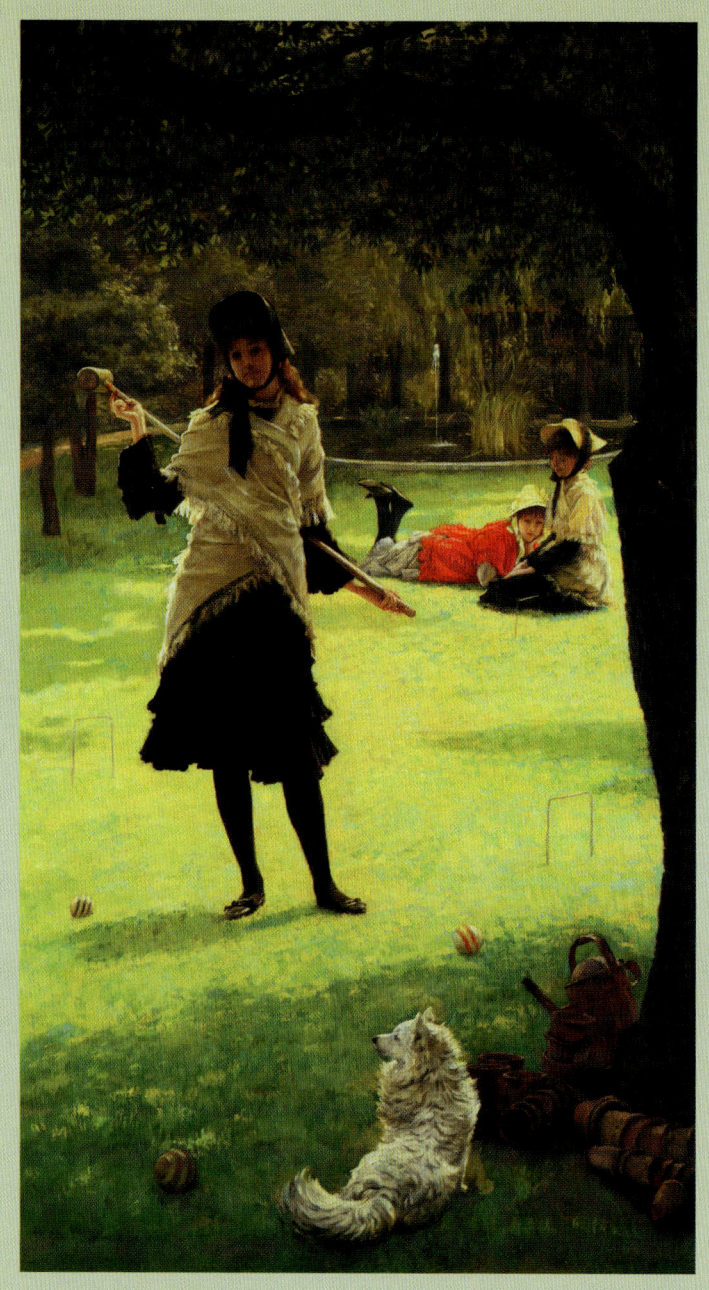

A game of croquet

The French artist James Tissot (1836–1902) is best known for his paintings of fashionable members of French and British society. His immense popularity arose from his ability to capture the subtleties and characteristics of the wealthy in Paris and London. Arriving in the latter city in 1871 after fighting in the Franco-Prussian War, Tissot befriended other artists and welcomed guests to his mansion in St John's Wood. His works reflect the influence of Realism, Art Nouveau and Impressionism, featuring a mixture of narrative realism and decorative effects, as in this scene. A girl stands on a summer lawn facing the viewer while holding a croquet mallet behind her back, with her friends relaxing on the grass behind her. On close inspection, it turns out that all three girls in the painting are the same model, in different clothes and poses. Equipment for the game of croquet – which had arrived in England from France in about 1860 – is around her on the grass, including three balls and stakes. A small white dog, probably a German spitz, sits in the shade of a large tree near a pile of terracotta flowerpots. The dog symbolizes leisure, and the setting is Tissot's own garden in London, with a colonnade and fountain in the background.

35

JAMES TISSOT
Croquet
1878
Oil on canvas
35¼ × 20 in
(89.8 × 50.8 cm)
Art Gallery
of Hamilton,
Ontario, Canada

GERMAN SPITZ

This breed is probably descended from larger spitz dogs brought from Scandinavia by the Vikings, although the earliest mentions of them in German literature date from 1450. The larger spitz dogs were originally kept on farms and used for herding and guarding, among other roles; gradually, some were bred to be smaller for other duties, especially as small companion dogs. There are now five varieties, which vary significantly in size. The German spitz seen here, the ancestor of the Pomeranian, is the smallest. Bred in all colours, it has long, straight hair with a thick, woolly undercoat. Most dogs of this breed are full of character and highly intelligent.

Earnest and alert

Born in Groningen in the Netherlands, Otto Eerelman (1839–1926) became best known for his depictions of dogs and horses. He longed from an early age to be an artist, and although his parents were against it, he eventually studied art and later painted history and genre scenes, portraits and detailed depictions of Dutch interiors. By the 1880s, having visited Brussels, Paris, Vienna and London, he had moved on to painting horse and dog portraits. He became a court painter for Queen Wilhelmina, an appointment that raised his reputation even more, and he became highly sought after by wealthy owners for his dog and horse paintings. For his dog portraits, patrons brought their faithful companions to his house on Elandstraat in The Hague, and before beginning to paint them, he trained each dog to sit for him. He painted various breeds but preferred larger dogs, such as St Bernards and the Leonberger seen here. He was uniquely accomplished in capturing the dogs' expressions and personalities, as well as the textures of their coats, clearly seen here. Using quick marks in watercolour and chalk pastel, he captured the softness of the fur, the protruding black nose and muzzle, and the distinctive features, including the gentle, earnest and alert expression of the eyes.

36
OTTO EERELMAN
Head of a Leonberger
c. 1880–92
Watercolour and chalk on paper
25½ × 19⅔ in (64.8 × 49.8 cm)
Rijksmuseum, Amsterdam, The Netherlands

LEONBERGER

This giant, muscular breed is named after the city of Leonberg in Baden-Württemberg, Germany. The fur is thick and soft, especially around the neck, and the dogs are usually intelligent, dignified and gentle. It is not clear whether the breed was developed in the sixteenth or the nineteenth century, but it seems to have been popular with several European royal and noble households, including the Metternich family, Napoleon II, Empress Elisabeth of Austria, Otto von Bismarck and Napoleon III. From the earliest times, these dogs were kept as family pets or search-and-rescue dogs, since they are agile, strong and good swimmers.

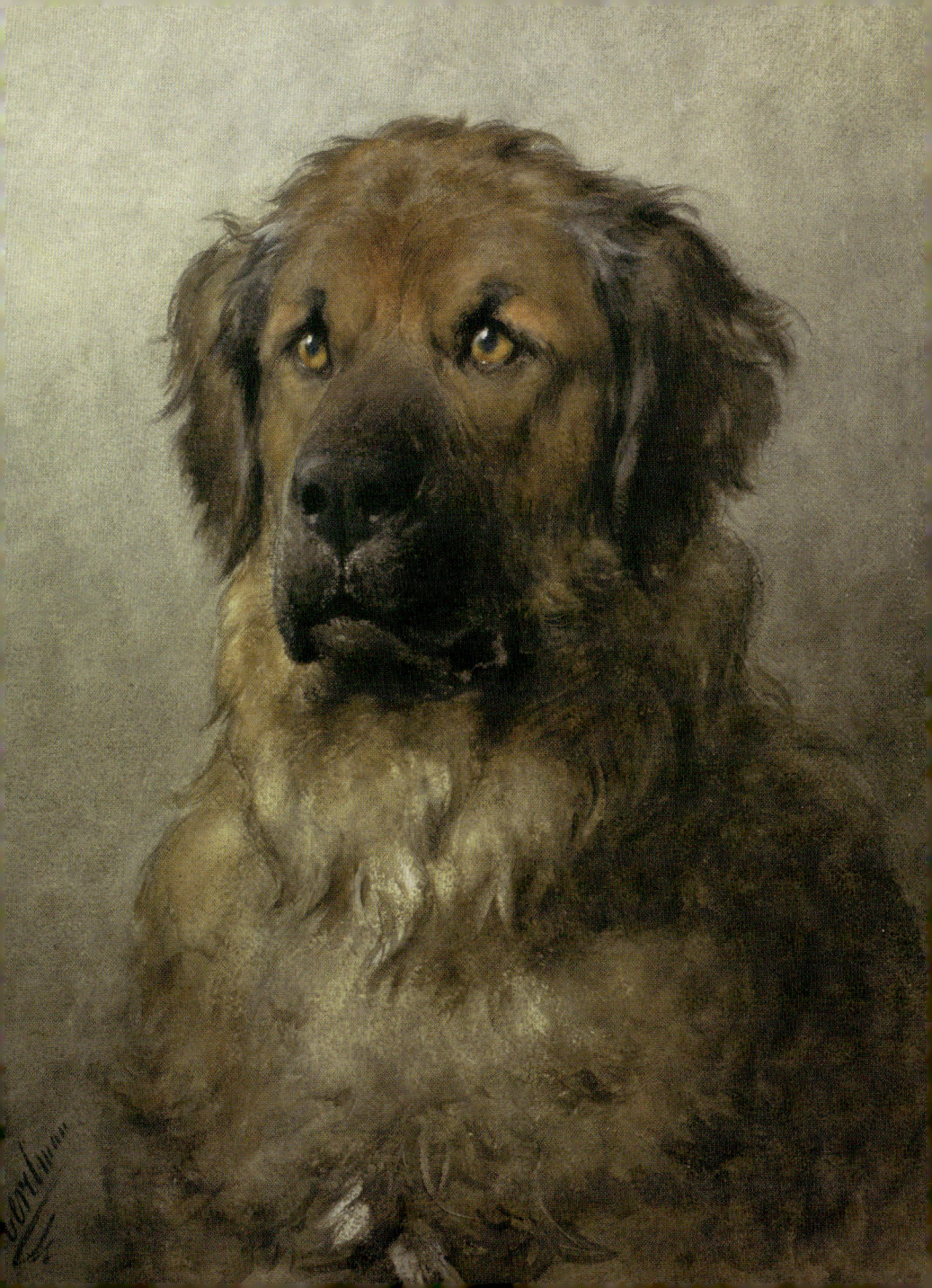

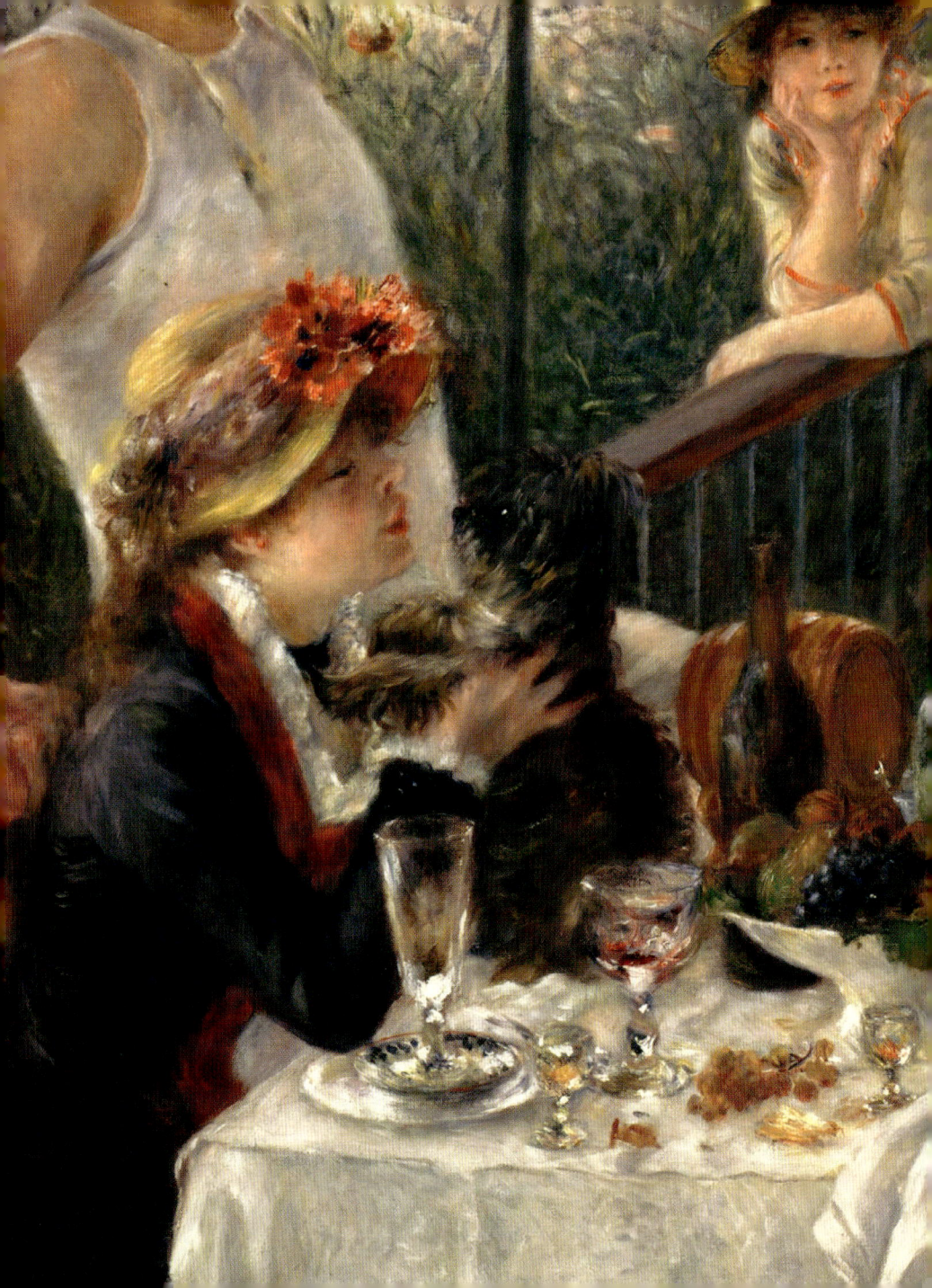

A special moment

A group of friends relax on a balcony at the Maison Fournaise restaurant by the River Seine in Chatou, France. Most of the models were friends of the artist, Pierre-Auguste Renoir (1841–1919). In the right foreground Angèle, one of his frequent models, turns her head to the viewer's right, while leaning over her in a striped blazer is Maggiolo, a journalist. In a singlet and straw boater, the painter Gustave Caillebotte (1848–94) sits and looks across the table at Aline Charigot (1859–1915), Renoir's future wife, who coos to her little fluffy dog, an affenpinscher. This cameo captures the relationship between a young woman and her pet – a naturally close moment, while all around is movement and chatter. On the table is fruit and wine. Behind Aline and her dog, the muscular Alphonse Fournaise Junior, son of the restaurant's owner, leans against the railing. Other friends fill the scene, including the actor Ellen Andrée, drinking from a glass, and the top-hatted Charles Ephrussi, a banker and editor of the *Gazette des Beaux-Arts*. This vibrant work was included in the annual Paris Salon in 1882, and identified by three critics as the best painting in the show.

37

PIERRE-AUGUSTE RENOIR

The Luncheon of the Boating Party

1881

Oil on canvas

51 × 68 in
(129.9 × 172.7 cm)

The Phillips Collection, Washington, DC, USA

Opposite: detail

AFFENPINSCHER

First depicted in fifteenth- and sixteenth-century paintings, affenpinschers are one of the oldest toy breeds in the world. They originated in Germany and the name means "mock terrier". Dogs portrayed in the fifteenth-century woodcuts of Albrecht Dürer are among the earliest visual examples of the breed. These little dogs were originally bred to catch vermin and were extremely good "ratters", for which they became particularly popular in southern Germany during the nineteenth century. The miniature schnauzer and the Brussels griffon were both developed from the affenpinscher. Their loyal, comical personalities meant that their popularity soon spread across the world.

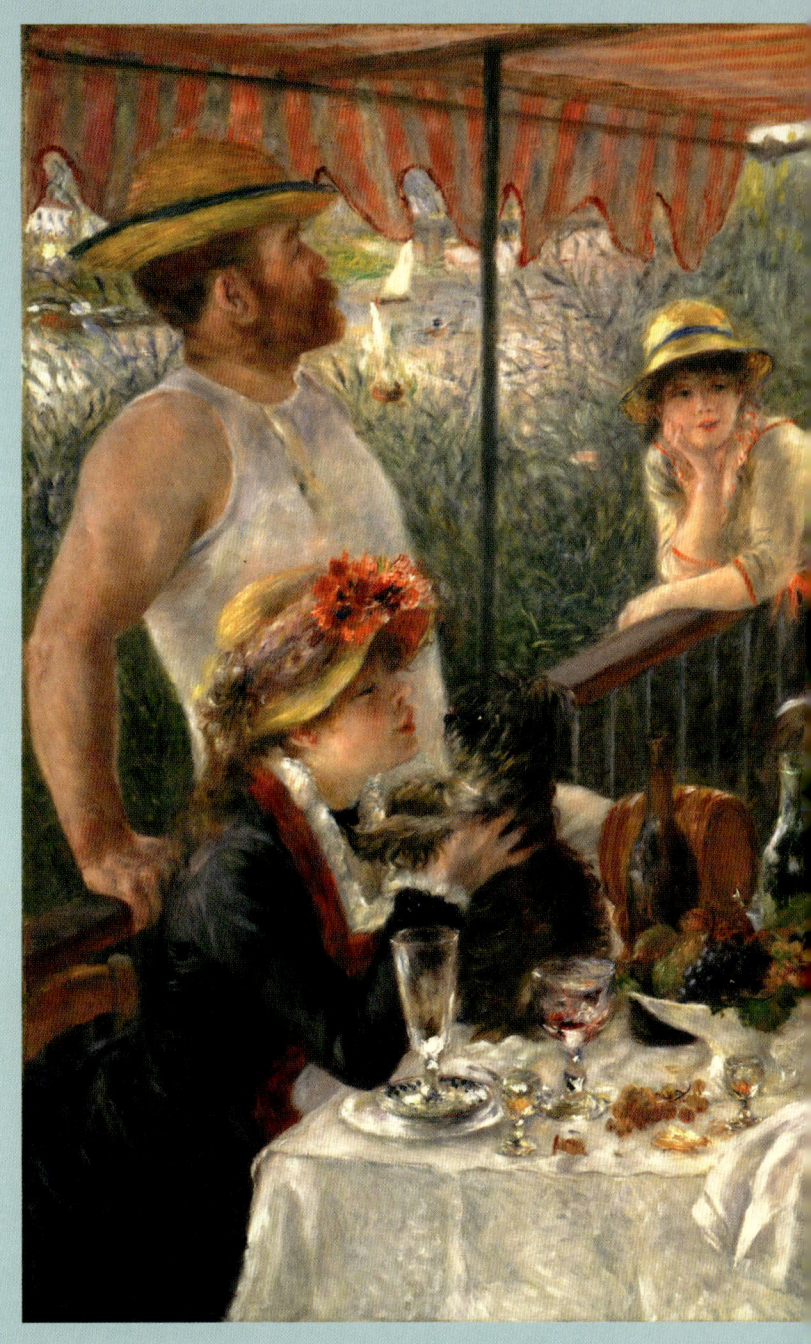

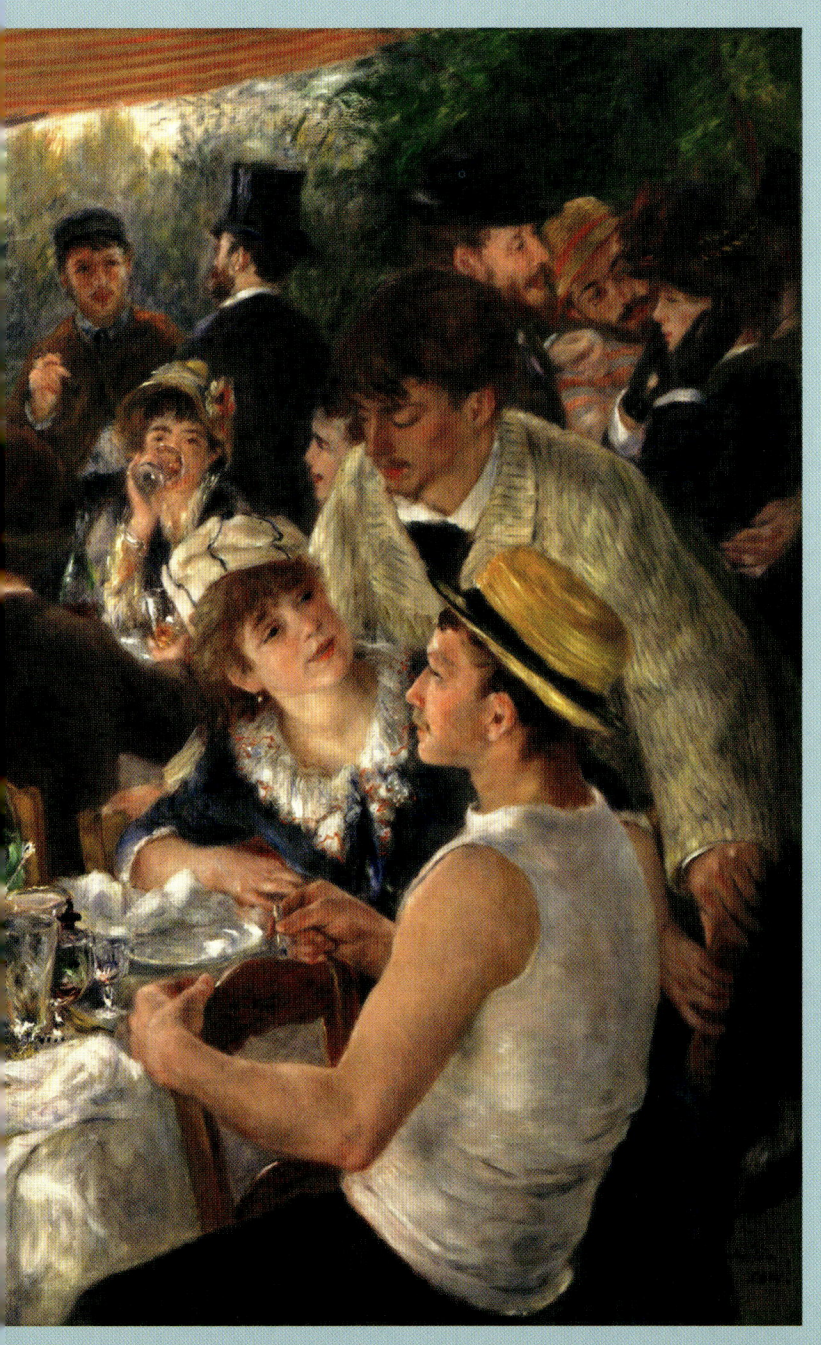

Spontaneity and empathy

Internationally acclaimed as a portrait painter, John Singer Sargent (1856–1925) was an American expatriate, born in Florence and trained in Paris, who lived mainly in London. This is one of his earliest portraits, of 12-year-old Eleanor Beatrice Townsend (1870–84), one of seven children born to a wealthy American couple. Rather than producing a staid image, Sargent has conveyed his young subject's personality, showing her holding her favourite pet dog wriggling under one arm and smiling slightly at the artist. Sargent – who was inspired especially by the Realist movement and the work of Diego Velázquez (page 60) – eschewed the exacting techniques of drawing and underpainting in favour of loose, fresh brush marks and a striking colour palette, conveying spontaneity and naturalism. Portrayed from the hips up and wearing a black dress with a creamy white collar and cuffs, a coral necklace and a wide coral-red sash, the pale-skinned, brown-haired, blue-eyed young girl looks confidently at the artist, whom she knows as a family friend. With equal fluid realism, Sargent has captured her little Yorkshire terrier. He depicts the soft, shaggy fur, dark eyes, pointed ears and shiny black nose loosely and expressively. Sargent was particularly sensitive to young people's feelings and uncertainties, and especially empathetic towards animals.

38
JOHN SINGER SARGENT
Miss Beatrice Townsend
1882
Oil on canvas
31¼ × 23 in (79.4 × 58.4 cm)
National Gallery of Art, Washington, DC, USA

YORKSHIRE TERRIER

In the nineteenth century, miners in Yorkshire, northern England, bred English terriers with Paisley and Clydesdale terriers, aiming to develop a ratting terrier, and in the late 1860s it is possible that the Maltese was used as well, resulting in an improved breed. The Yorkshire terrier was introduced to North America in 1872. Among the smallest of dog breeds, it has a long, silky coat that is tan on the head and dark steel-grey on the body; the tan colour is dark at the roots, lightening at the tips. Playful and energetic, these little dogs are usually kept as companions.

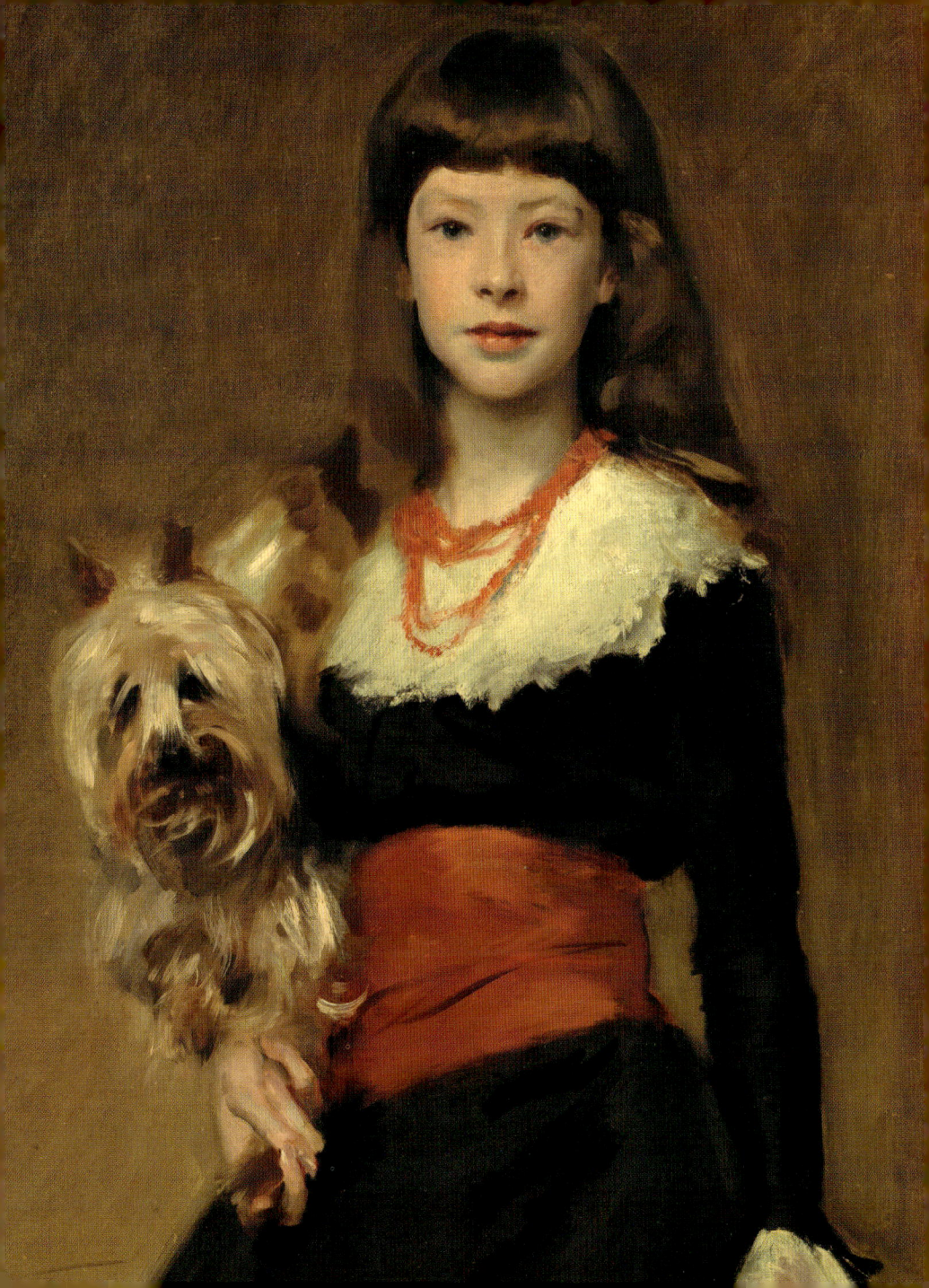

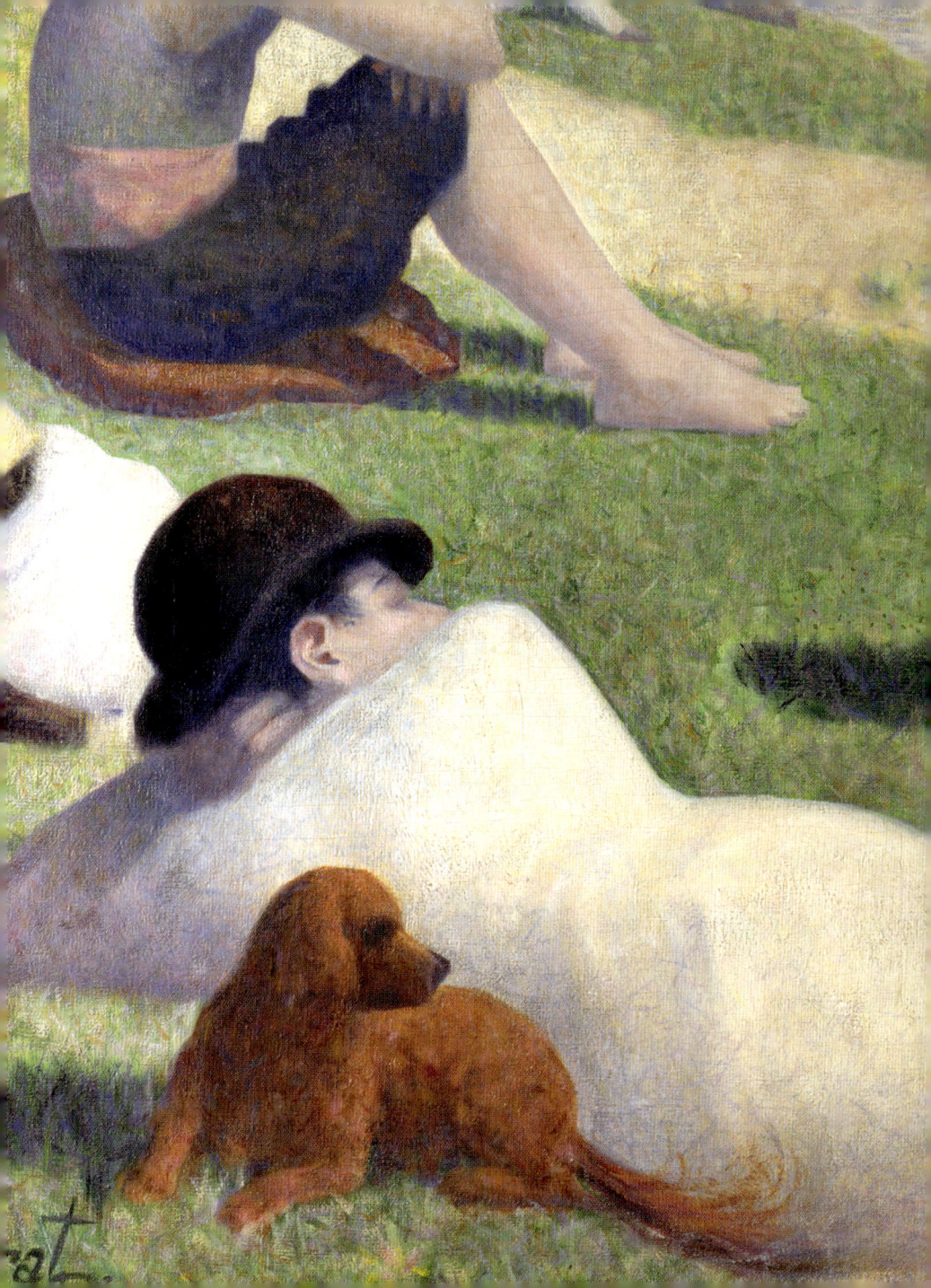

Watching the river

Following the Impressionists, Georges Seurat (1859–91) devised the painting techniques known as chromoluminarism and pointillism, which altered the direction of modern art by initiating Neo-Impressionism. This is a suburban scene of men and boys relaxing in the sun on the banks of the River Seine, between the bridges at Asnières and Courbevoie, northwest of Paris. In the background is a railway bridge that partly hides a parallel road bridge, and the chimneys of the gas plant and factories at Clichy, where some of the men may work. In the baking heat of a summer's day, a haze softens the edges of the trees in the middle distance and washes out colour from the bridges and factories in the background. Some of the men's clothes are piled beside them, two boys are in the water and a small cocker spaniel curls up by its owner, alert to activity on the river. The image seems motionless, as the men rest in the heat, tired but in companionable silence. Seurat described the complex brushstrokes and the meticulous application of colour he uses here as the "balayé technique", for which he used a flat brush to apply cross-hatched strokes of colour that become smaller as they approach the horizon.

39
GEORGES
SEURAT
Bathers at Asnières
1884
Oil on canvas
79 × 118 in
(201 × 301 cm)
The National
Gallery, London,
UK

Opposite: detail

COCKER SPANIEL

While their origins are unknown, "spaynels" are mentioned in fourteenth-century writings and they are commonly thought to have originated in Spain. There are two breeds of cocker spaniel: the American and the English. The breed was first developed as hunting dogs in the United Kingdom, and the term "cocker" derived from the dogs being used to hunt Eurasian woodcock. Later, some cocker spaniels were taken to the United States, where they were bred to a different standard so as to be successful in hunting the American woodcock. However, with their almost constantly wagging tails, they proved such charming companions that they were soon kept mainly as pets.

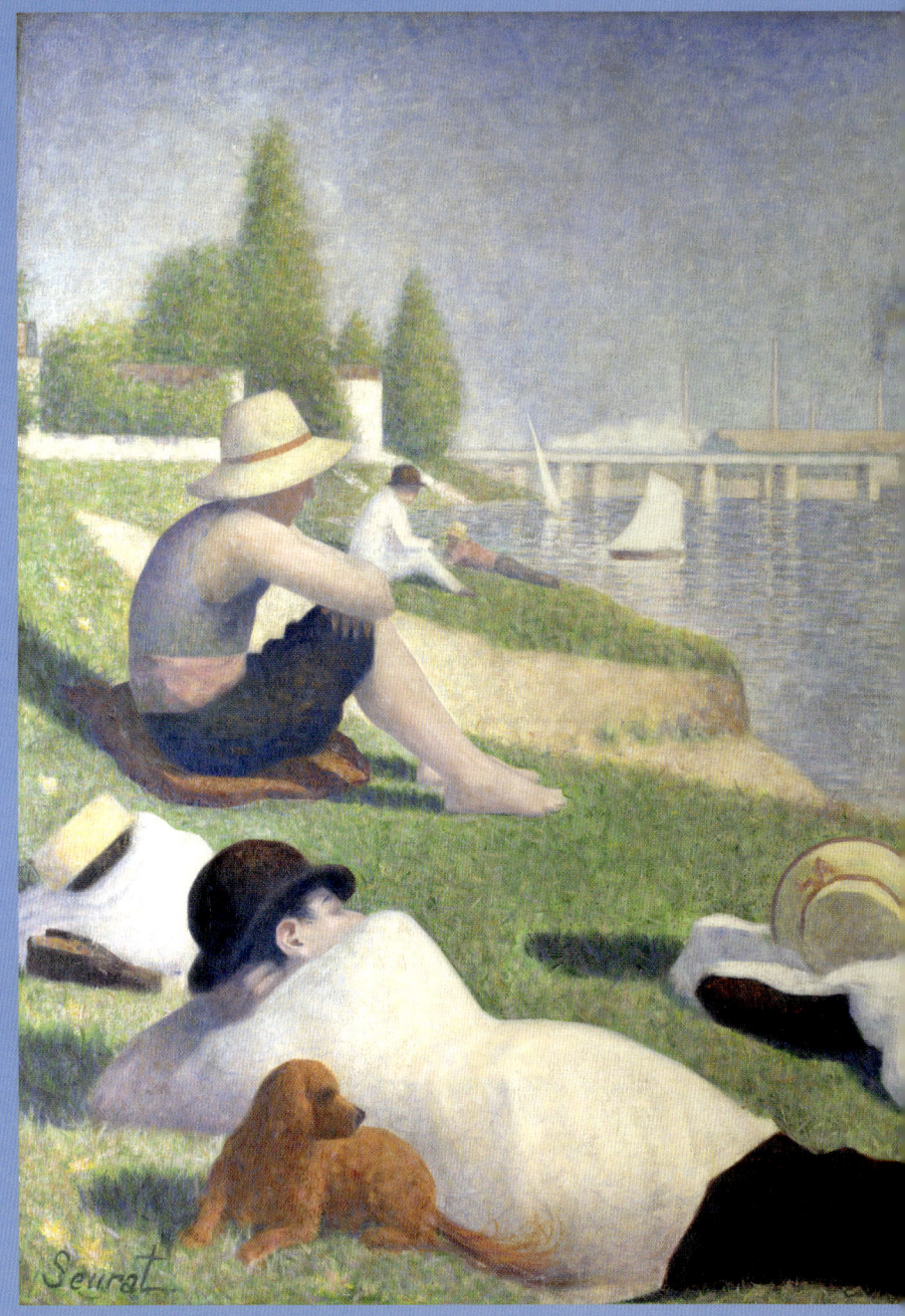

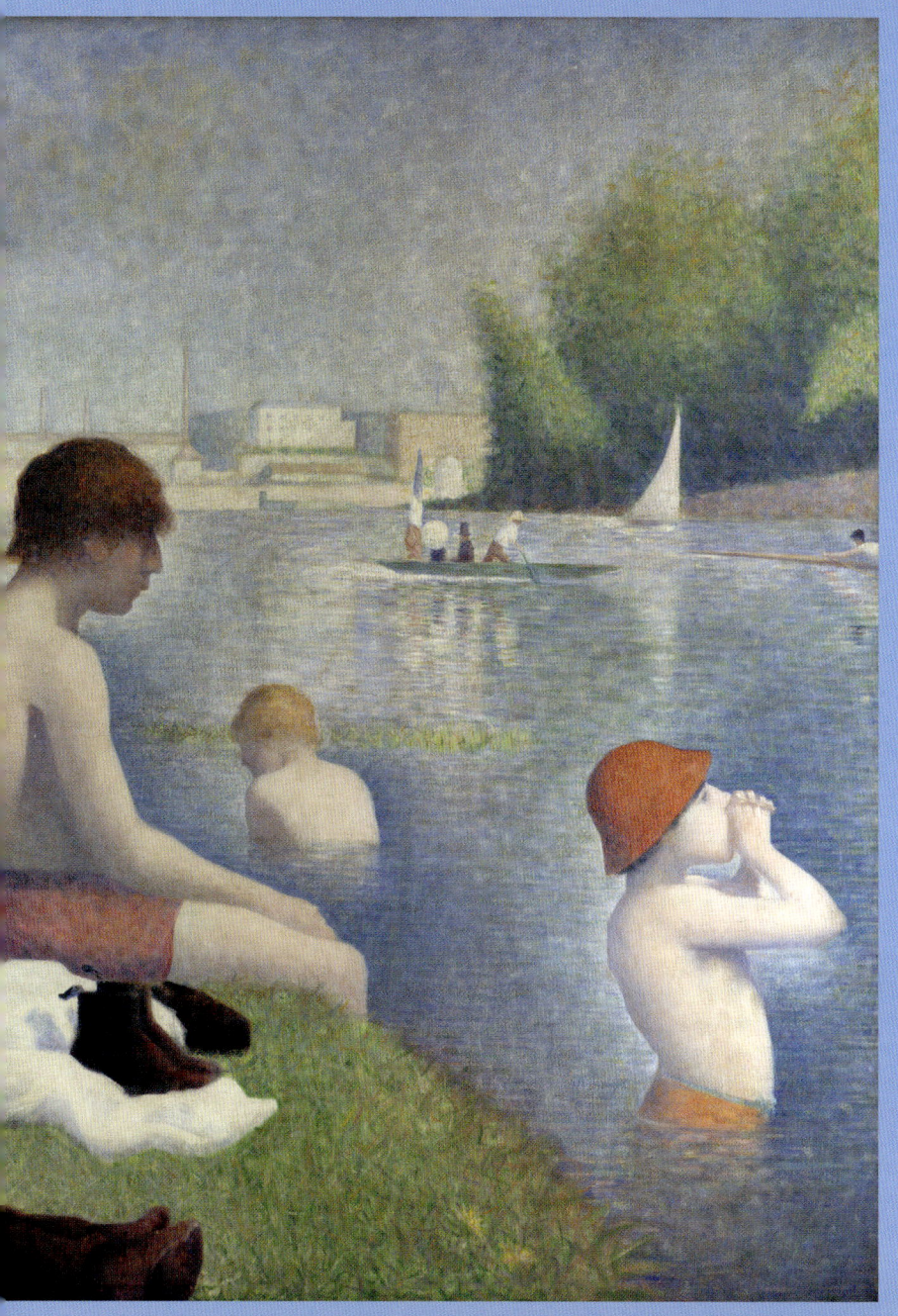

Bathed in light

Seated side on to the viewer, reading a book and wearing a pale blue dress, is Susan Hannah Macdowell (1851–1938), wife of the artist Thomas Eakins (1844–1916). On the floor beside her, the couple's Irish red and white setter Harry stretches out on a rug, supremely relaxed. For six years from 1876, Eakins taught Macdowell at the Pennsylvania Academy, and they married in January 1884, just before he began painting this image. Eakins received little recognition for his art during his life, and barely sold any artworks, but is now acknowledged as one of America's most important artists. A realist painter, sculptor and photographer, he worked in a style that was not popular, and although he transformed the Pennsylvania Academy into the leading art school in America, he was later forced to resign for allowing female students to paint nude models. However, in more recent years, his works have become greatly admired for his focus on light. Here, both Susan and Harry look at ease. Light illuminates them from a skylight above. Macdowell was also a talented painter and photographer, and this room was their studio in Chestnut Street, Philadelphia, where the three of them lived from 1884 to 1886. To produce his paintings, Eakins worked exactingly from life and from photographs.

40

THOMAS EAKINS

The Artist's Wife and His Setter Dog

c. 1884–9

Oil on canvas

30 × 23 in
(76.2 × 58.4 cm)

The Metropolitan Museum, New York, USA

IRISH RED AND WHITE SETTER

Known for their vibrantly coloured, medium-length coats, and their energy, enthusiasm and endurance, Irish red and white setters are often also described as affectionate, intelligent and eager to please. They were first written about in 1570, called "setting" dogs, and were used by hunters for centuries. This was long before the pointer breed was known, and these setters were valued for their ability to locate game, their lightness of foot and their speed. They are generally a rich chestnut or mahogany-red, partially red with white patches, or mainly white. Medium to large dogs, they are athletically built and have some feathering on their ears, chest, legs and tail.

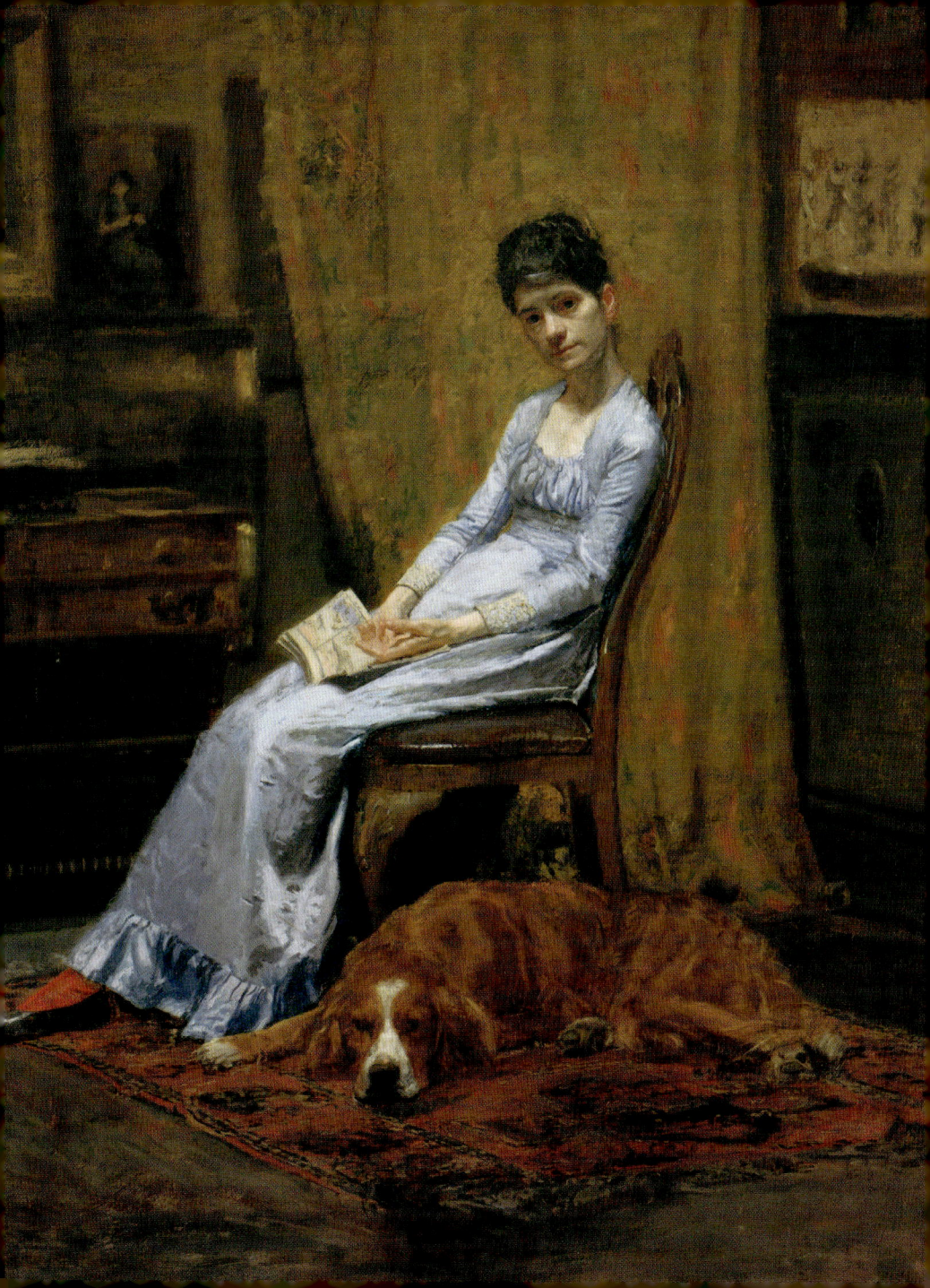

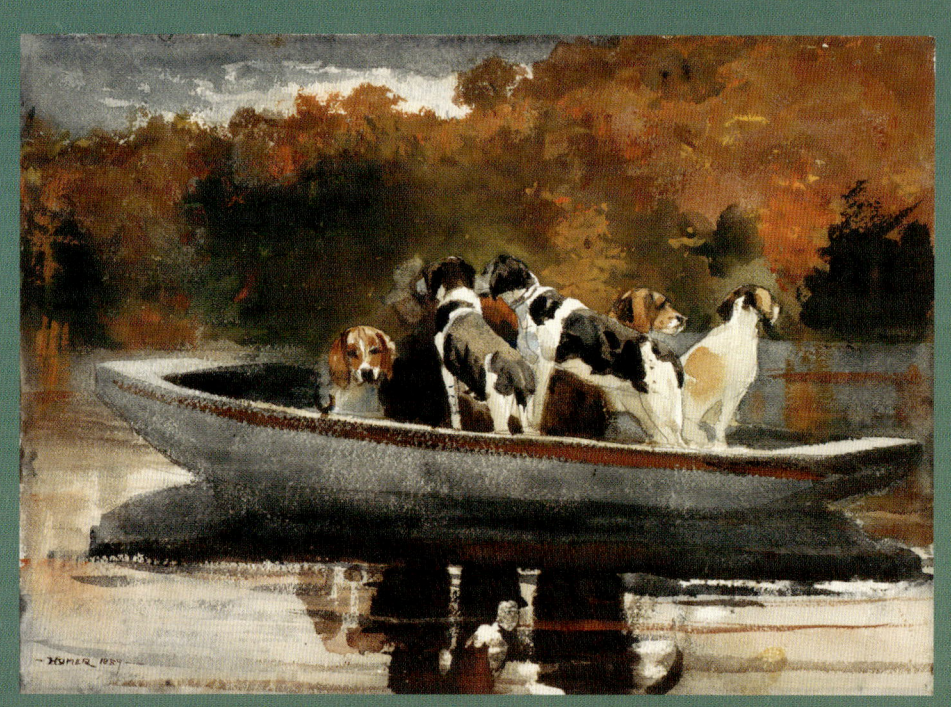

Ready to run

L argely self-taught, the Boston-born artist Winslow Homer (1836–1910) painted his native landscapes, often exploring themes of mortality through images of a turbulent stretch of the northern Atlantic. He became one of the leading painters of nineteenth-century America. He worked in both oils and watercolours, and this example of the latter depicts five dogs crowded into a boat, possibly waiting for commands or relaxing before a deer hunt. These American foxhounds were trained to race ahead of hunters, find deer and drive them into the water. Here, Homer used a muted palette, blending wet-into-wet and wet-on-dry. The autumnal trees in the background consist of muted tones of rusts, browns and greens, while thinner layers below leave some white paper showing through to suggest reflections on the water. To create these reflections, and the dogs and boat, Homer applied the paint, then scraped and sponged before repainting. Originally, he had painted a sixth dog in the upper left of the boat, but he removed it. For the background, he made sketches of the Adirondack Mountains in New York State. His innovative approach to light and shadow using loose brushwork brought atmosphere and drama, spontaneity and dynamic energy to his work.

41

WINSLOW HOMER

Hunting Dogs in Boat (Waiting for the Start)

1889

Watercolour with sponging and scraping over graphite on paper

14 × 20 in (35.6 × 50.8 cm)

Rhode Island School of Design Museum, Providence, USA

AMERICAN FOXHOUNDS

Closely related to the English foxhound, the American foxhound is a scent hound, bred to hunt foxes and deer. The breed originated in the US states of Maryland and Virginia, where George Washington lived, and it is now the state dog of Virginia. With his deep love of both dogs and hunting, Washington bred the American foxhound to run faster and have more stamina than the dogs he already owned. These long-legged dogs have medium-length coats, and although the combination of black, white and tan is predominant, they can be of any colour. They are docile, amiable, easy-going and full of energy.

Mysterious, exotic and sacred

This is one of the works that Paul Gauguin (1848–1903) painted in Tahiti and showed at his exhibition of 1893 in Paris. Gauguin came to art late in life, and in April 1891 he embarked on his first visit to the Pacific island of Tahiti, seeking a simpler way of life than he had in Paris. He took inspiration for his imaginary scenes from aspects of life that he looked for around him, as well as from local stories of history and ancient religious traditions. This is one of his mysterious, "primitive-style" paintings that were unlike any being produced elsewhere, with their sense of flatness, bright colours and flowing lines. In the left foreground, a reddish dog sniffs the ground. Further back, slightly to the right-hand side, two women in traditional dress are seated on the ground; behind them is a tree and in the background three women are worshipping a large Māori statue. There is no sky, but instead the composition is built up of a succession of coloured planes, in red, green and gold. When Gauguin exhibited this work in Paris, his red dog provoked much sarcasm for being crudely drawn and painted. Nonetheless, Gauguin considered *Arearea* to be one of his best paintings.

42
PAUL GAUGUIN
Arearea
1892
Oil on canvas
30 × 37 in
(75 × 93 cm)
Musée d'Orsay,
Paris, France

Overleaf: detail

TAHITIAN DOG

The Tahitian dog, also known as the Ma'ohi or the Polynesian dog, is an ancient breed originating from the islands of French Polynesia. These small to medium-sized dogs have thick coats and pointed ears, and are known for their intelligence, agility and loyalty. Used for hunting, fishing and guarding, they were also considered sacred and used in religious ceremonies, often being buried with their owners as a symbol of loyalty and companionship. Only certain families were allowed to breed them, and strict rules and traditions were followed to ensure their purity. They were often given as gifts to chiefs and other high-ranking members of society.

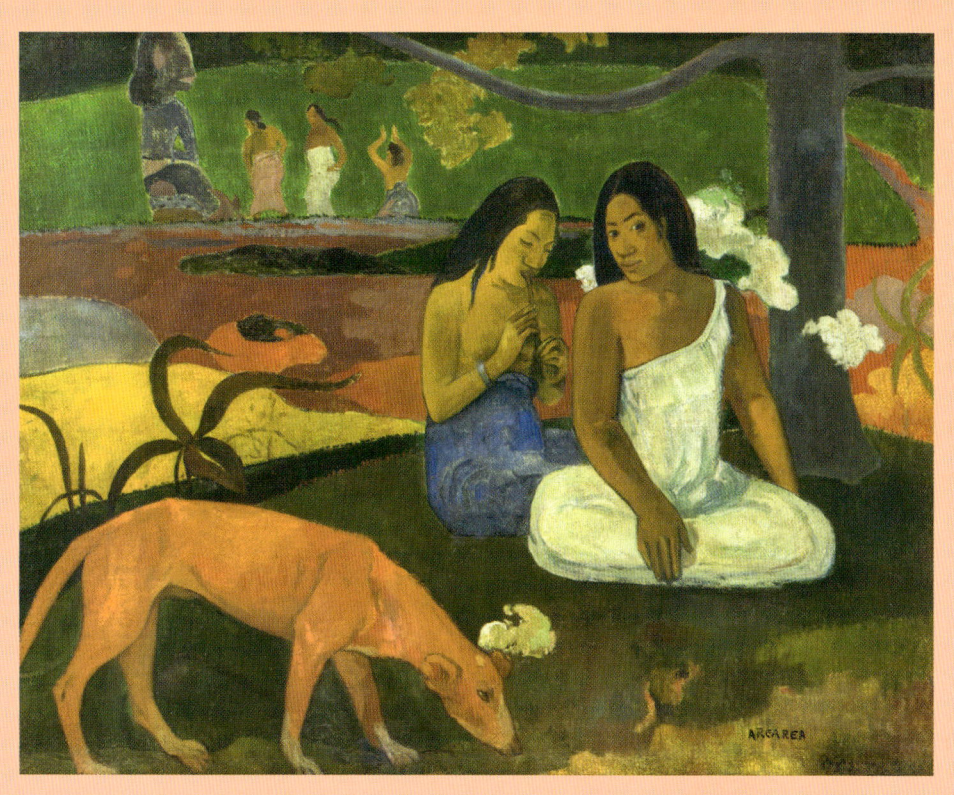

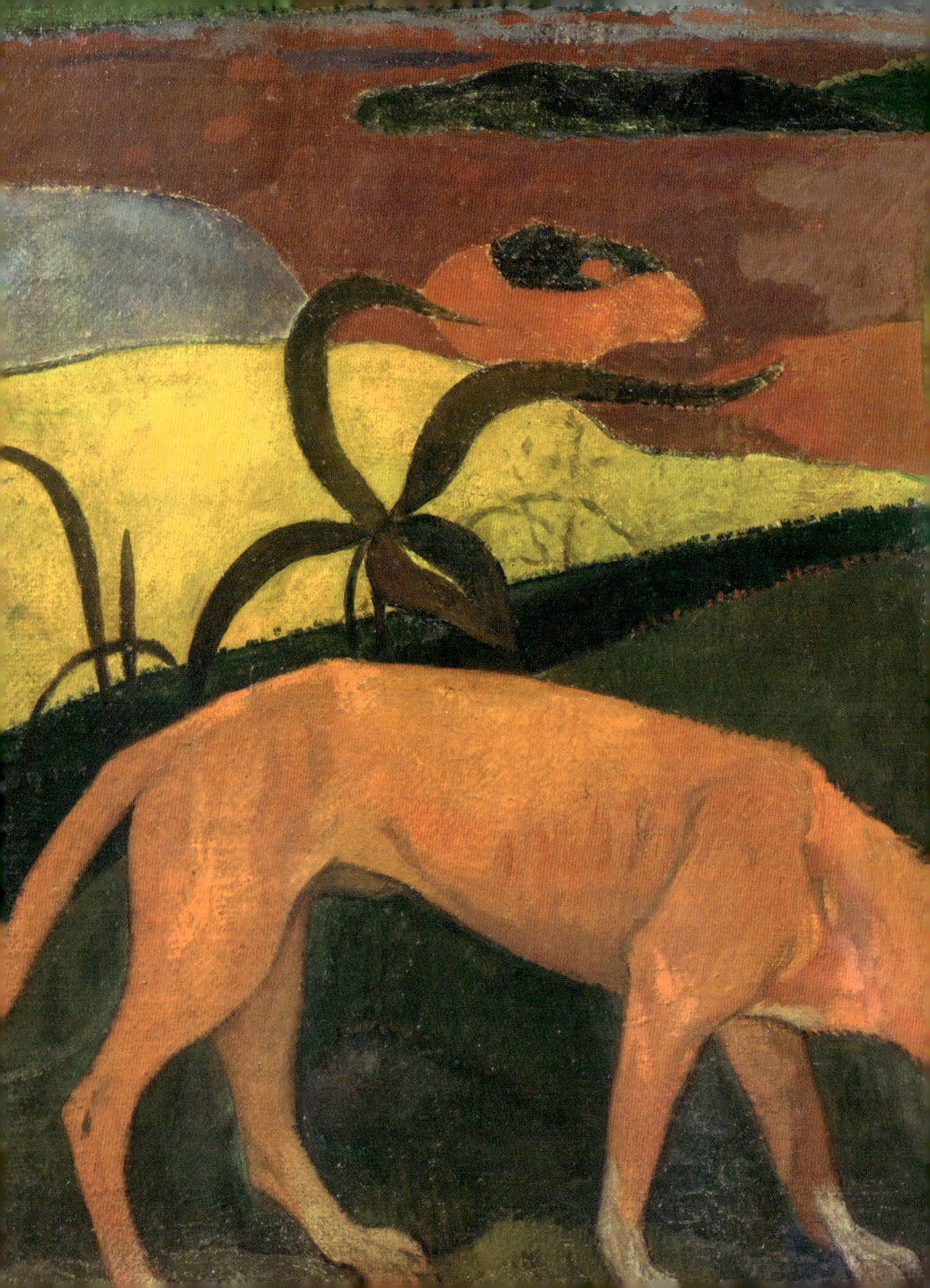

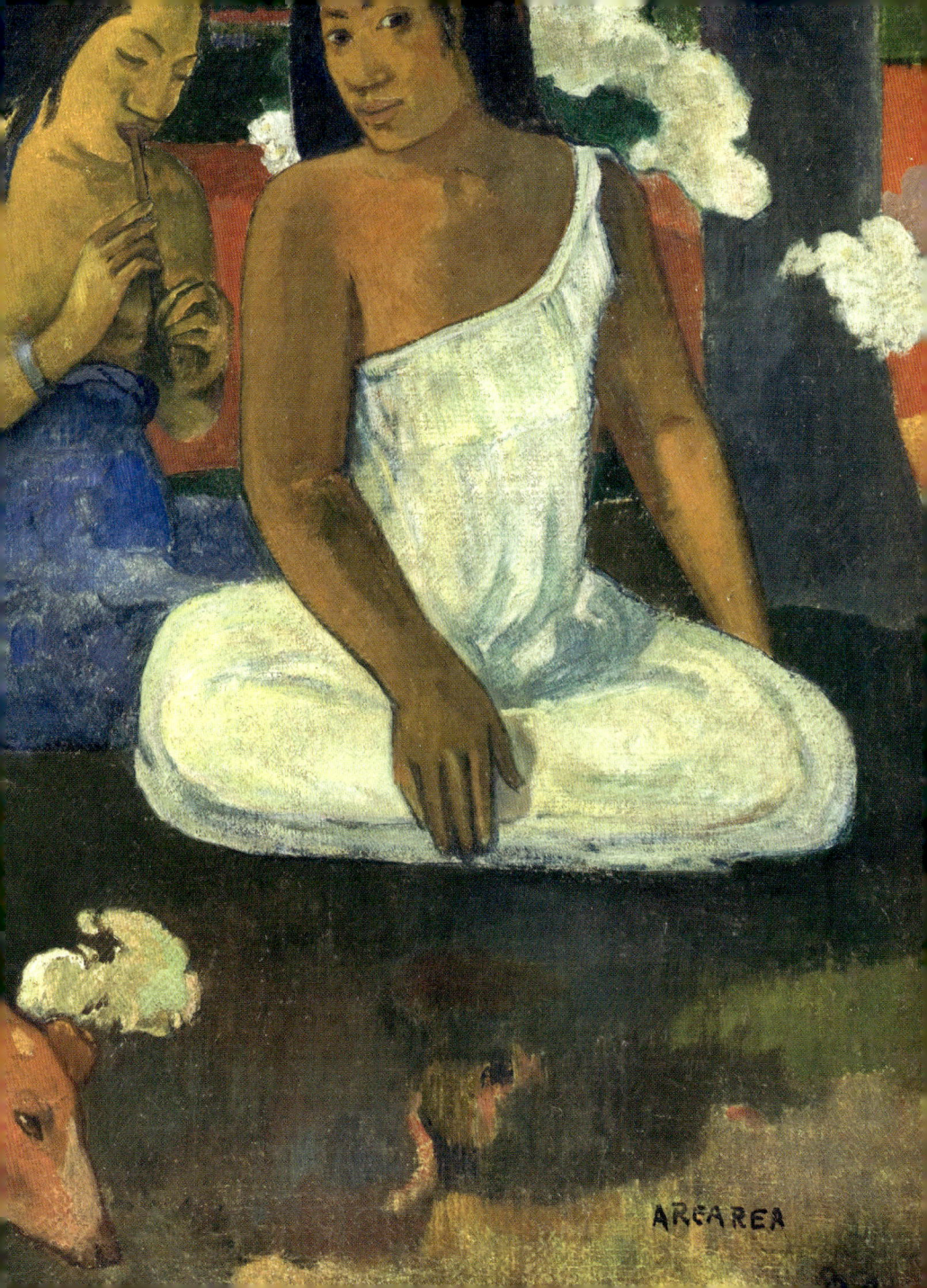

Sit!

In the late nineteenth and early twentieth centuries, Valencian-born Joaquín Sorolla y Bastida (1863–1923) was one of the most successful Spanish painters. Indeed, until 1910, when Pablo Picasso (1881–1973) overshadowed him, Sorolla was the most famous Spanish artist in the world. Having started by studying drawing at the age of 11, he was painting at the Academy in Valencia in his late teens, and soon afterwards he began exhibiting in Madrid and sending large, colourful paintings on Spanish themes to major exhibitions across Europe and the Americas. He won prestigious awards, and for his first exhibition in London in 1908 he was advertised as The World's Greatest Living Painter. He was even summoned to the White House to paint the American President. Painting in a broadly Impressionist style, and especially capturing the play of light, here he depicts a Jack Russell terrier using a restricted palette and loose, directional brushstrokes. Since this is such an intimate portrait and the dog is looking happily at the artist, it is likely that it was either Sorolla's family pet or the pet of a friend or relative. The dog has clearly been told to sit but cannot wait to move and is waiting for the command to do so, probably wagging its tail all the while.

43
JOAQUÍN
SOROLLA
Y BASTIDA
Portrait of a Jack Russell Terrier
1909
Oil on canvas
18 × 18 in
(45.7 × 45.7 cm)
Private collection

JACK RUSSELL TERRIER

This small terrier is a British breed, the origins of which can be traced to the now extinct English white terrier. Smooth or rough-coated, these little dogs were bred in Devon, southwestern England, in the early nineteenth century by a vicar called John "Jack" Russell, who wanted a small, tenacious fox-hunting dog. These little dogs could keep up with horses on the chase and run into confined spaces, so they were successful in hunting foxes and other small animals. They are lively, fun and intelligent, recognizable for their mainly white bodies with patches of brown or black, and their alert triangular ears.

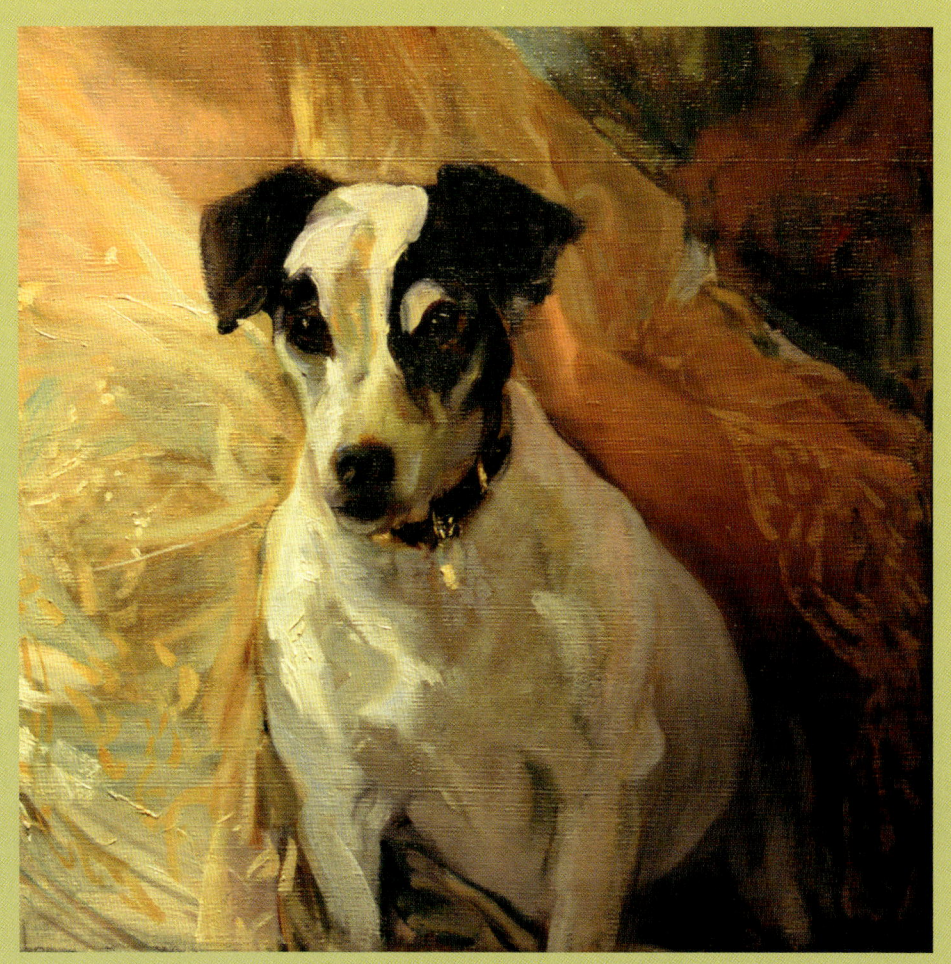

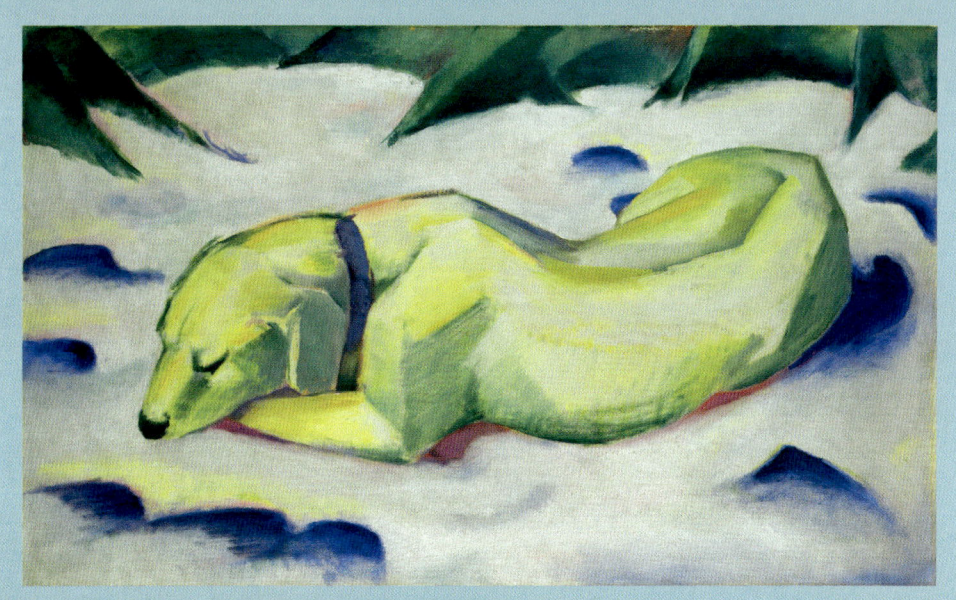

Purity and spirituality

Recognized for his vibrant, abstracted depictions of animals, the German painter and printmaker Franz Marc (1880–1916) was a pioneering Expressionist artist. In 1911 he co-founded the influential avant-garde group Der Blaue Reiter (The Blue Rider), which championed the bold, non-naturalistic use of colour and form. His paintings of horses, deer, foxes, dogs and other animals in bright colours and abstracted shapes expressed a sense of spiritual harmony with the natural world. Marc was an expert in animal anatomy, so here he deliberately simplified the shape of the dog. The painting is of his own white shepherd dog, Russi, in the January snow near the village where he lived. He commented at the time that he found the snow "too pure white and blue", so he painted the entire composition in yellow, blue and green. The dog lies in the snow surrounded by trees in a simplified, pared-down style. The curves of its body reflect the shapes in the landscape, creating a sense of harmony and peace. To illustrate what he perceived as animals' purity and spirituality, Marc often depicted them lying on the ground asleep. By placing Russi in the centre of the composition and at eye level, Marc demonstrates the affectionate, respectful relationship between him and his dog.

44

FRANZ MARC

A Dog Lying in Snow

c. 1911

Oil on canvas

24⅔ × 41⅓ in (62.5 × 105 cm)

Städel Museum, Frankfurt, Germany

WHITE SHEPHERD

One of the most intelligent dog breeds in the world, the white shepherd is a variety of the German shepherd that was first bred in Europe in the late nineteenth century. It is not albino, but rather carries the recessive gene for its white coat. Physically, white shepherds share many characteristics with their German shepherd counterparts. Medium-sized, they have sturdy, well-proportioned, athletic bodies with distinctive wedge-shaped heads, erect ears, a thick, double coat and curving tails. Loyal and eager to please, they are calm, gentle and affectionate companions while also having the herding and guarding instincts of their German shepherd heritage.

Dog-walking

This work, painted by the Italian Futurist artist Giacomo Balla (1871–1958) two years before the First World War broke out, exemplifies the Futurists' fascination with movement, speed and the depiction of modern life. They wrote in their manifesto: "All things move, all things run, all things are rapidly changing ... moving objects constantly multiply themselves ... a running horse has not four legs, but twenty." Here, a woman in dark clothing and her dachshund are going for a walk. Through several overlapping elements, Balla conveys a sense of speed and vitality on a static canvas. Born in Turin, the artist was inspired by dynamism and by the rapid technological advancements of his time. So, while he draws on Impressionist depictions of everyday life, he also shows the influence of chronophotographic studies of animals in motion, created by Eadweard Muybridge (1830–1904) and Étienne-Jules Marey (1830–1904). The close-up of the long-haired dachshund and the cropping of the owner capture a sense of the energy and dynamism of everyday life. To achieve this effect, the woman has several feet and the dog at least eight tails, many ears and legs, all painted in a flurry of layers, with four leads swinging between them.

45
GIACOMO BALLA
Dynamism of a Dog on a Leash
1912
Oil on canvas
35⅓ × 43¼ in
(89.8 × 109.8 cm)
Buffalo AKG
Art Museum,
New York, USA

DACHSHUND

With short legs and a long body, the dachshund (from the German *dachs*, meaning "badger", and *hund*, "hound") is often nicknamed sausage dog, wiener dog or badger dog. Dachshunds can have smooth, wiry or long hair, and they were originally bred in about the fifteenth century in Germany. Their primary purpose was to hunt small animals, particularly badgers. They have silky, floppy ears, a long nose and large, paddle-shaped front paws that are great for digging. They are bright, loyal, courageous, energetic and sometimes stubborn, and they make extremely loyal companions.

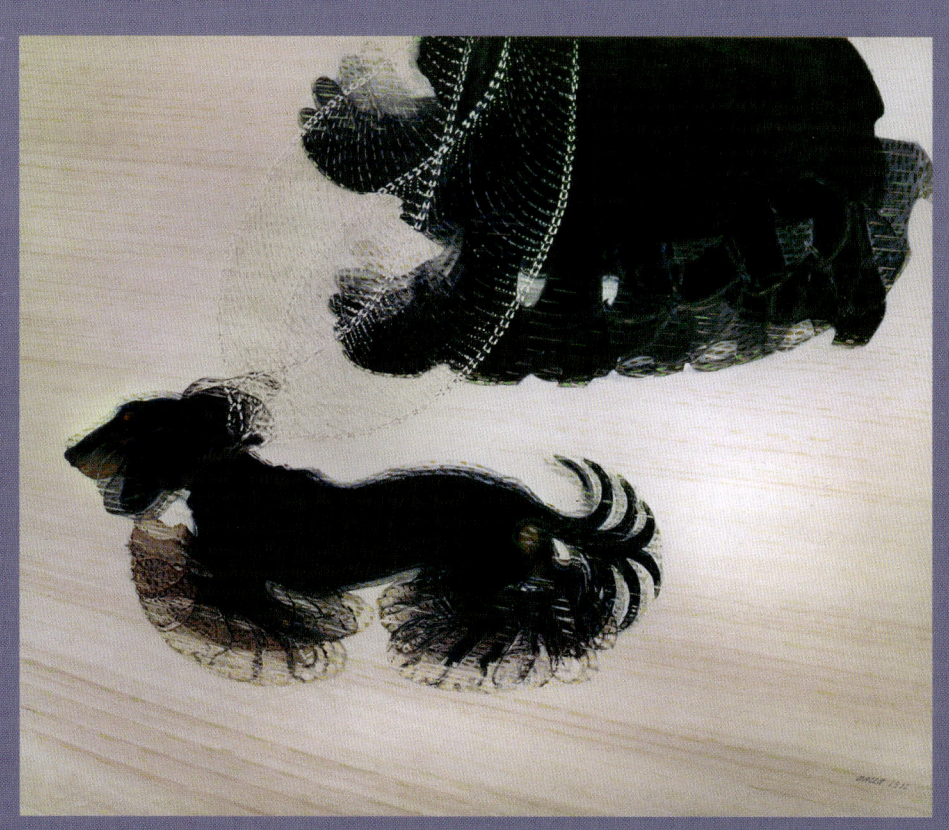

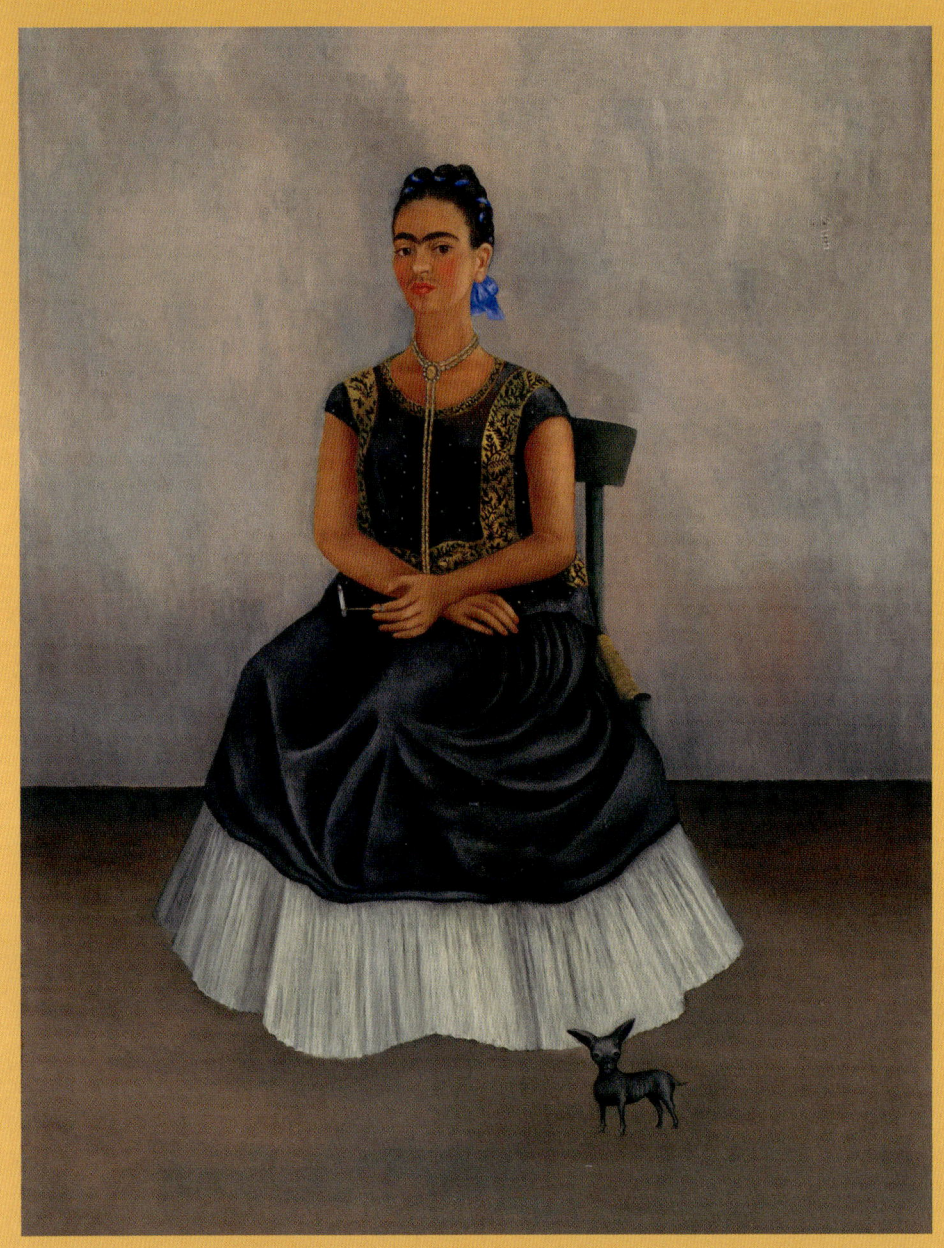

Aztec god

The deeply personal paintings of Frida Kahlo (1907–54) made her one of the most recognized twentieth-century artists. Throughout her life, she overcame immense physical and emotional adversity, including polio at the age of six, a devastating bus accident at 18 and a tumultuous marriage to the muralist Diego Rivera (1886–1957). These experiences imbued Kahlo's self-portraits and allegorical works with vivid, unflinching honesty and psychological intensity. Her painting style blended Mexican folk-art traditions with avant-garde ideas, often incorporating symbols of her Indigenous Aztec heritage, her chronic pain and the complexities of gender and national identity (her father was German and her mother Mexican). Her accident left her unable to bear children, so, as substitutes, she collected many pets, including monkeys, a deer, birds and dogs. Here she has painted herself with her favourite Xoloitzcuintli dog. Also called the Itzcuintli or the Colima, this rare breed of hairless dog was prized by the Aztecs, a fact that appealed to Kahlo, who often proudly expressed her Mesoamerican heritage. Here, she depicts herself sitting against a plain background, holding a cigarette, wearing her customary traditional Mexican dress. The tiny dog in front of her was her favourite, named Mr Xoloti after an Aztec god who represented lightning and death.

46
FRIDA KAHLO
Itzcuintli Dog with Me
1938
Oil on canvas
28 × 20⅓ in
(71 × 52 cm)
Private collection

XOLOITZCUINTLI

Commonly known as the Mexican hairless dog, the Xoloitzcuintli is an ancient breed. Archeological evidence of these dogs has been found in Colima, Mayan, Toltec, Zapotec and Aztec tombs, dating the breed to more than 3,500 years ago. Long regarded as guardians and protectors, these dogs were revered by ancient civilizations and believed to protect homes from intruders and evil spirits. The name Xoloitzcuintli derives from two Aztec words: Xolotl, the god of death, and *itzcuintli*, meaning "dog". Xoloitzcuintli are affectionate, playful and warm to the touch. Although described as "hairless", some actually have a short, fine fur coat and all are known for their loyal, affectionate temperament, intelligence and energy.

Waiting and watchful

Expressing themes of solitude, detachment and remoteness, the American artist Edward Hopper (1882–1967) painted this a year after the story "Lassie Come Home" by Eric Knight (1897–1943) was published in the *Saturday Evening Post*. Knight's story explores a rough collie's trek over many miles to be reunited with the boy she loves, and this atmospheric image could allude to that. In a scene with no sky, a white house is surrounded by dusky-blue trees. Long, dry grass grows up to the doorstep, which is occupied by a man, and both he and the woman nearby seem detached and preoccupied. Or perhaps they are listening to a whippoorwill, a native American bird that – according to folklore – heralds a death in the family of anyone who hears it. As is customary with Hopper, the realistic depiction of figures and surroundings is ambiguous, conveying the strangeness of ordinary settings. His wife, fellow artist Jo Nivison (1883–1968), always modelled for his female figures. He described the painting: "Pieced together from sketches and mental impressions ... The dry, blowing grass can be seen from my studio window in the late summer or autumn. In the woman, I attempted to get the broad, strong-jawed face and blonde hair of a Finnish type of which there are many on the Cape. The man is a dark-haired Yankee."

47
EDWARD HOPPER
Cape Cod Evening
1939
Oil on canvas
30 × 40 in
(76.2 × 101.6 cm)
National Gallery of Art, Washington, DC, USA

Overleaf: detail

ROUGH COLLIE

Medium-sized to large dogs, collies are known for their long, flowing coats and gentle temperaments. There are two varieties: smooth and rough. The former has a short, flat coat, while the latter has long, thick hair that requires regular grooming. Generally believed to have been popular with the ancient Romans and to have spread to Britain and beyond in about 500 BCE, collies were not recognized as a distinct breed until the eighteenth century. With their intelligence, enthusiasm, sensitivity and affability, they have traditionally been popular pets; being easy to train and having great stamina and agility, they have also been bred as herding dogs.

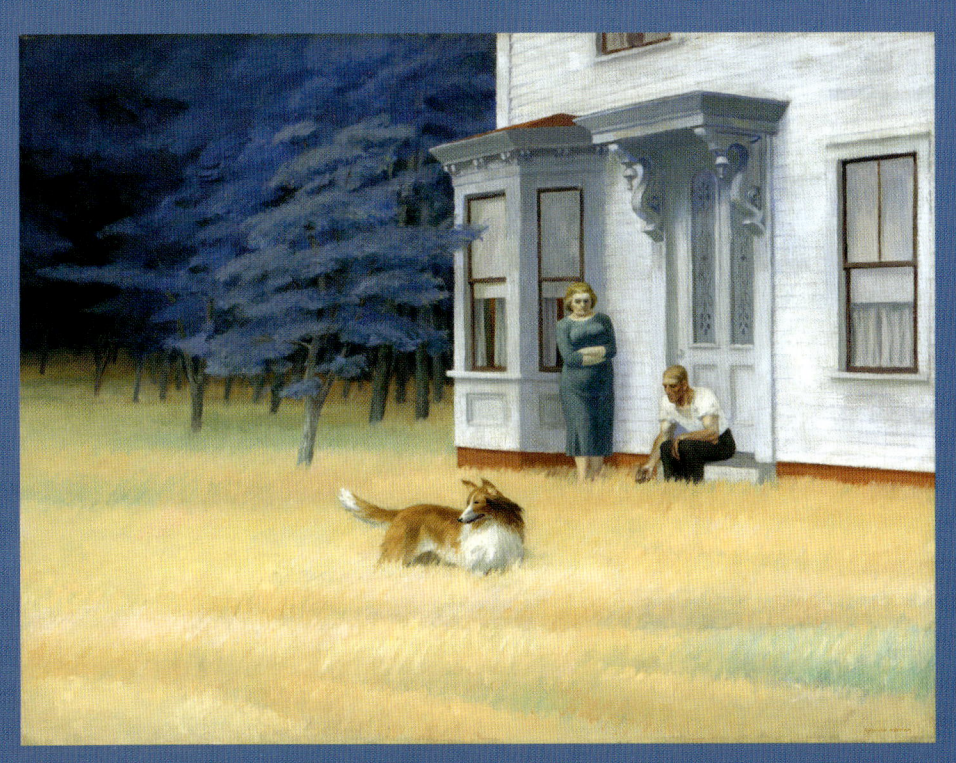

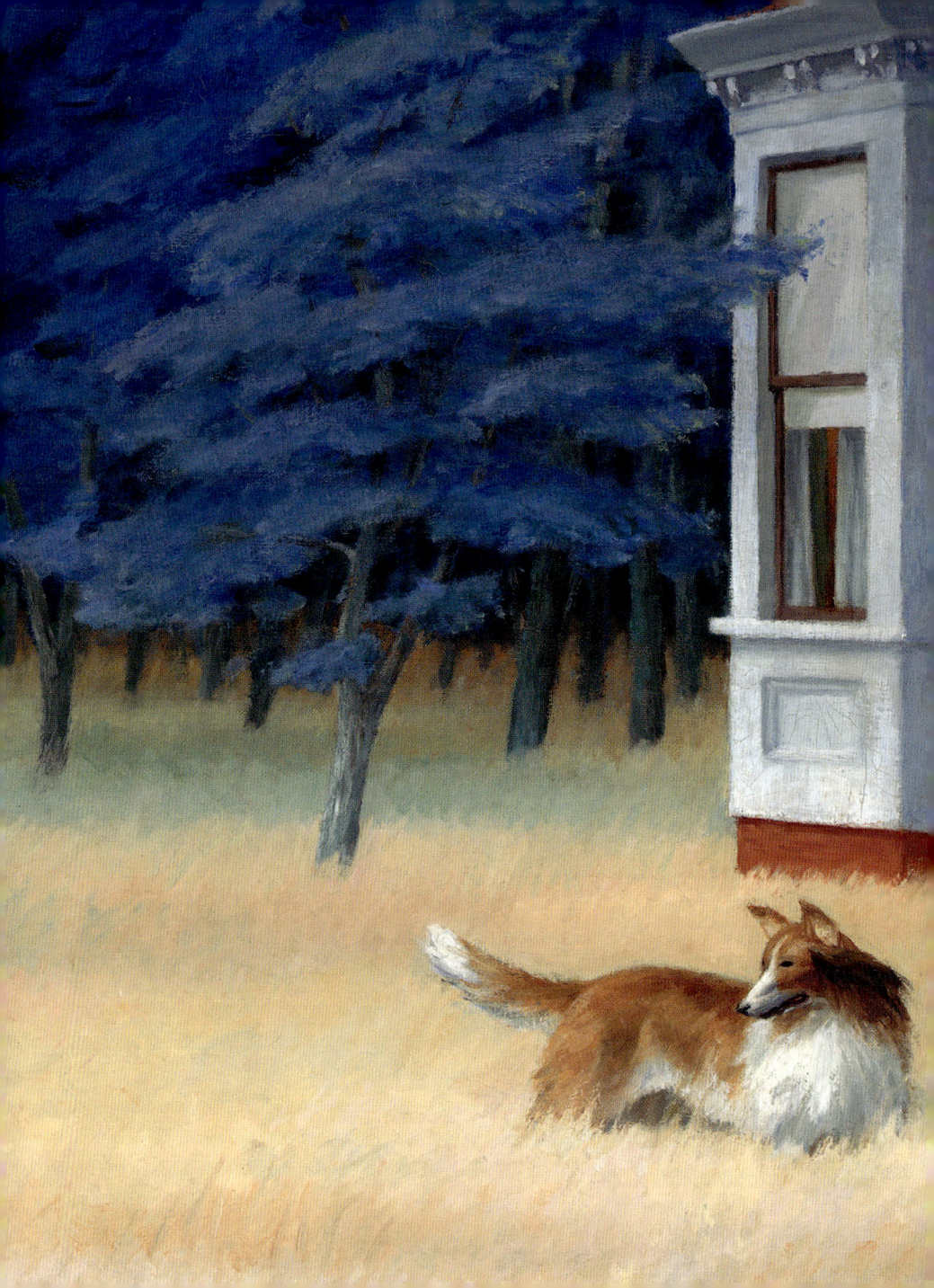

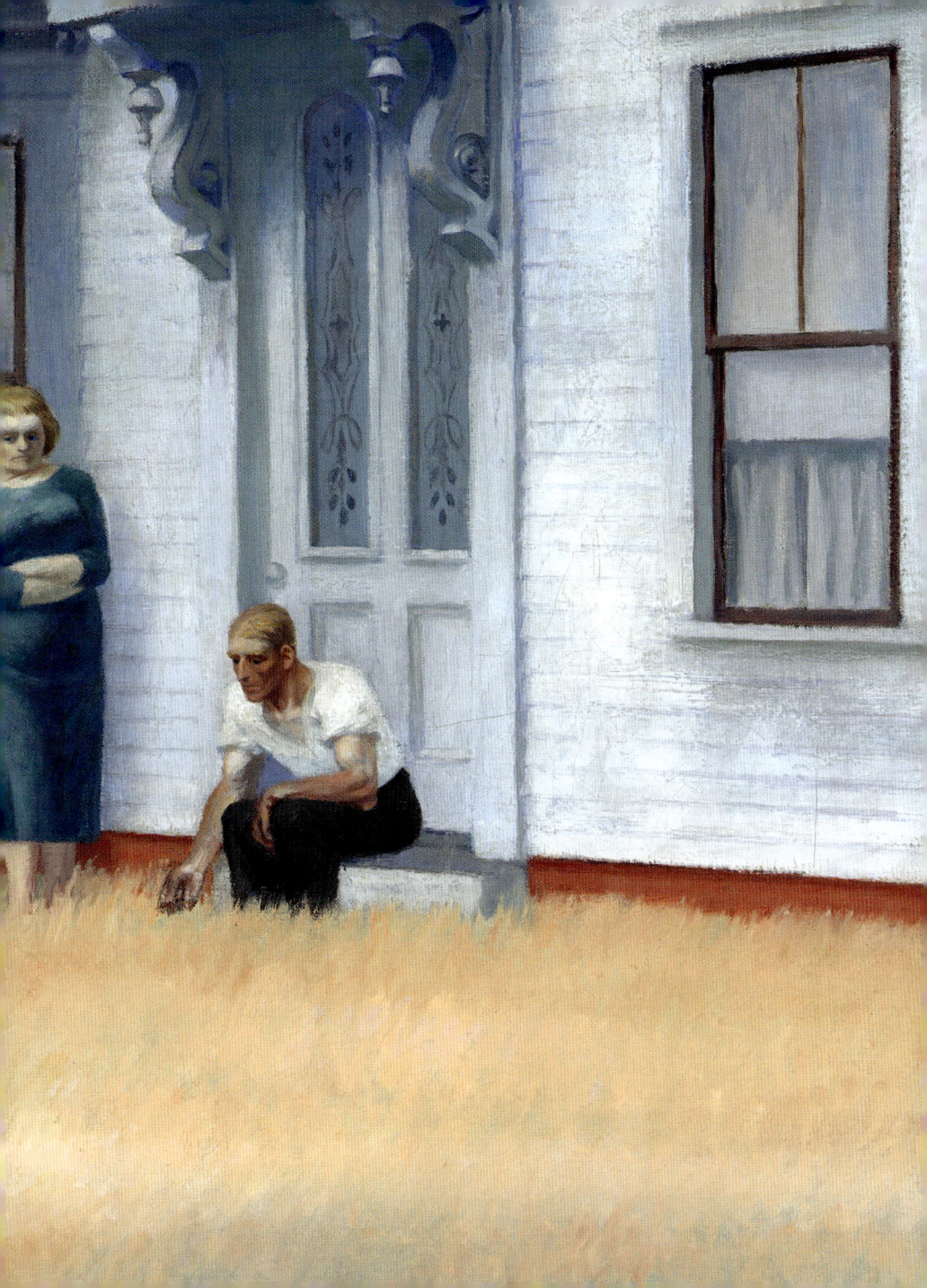

West meets East

The Japanese artist Hashimoto Kansetsu (1883–1945) worked in a range of styles. He was educated in Chinese classical literature, then studied traditional Japanese painting styles, and although at the time much Japanese art was becoming influenced by the West, he began by adhering largely to the style of the Edo Period (1603–1867). Fascinated by Chinese culture, he visited China often, and many of his artworks were inspired by the scenery and literature of that country. This painting reflects several of the styles he followed, including *nihonga* (using organic pigments and occasionally ink on silk or paper), *shijō* (a mix of realism with traditional Japanese painting techniques, expressing inner spirituality, often light-heartedly), *kanō* (the traditional painting style of the time) and *nanga* (known as "literati painting", a style among Japanese artists who considered themselves intellectuals, and who admired traditional Chinese culture). *Nangi* paintings were usually monochrome, but sometimes included light colour. Kansetsu's astute observational skill can be seen in this image, which he simplified to create a delicate, asymmetrical composition. He had many pets, and this painting, which comprises a pair of two-panel screens, depicts three elegant borzois wearing collars, with red peonies nearby. It is likely that the dogs were his pets and are shown in his own garden.

48
HASHIMOTO KANSETSU
Dogs from Europe
1941
Colour on silk, pair of two-panel screens
Each screen
64½ × 72 in
(164 × 183 cm)
Adachi Museum of Art, Yasugi, Japan

Opposite: detail

BORZOI

The borzoi or Russian hunting sighthound is a Russian breed of hunting dog. Formerly used for wolf-hunting, it was known as the Russian wolfhound until 1936. The breed originated in the sixteenth century through the mixing of Saluki and European sighthounds with thick-coated Russian breeds, and before the Russian Revolution of 1917, borzois could not be bought, but only given as gifts by the tsar. Resembling some Central Asian breeds, such as the Afghan hound, the Saluki and the Kyrgyz Taigan, these dogs have silky, flat and wavy, or slightly curly coats. They are calm and affectionate but can be stubborn and need stimulation.

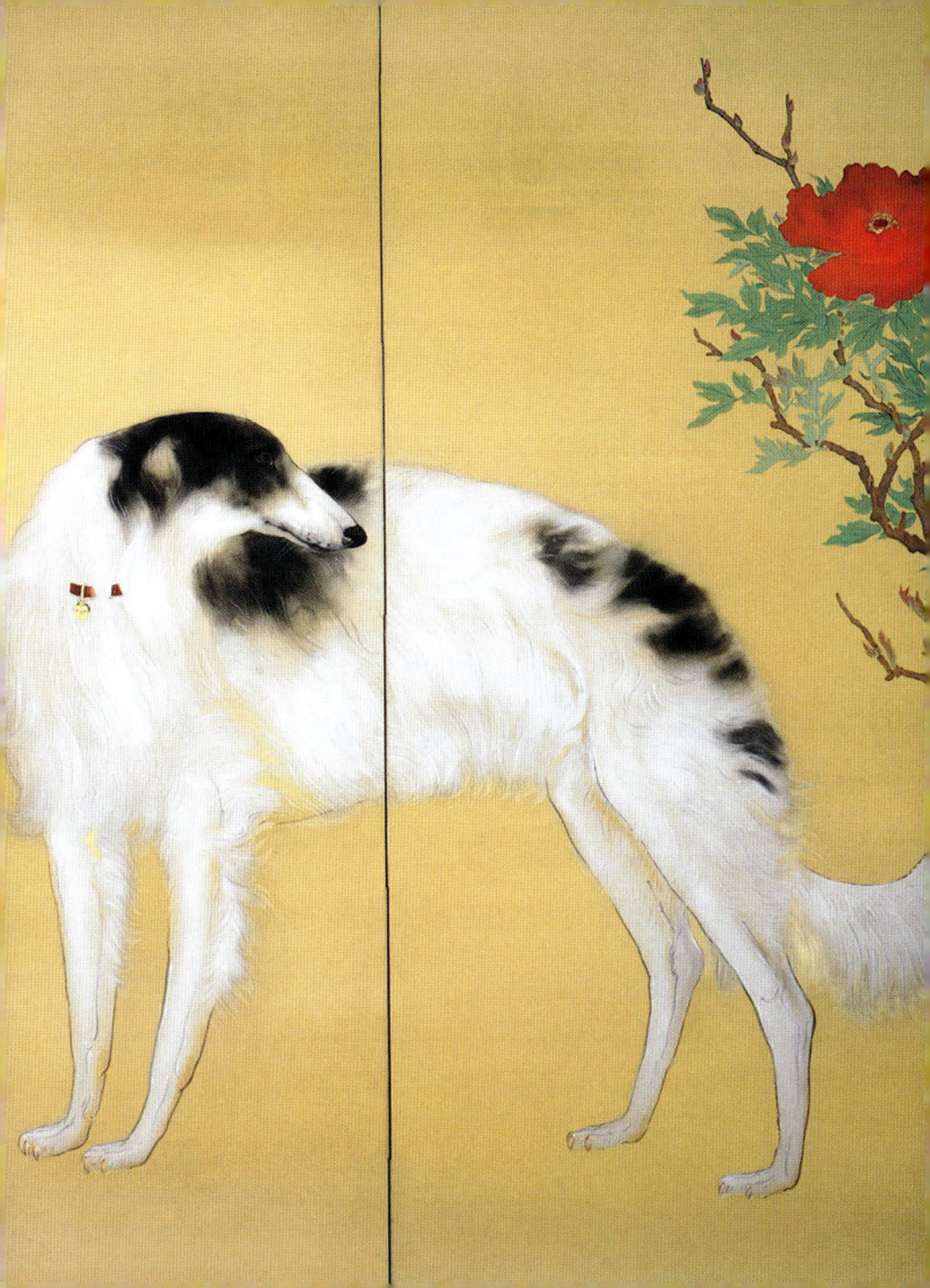

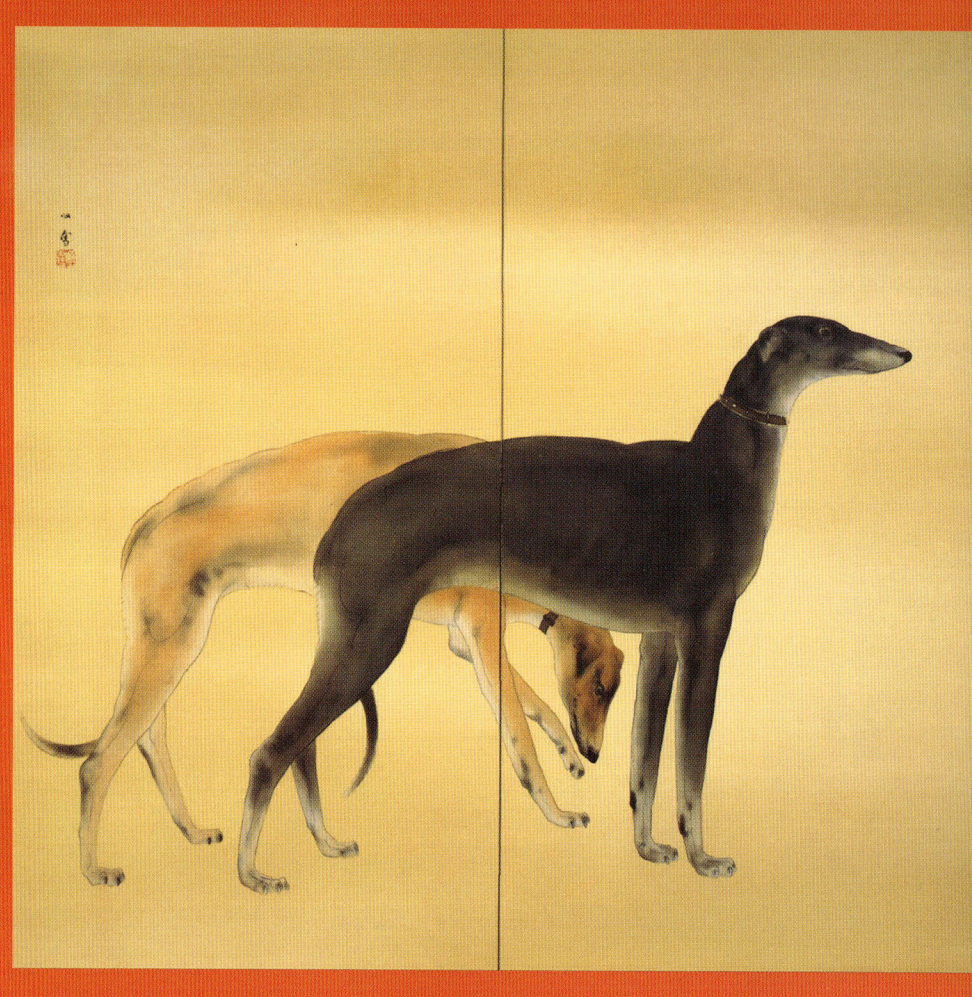

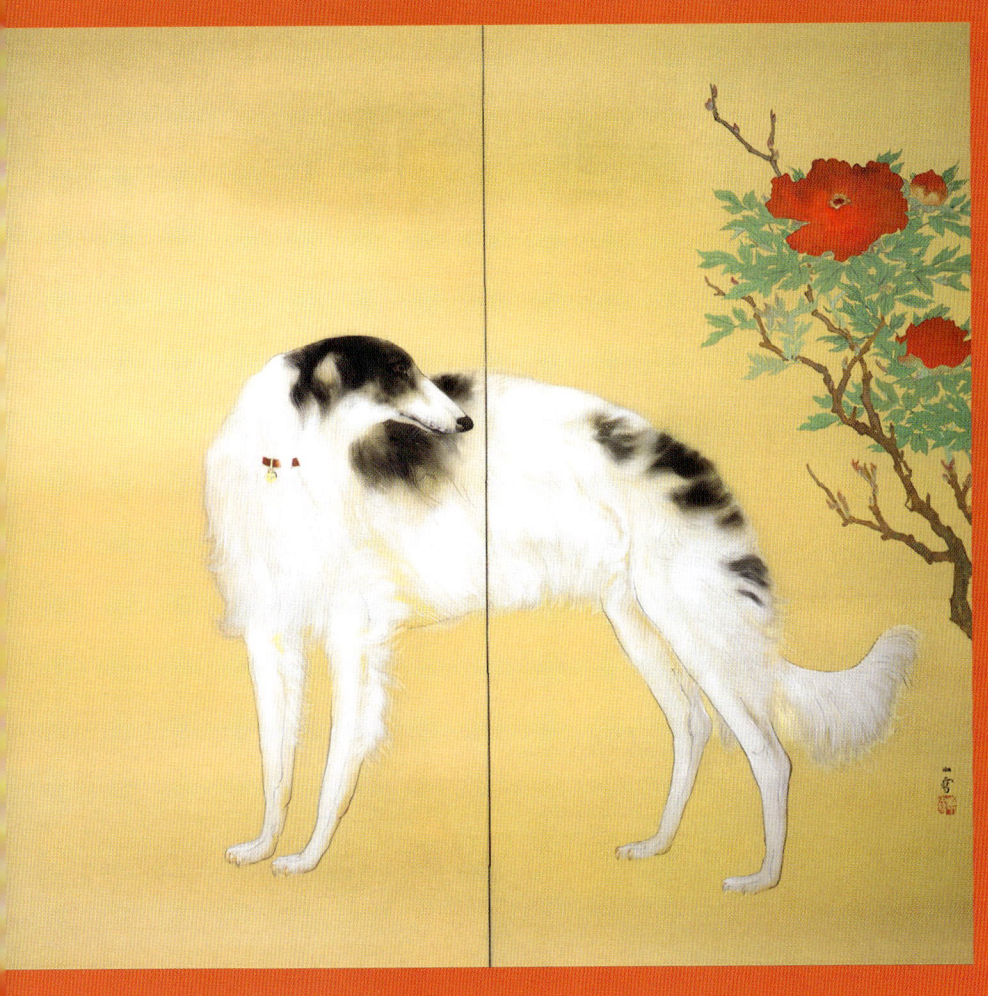

Wedding present

Recognized for his direct observations of anatomy and psychology, the British artist Lucian Freud (1922–2011) was one of the most celebrated portraitists of the late twentieth century. Painting only those close to him, he became notorious for the extremely long sessions on which he insisted with his sitters. His portraits never flattered, and they seem to continue some of the psychoanalytic practices of his grandfather Sigmund Freud (1856–1939). Here, a young brown-haired woman sits on a couch in front of draping curtains, wearing a soft yellow robe that blends with the subtle tones of her surroundings. She looks directly at the viewer, but her expression is hard to read. Her robe falls off her right shoulder, exposing her breast, while her right hand holds her left breast over her robe. Meanwhile, echoing the shape of her leg, her white dog snuggles comfortably next to her, leaning his head on her lap, his ears alert. She is Kitty Garman (1926–2011), Freud's first wife, who at the time was pregnant with their second child, and the dog is one of two bull terriers the couple were given as a wedding present. Minimizing tonal contrasts, Freud applied paint with linear precision, building up subtle shading to evoke a sense of stillness.

49
LUCIAN FREUD
Girl with a White Dog
1950–1
Oil on canvas
30 × 40 in
(76.2 × 101.6 cm)
Tate Britain, London, UK

BULL TERRIER

Bull terriers can be independent, calm, stubborn, brave and spirited. The most recognizable feature of this breed is the egg-shaped head. When viewed from the front, the top of the skull and face is almost flat, and they have uniquely shaped triangular eyes. Their bodies are strong and muscular. In the early nineteenth century "bull and terrier" breeds were developed to control vermin and participate in animal-based blood sports. These dogs were developed from the Old English bulldog and the Old English terrier (both now extinct). So the bull terrier combines the speed and dexterity of lighter terriers with the resolve of the bulldog.

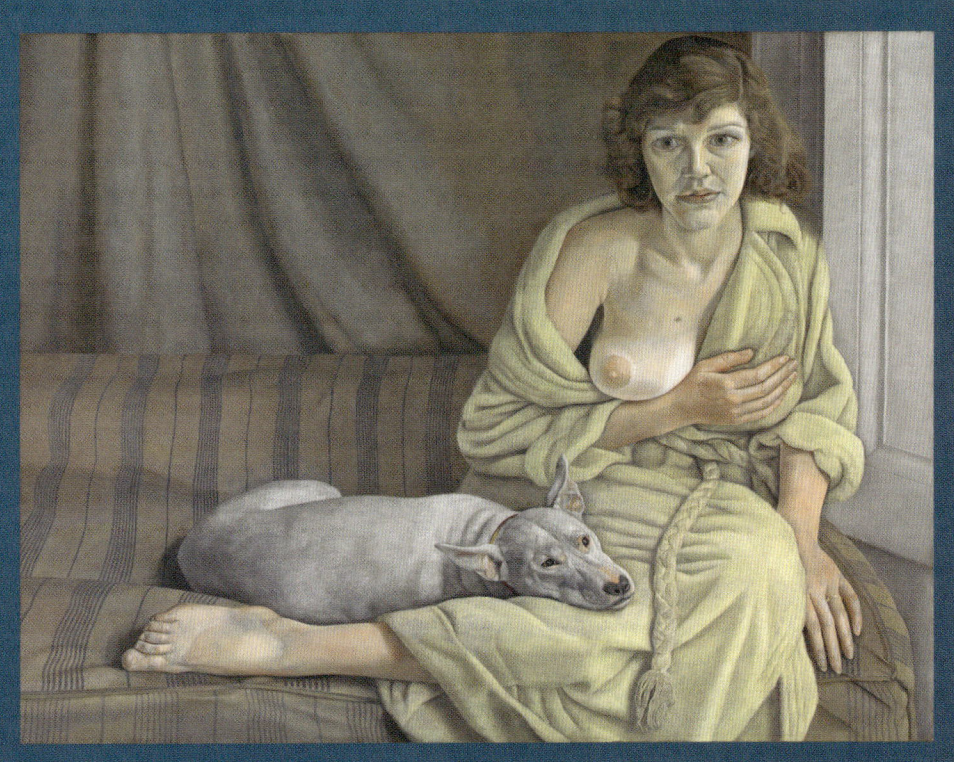

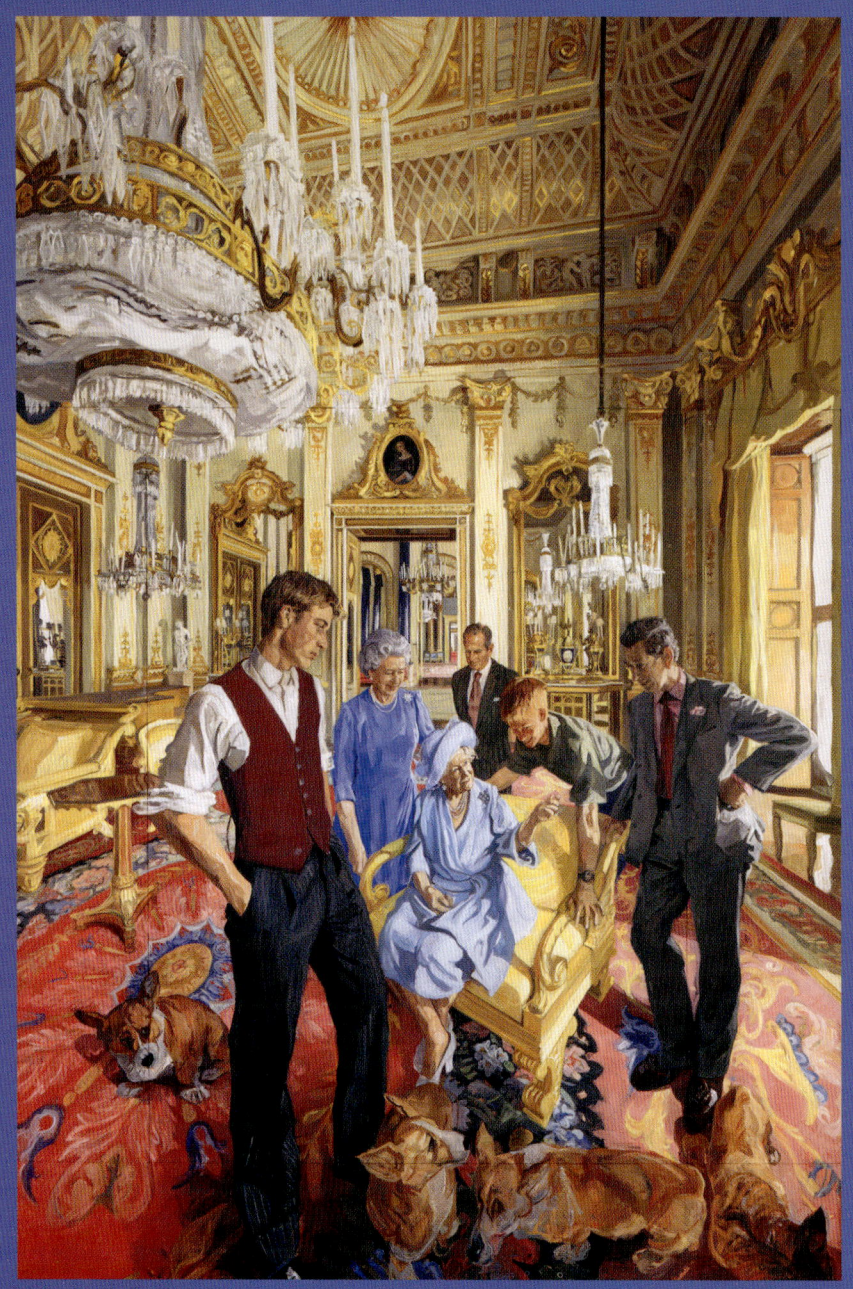

Family involvement

In 2000 the British artist John Wonnacott CBE (b.1940) was commissioned to paint a portrait of the British Royal Family in honour of Her Majesty Queen Elizabeth, the Queen Mother's hundredth birthday. The result was a monumental portrait, comprising all the main members of the Royal Family at the time – four generations of royalty – including Queen Elizabeth II, Prince Philip the Duke of Edinburgh, Prince Charles (later King Charles III), the princes William and Harry, as well as four of the Queen Mother's pet corgis. Wonnacott created an almost bird's-eye view in a work that reflects his fascination with Old Master painting, along with the influence of his friends in the School of London. The figurative, documentary style opposed contemporary trends in art. The Queen Mother dominates, sitting on a golden couch. Next to his father, Prince Harry leans on his great-grandmother's chairback. In the foreground, Prince William stands amid the corgis, which mill about, wanting to be part of the scene. The two queens wear blue, and the Queen and Prince Philip are set back in the opulently decorated room, recalling the sovereigns in *Las Meninas* (page 60). Also echoing Velázquez, this painting conveys naturalism and informality, and even the position of the dogs evokes that seminal royal portrait.

50

JOHN WONNACOTT

The Royal Family: A Centenary Portrait

2000

Oil on canvas on foamboard

144¼ × 98⅛ in (366.3 × 249.3 cm)

The National Portrait Gallery, London, UK

Overleaf: detail

PEMBROKE WELSH CORGI

The name "corgi" derives from the Welsh words *cor* and *ci* (which mutated to *gi*), meaning "dwarf" and "dog" respectively, and the Pembroke Welsh corgi is a small type of herding dog. The origin of the breed is not confirmed, but a cattle dog was referred to in laws in 920 CE, and they were possibly taken to Wales by Flemish weavers at around that time. Descending from the spitz family, these dogs were often described as "heelers" because they nipped at cows' heels to keep them moving. As pets, they have a great desire to please, and love to be involved with their humans.

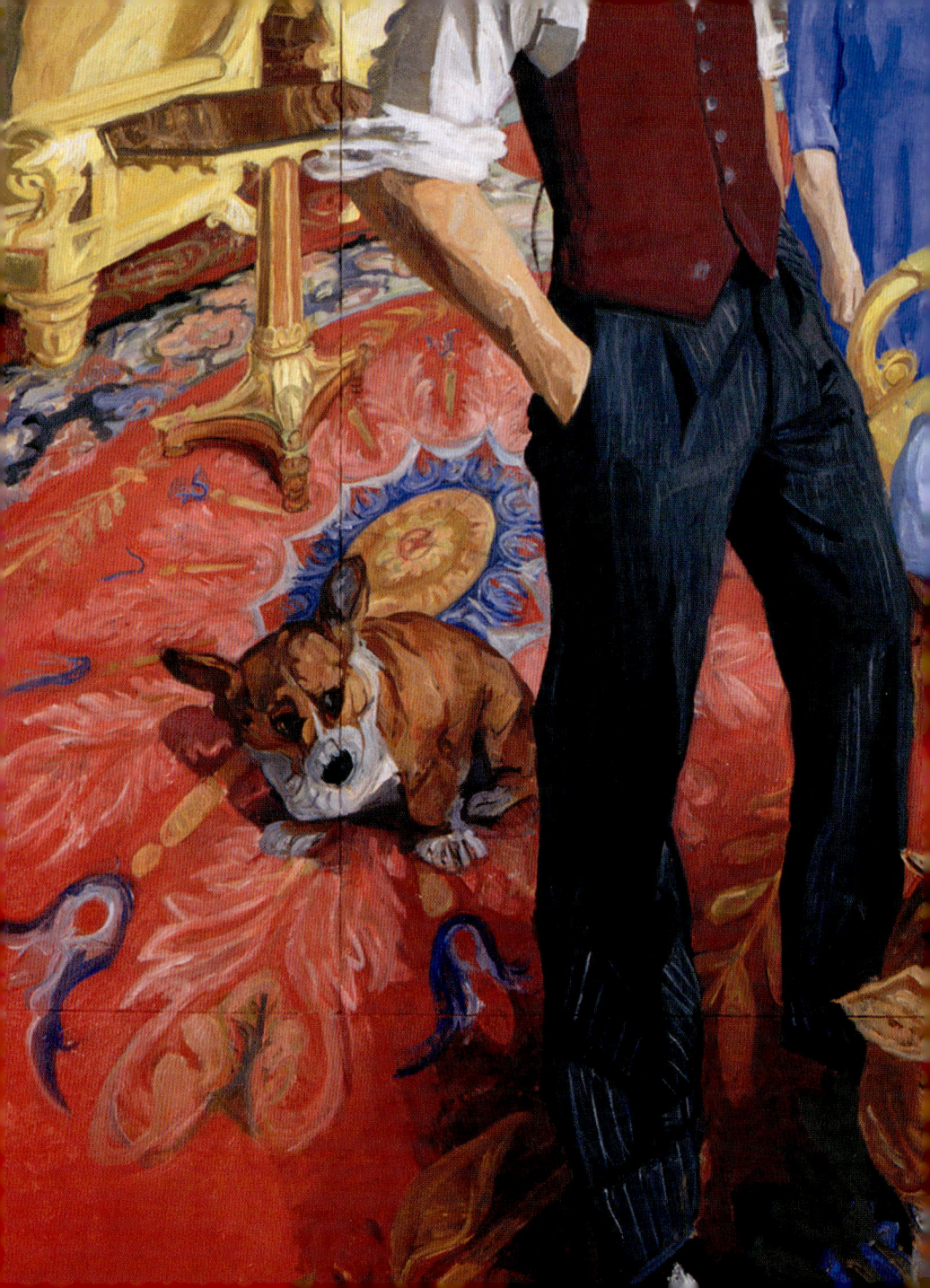

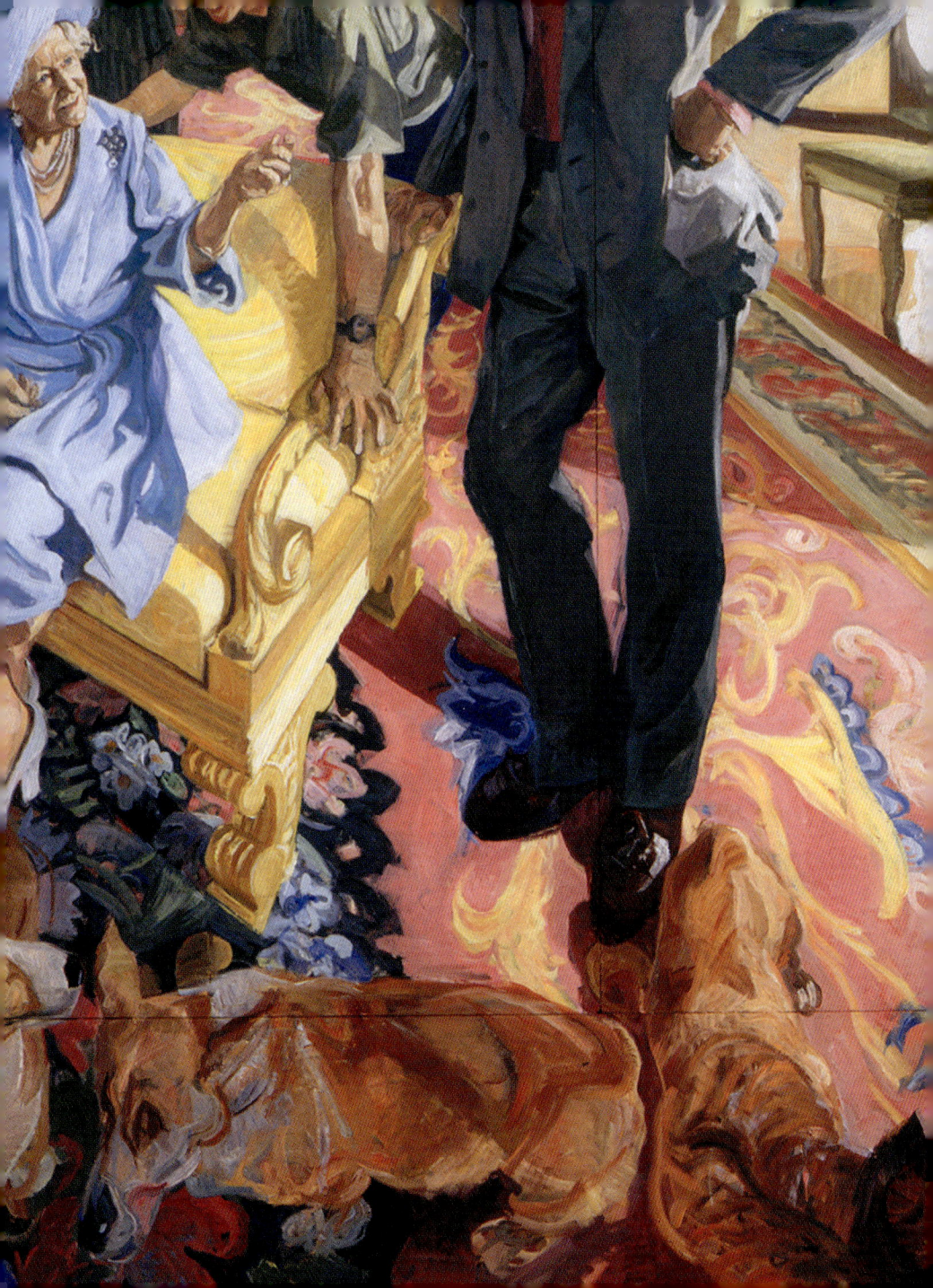

Index

Acknowledgements

It's my belief that two of the most wonderful aspects of this world are dogs and art; I have an overwhelming passion for both. So this book was a dream to research and write. What made it even better was working with Mark Fletcher – I always know that when we work together, the experience will be a pleasure and the book excellent! Special thanks to you, Mark, for always being positive, thoughtful, supportive and perceptive.

With gratitude to Gemini Books for believing in the book and making it happen; to Rosanna Fairhead for astute observations and understanding; to John Round for the uplifting design and layouts; and to Patricia Burgess for proofreading and Pauline Hubner for indexing.

I am grateful to the owners and custodians of all the artworks featured, for the privilege of allowing us to reproduce them.

And, of course, to dogs everywhere!

Picture Credits

Published in 2025
by Gemini Gift Books
Part of Gemini Books Group

Based in Woodbridge and London

Marine House, Tide Mill Way,
Woodbridge, Suffolk IP12 1AP
United Kingdom

www.geminibooks.com

ISBN 978-1-78675-191-1

A CIP catalogue record for this book is available from the British Library.

Manufacturer's EU Representative: Eurolink Compliance Limited, 25 Herbert Place, Dublin, D02 AY86, Republic of Ireland. admin@eurolink-europe.ie

Printed in China

10 9 8 7 6 5 4 3 2 1

Frontispiece: Utagawa Hiroshige II, *French Woman, Her Child and Pet Dog*, 1860 (page 97)

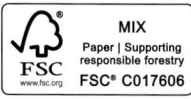